ASTROLOGY 4 PURPOSE, POWER & PERSPECTIVE

A Primer for the Seven Rays & the Work of Alice Bailey

JOHN LAWRENCE MAERZ

Published in the United States by
Emotional Troubleshooter, LLC
ISBN 978-0-9864364-8-2
Library of Congress: 2021915322

TABEL OF CONTENTS

Introduction..12

THE LANDSCAPE

THE TRIPLICITES

Cardinal...15
Fixed...15
Mutable...15

THE ELEMENTS

Fire..16
Earth...17
Air...17
Water..18

SIGN QUALITIES

Qualities Chart...20
Axis Signs & Balance..22
Balancing the Pendulum..25
Aries/Libra Axis..27
Taurus/Scorpio Axis...29
Gemini/Sagittarius Axis..31
Cancer/Capricorn Axis..32
Leo/Aquarius Axis...33
Virgo/Pisces Axis..35

THE PRIMARY HOUSES OF SELF

First House..38
Second House..39
Third House...39
Fourth House..40

Fifth House..41
Sixth House...42

THE EXTERNAL OR MIRROR HOUSES

Seventh House...44
Eighth House...45
Ninth House..46
Tenth House..47
Eleventh House..48
Twelfth House...48

THE VISITORS

Mercury..56
Venus..57
Mars..62
Jupiter..64
Saturn...66
Uranus..69
Neptune..71
Pluto...73
Sun...75
Moon..76
Vulcan..78

CONCEPTS

Involution –Evolution...80
Cycles & Phases..83

THE MAJOR ASPECTS

How Do They Work?...88
Conjunction...89
Opposition...90

Square…………………………………………………………..91
Trine…………………………………………………………….92
Sextile………………………………………………………...93
Inconjunction & Quincunx…………………………………………..94

WAXING & WANING ASPECTS

How Do They Work?………………………………………………95
Waxing & Waning Trines…………………………………………..97
Waxing & Waning Sextiles……………………………………...98
Waxing & Waning Inconjuncts & Quincunx……………………………...99

THE MINOR ASPECTS

What's the Difference?……………………………………………100
Semi-Sextiles & Sesquiquadrates…………………………………...100
Semi-Sextiles………………………………………………….101
Quintiles……………………………………………………..101
Noviles………………………………………………………101
Septiles……………………………………………………...101
Aspects & Their Cycle of Transition…………………………………102
Waxing or Sowing Cycle……………………………………………102
Waning of Reaping Cycle…………………………………………...103
Void of Course Moon & Planets………………………………………105

NODES & DECLINATIONS

Nodal Discrimination………………………………………………109
Aries & 1st House……………………………………………….109
Taurus & 2nd House…………………………………………...110
Gemini & 3rd House………………………………………………111
Cancer & 4th House……………………………………………..112
Leo & 5th House………………………………………………..113
Virgo & 6th House………………………………………………114
Libra & 7th House……………………………………………….114
Scorpio & 8th House…………………………………………….115

Sagittarius & 9th House...116
Capricorn & 10th House..117
Aquarius & 11th House..118
Pisces & 12th House..119

TANGENT SUBJECTS

Understanding & Discriminating Declinations.......................................120
Retrogrades & The Planets..122
Planets in Mutual Reception..124
Final Dispositors...125
Planetary Pictures...129

AN ALTERNATE LANDSCAPE

Beyond Flat Earth..132
At the Crossroads: A Necessary Choice...133
An Upgrade in Rulerships...135
Esoteric Mercury..137
Esoteric Venus..138
Esoteric Mars..139
Esoteric Jupiter...140
Esoteric Saturn...142
Esoteric Uranus..143
Esoteric Neptune..145
Esoteric Pluto...146
Esoteric Earth...148
Esoteric Vulcan..148
Esoteric Sun & Moon...149

THE SEVEN RAYS

Ray One...151
Ray Two...152
Ray Three..153
Rays of Attribute...154
Ray Four..154
Ray Five...156

Ray Six...157
Ray Seven..158
Sacred & Non-sacred Rulerships...160
Finding the Seven Rays in the Chart...160
Component Signs..160
Ascendant Sign Component...161
Sacred & Non-Sacred Positioning..162

PART II
RAY APPLICATIONS BY SIGN & HOUSE AXIS

1 - ARIES & THE ASCENDANT / SEVENTH HOUSE AXIS

Mercury...164
Venus...165
Mars...165
Jupiter...166
Saturn...167
Uranus...169
Neptune...170
Pluto..171
Vulcan...172
Moon..173

2 - TAURUS & THE SECOND / EIGHTH HOUSE AXIS

Mercury...173
Venus...174
Mars...175
Jupiter...175
Saturn...176
Uranus...176
Neptune...177
Pluto..178
Vulcan...178

Moon...179

---

3 - GEMINI & THE THIRD / NINTH HOUSE AXIS

Mercury...179
Venus..180
Mars..180
Jupiter..181
Saturn...182
Uranus..183
Neptune..183
Pluto...184
Vulcan..185
Moon..185

---

4 - CANCER & THE FOURTH / TENTH HOUSE AXIS

Mercury...186
Venus..187
Mars..188
Jupiter..189
Saturn...190
Uranus..190
Neptune..191
Pluto...192
Vulcan..193
Moon..193

---

5 - LEO & THE FIFTH / ELEVENTH HOUSE AXIS

Mercury...194
Venus..196
Mars..196
Jupiter..197
Saturn...198
Uranus..199

Neptune..200
Pluto...201
Vulcan..202
Moon..202

6 - VIRGO & THE SIXTH / TWELFTH HOUSE AXIS

Mercury...203
Venus..205
Mars...206
Jupiter..207
Saturn..208
Uranus...209
Neptune...210
Pluto...211
Vulcan..212
Moon..213

7 - LIBRA & THE SEVENTH / FIRST HOUSE AXIS

Mercury...214
Venus..215
Mars...216
Jupiter..217
Saturn..218
Uranus...219
Neptune...220
Pluto...221
Vulcan..222
Moon..223

8 - SCORPIO & THE EIGHTH / SECOND HOUSE AXIS

Mercury...224
Venus..225
Mars...226

Jupiter...227

Saturn...228

Uranus...230

Neptune..231

Pluto..232

Vulcan...233

Moon...234

9 - SAGITTARIUS & THE NINTH / THIRD HOUSE AXIS

Mercury..235

Venus..236

Mars...237

Jupiter..238

Saturn...240

Uranus...241

Neptune..242

Pluto..243

Vulcan...245

Moon...246

10 - CAPRICORN & THE TENTH / FOURTH HOUSE AXIS

Mercury..247

Venus..248

Mars...250

Jupiter..251

Saturn...252

Uranus...254

Neptune..255

Pluto..256

Vulcan...257

Moon...258

11 - AQUARIUS & THE ELEVENTH / FIFTH HOUSE AXIS

Mercury...260
Venus...261
Mars...262
Jupiter..263
Saturn..265
Uranus...266
Neptune...267
Pluto..268
Vulcan..269
Moon..270

12 - PISCES & THE TWELFTH / SIXTH HOUSE AXIS

Mercury...271
Venus...272
Mars...274
Jupiter..275
Saturn..276
Uranus...278
Neptune...280
Pluto..281
Vulcan..283
Moon..285
Summary of Part II..286
References & Helpful Reading Material................................287

APPENDIX

Short House Meanings...289
Family Members by House...290
45 Degree Chart..291
Phase Wheel...292
Ray Correspondences..293
About the Author..295

ASTROLOGY 4 PURPOSE, POWER & PERSPECTIVE

A Primer for the Seven Rays & the Work of Alice Bailey

INTRODUCTION

After fifty-two years of working with astrology I have found that the perspective that is still held by astrologers and their clients remains the same: your sign tells you who you are and what you should expect to occur in your life. For our western population that is so concerned with gaining and maintaining control of their lives, this seems to be a logically assumable perspective for people to have. Yet, and along the same lines, many people use the qualities attributed to their sign as an excuse for why they can or can't be or do what they say they want. Others flaunt their sign's qualities as a reason for why others should give them deference for their assets or detriments. Others simply use the sign as an identity to describe and solidify a preferable or forgivable image of themselves.

All these interpretations present a fated set of circumstances etching in stone, at least from a perceived security perspective, what a person should think about themselves and what they should expect of life. Few people, let alone astrologers, can predict, or more likely guess, the choice and circumstance that any individual will either make or fall into with any high degree of accuracy. The better the astrologer, the better the odds but no one can predict with any guarantee that what they say is true or will happen. Because each individual has their own experience, their choices are just that, individual. And the most important variable a client can possess is their choice. All the best astrologer can do is offer a fairly accurate likelihood of future events depending on the client's chart and current circumstance.

These and most of the astrological experiences I have had over many years of experience have brought me to a point where I have chosen to use my client's individual perception of their experience and understanding as simply a starting point for preparing them for the oncoming energies. This has been chosen in lieu of giving them the usual presentation of a perceptual envelope limited to what their sign dictates they should be and do coupled with their limited and fearfully predictable imagination of what they *think* they know and focused on preventing what they fear the most. In short, I have learned not to allow myself to be limited to operating within *their* framework of expectation but in the realm of expanded possibilities much more than what conventional astrology might say is inevitable.

Many times, the client will have little or no understanding of the next step up toward what they could be becoming and learning about themselves and how their perception of the world might change. Their need for control usually keeps them within very tight boundaries where they feel safe in their perceived ability to control future circumstances. My task is to help them see the advantages of moving past their comfort zone. After all, they came to me either to find a better way toward their goals or to gain confirmation that what they've chosen to do is "right" for them. Neither choice has anything carved in stone but their hopes in consistency remain the same. Many clients will also ask the same questions but in different ways to elicit an answer that agrees with what they want to hear. The answer is usually not in keeping with what they want but they must remember that their inability to see beyond their current landscape is the reason that they have come for counseling.

My perspective on astrological counseling is simple but unique. Our Sun sign is not who we *are* but who we are to *become*. That is, why would we have been born under our Sun sign if we've already mastered the qualities that the sign is described by? Most astrology supporters think that they *are* what their Sun sign describes. People who have no faith in astrology see that the qualities that are supposed to describe them almost entirely miss the mark justifying their lack of trust or belief in the science. Additionally, most people see the miniscule information provided in most of the published astrology columns severely lacking anything tangibly useful if not entirely off the mark. There's a very solid reason for this.

People who are born under a specific sign have the potential for the sign's qualities in their makeup, but those qualities are unfocused and undeveloped. Because they *are* present and undeveloped, they are more easily spotted as the sign by others who know how the sign operates and assesses them as being imbalanced. The rationale behind this is that when we *know* and *properly use* the sign's qualities, they become seamless and virtually invisible to the onlooker. So, we as laymen, see the person's birth sign qualities because they stick out like a sore thumb due to the fact that they haven't been integrated or refined into the personality. When we're born under a sign, we're learning to develop and integrate their qualities. I would then say that I would then say that I'm *learning* to be a Libra and *not* that I *am* one. Our Sun sign simply tells us what we should be focusing and working on in order to ascend to our fullest potential for awareness.

The rest of the planets will operate in a similar manner in each sign they're found in. The planet's individual meanings and catalyzing qualities will remain the same, but each in sign they will take on a "coloring" of characteristics more aligned with the sign and what we need to experience from a karmic perspective. When I speak of karmic, I merely mean that the planets will aid the client in realizing and using the energy of the Sun sign according to what they have not yet mastered and what the residue of their past lives has not exposed the soul to yet. In a very mundane sense, this is like retrieving and eating leftovers from our refrigerator. We need to recombine them to gain a "full flavor" of all the possible perspective tastes.

There are many other facets of astrology that I will explain both from a conventional and goal-oriented perspective from what we might consider the soul's perspective. This assumption on my part has no special knowledge about anyone's soul purpose but with a pragmatic approach delineating why I believe a particular planet might be in a particular sign, house and aspect from a growth-oriented perspective. With all this in mind, let's begin.

THE LANDSCAPE

THE TRIPLICITIES & ELEMENTS

These will be a mix of conventional concepts. Let's start with *triplicities*. There are three ways that action can occur. We can initiate something or we can concentrate and continue something already begun or we can react to something by attempting to change it.

CARDINAL

In astrology we call an initiator someone who is *cardinal*. These are the people that get things rolling. They're the ones that start a conversation at a cocktail party or begin work that their boss has outlined for them. In a group, they are the ones who suggest or take action to get the group moving. In life and business, these are the shakers and the movers.

FIXED

Someone who concentrates or keeps the ongoing action continuous are called *fixed*. These are the people who are consistent, tenacious, persistent and steadfast. They're the ones who keep the cocktail party conversation going by adding useful information stabilizing the flow. They make sure that if a boss has dictated a policy for work that they will stay applied and diligent. They keep the rudder steady and the ship on course and add things that will intensify their path to the objective.

MUTABLE

A person who is *mutable* can be an agent of change and someone who is likely able to change the ship's course enabling the avoidance of storms, faux pas and undesirable outcomes. Their tendency is to make changes and adjustments in the action that is occurring whether it is needed or not. They are the ones who react to the conversation at the party by changing the subject if it is headed in what looks like a bad direction. They often react to circumstances but don't necessarily do anything about fixing them. They usually require an outside force to get them moving.

All three of these approaches have their best applications but can produce difficulties in circumstances that need a different type of energy. For example, if consistency is needed, a *mutable* approach would be counterproductive. If a situation is stagnant, there, a *mutable* or *cardinal* could be useful. Different life situations require different types of approaches in the application of energy. When we get to looking at the planets and the signs they're in, we will see how they can be conducive or counterproductive. The *triplicities* give us those options.

THE ELEMENTS

This is probably what most people know about astrology besides their Sun signs. The elements are how planets and house cusps (starting points) are "colored with perspective." An element is the basis through which the functioning of a planet or house is derived and perceived showing how its energy will be expressed. Simply put, does it motivate you? Is it practical? Does it seem theoretically feasible? Do you feel it? These are the general perspectives driven by the elements fire, earth, air and water or energy, tangibility, mentality and feeling. These four elements are coupled with the three triplicities and form twelve combinations known as the signs. Before we look at each of the twelve signs, let's look a little more closely at the elements.

FIRE

When we speak of passion, an image of personal intensity is usually elicited from within our psyche. Fire usually encompasses a component of intense or overpowering impulse and drive. The impulse comes from a place without words or thought. The triplicity determines the degree of consistency. The impulse is usually converted into physical action before the thought process even comes into play. The lower vibration is gross and comes from a gut instinct. The higher vibration is much more subtle and comes from intuitiveness. Intuitive fire is said to drive the spirit.

Fire produces spontaneous courage, especially, in light of the fact that the impulse manifests before the mental rationalization of fear is able to take place. It also pushes its possessor beyond their limits, often to a point of self-destructiveness if not compensated for by other factors. Fire people do not know their limits. Heat and purgation are the children of fire. Oxidation is a function of fire whether it occurs as a slow burn or explosive disintegration. Our physical limits and endurance are a function of the fire we employ.

Conscious direction of fire is a task that challenges us all. The other elements must be possessed in a balance to keep fire within our survivable limits. With too much fire, a person will flame out. With too little, life will be near dead and never progress.

People who possess a great deal of fire in their makeup have a vibration akin to a low rumble accompanied by heat. There is a feeling of great force and potential just below the surface.

EARTH

Earth is the home of tangibility. When something has an earthy quality to it, we find ourselves saying, "I'm from Missouri, show me", or how practical is it or what can you do with it? Earth deals directly with the senses. That is, if we can see it, touch it, feel it, hear it, or taste it, it has a valid quality to be part of our world.

Earth is cool, dry and moves very slowly. It occurs in layers and constantly regenerates itself. Gathering for manifestation is a natural force. Earth relates to anything that has form and inertia.

Creating or building something comprised of earth serves as a confirmation of our existence. The physical earth is proof to our senses and evidence of our perception of ourselves. Earth validate itself through the senses. This is the validation of its worth to the rest of the world. It is the densest of the elements and serves as a foundation on which the other elements may build. It is the last remaining element of existence when we leave this world and it is the most tangible testimony that we've been there. For earth, tangibility is the most solid consequence of our actions.

People who possess a great deal of earth in their charts have a vibration that is slow and cool. They convey a feeling of "immovability" and no matter what of them might be removed there would still remain a tangible history and residue.

AIR

Air is invisible but the most necessary element perpetuating movement through our existence. Evidence of its existence can only be seen in its movement through the other elements. Air accelerates the action of fire, reduces the density of earth and enables the movement of water. Air is the conductor of thought. It is the medium through which change is directed or reacted to.

Air is the vehicle of thought and thought is the consequence of mind. But the mind is only a tool creating our ability to frame the perception of what we have sensed through the other elements. It is transient and elusive and changes with its exposure to the other elements.

Air contains the ability to rationalize, analyze and study perceptions and concepts. It is the basic medium for all types of conscious communication and exchange of ideas and perceptions. It brings our focus and awareness to our social exchanges as perceived through the constructs of time. It allows for the comparison and free flow of memories. Thinking operates in a linear fashion and does not led itself easily to deciphering intuition which operates independently of time.

People who possess a large amount of air energy in their charts appear to be hot and electric. They convey a feeling of constant movement sometimes so much so that they may seem to border on instability. They usually appear to be quick, verbal and projective.

WATER

Water is the lubricant of life. It is the vehicle of feeling and immersion. Feelings will swell and ebb like the tide. They are involuntary unless they arise attached to a thought connected to a memory. They are then called emotion. Sometimes those swells reach the level of a tsunami. Other times, they are as subtle as the rings generated by a leaf falling on water.

Water can act as an insulator or as a conductor. It will also be susceptible to changes in its intensity like moving from ice through liquid to a gas with the same immoveable and movable qualities existing on either pole. But given to no outside change, it will always return to its placid and liquid state.

Aside from fire or air, water has the ability to break down anything of a tangible nature. Water is also permeative toward anything it touches but in varying degrees depending on the object's density and solidity.

Water is the vehicle by which memory is stored and submerged in the unconscious. Our youngest memories are preverbal. That is, they were encountered before language became a tool to discriminate between them. Water exists at the depth where our dreaming occurs. This is also the place where empathy originates from. Empathy is an *involuntary* feeling which *everyone* has but might not perceive or recognize. It is one of the deepest human connections we can have with any other entity.

People who possess large amounts of water in their charts are not only extremely feeling oriented but are often paranoid about being used by their feelings. Because the water element emanates from and operates below the level of consciousness, feelings of insecurity often drive a person with heavy water to be secretive in order to avoid being manipulated or controlled through what they feel they can't control in themselves: their feelings.

The elements are a tremendously influential force on any planet or house cusp they are found on. They color, temper and even shape our perspective on the how the house issues will play out and what the planetary energies will contribute to the current and future situations. The triplicity they're found in will determine whether they are initiative, concentrative or changeable.

SIGN QUALITIES

Although the list below only includes twelve general subjects that become observable when dealing with each sign, there are many, many more ideas and perspectives that can be connected to each sign. Remember, the twelve signs represent *all* the aspects we deal with in life. That is a massive amount of issues and subjects to be covered and dealt with. Remember also, that what we see of any planet in any sign is, generally, what is needing to be integrated or out of balance and obviously being worked on. The chart will always be a work in progress moving toward awareness.

You may have noticed that I didn't say each *Sun* sign. Depending on where the Sun falls in most charts, these qualities may not be observed as clearly as if he were the only planet positioned in them. There are nine other planets that can be positioned in twelve different signs and houses. If one of those planets is posited in a different sign and in a more prominent house in the chart than the Sun, the sign the Sun is in may not be as obvious to the onlooker. Sometimes the Sun and his work are not intended to be in the limelight for all to see. Sometimes the work needs to be done internally and from a darker more undeveloped portion of the chart.

With these factors in mind, let's continue developing the aspects of our astrological landscape with looking at a few of the qualities each sign brings forward.

ARIES - *Impulsive Doing – Cardinal-Fire*		
Independence	Pioneering	Competition
Bluntness	Impulse	End Justifies Mean
Projection	Assertion	Initiation
Excessive	Impatience	Fearless
TAURUS - *Concentrated Tangibility – Fixed-Earth*		
Practical	Tangible	Identity
Patience	Evidence	Possessions
Abilities	Tenacity	Stoic
Consistent	Impenetrable	Deliberate

GEMINI - *Flexible Exchange – Mutable-Air*		
Flexibility	Communication	Language
Ungrounded	Photography	Comparison
Exchange	Point of View	Asexual
Information Overload	Writing	Polarity
CANCER - *Generated Feeling – Cardinal-Water*		
Nurturance	Family	Possessive
Emotional	Security	Controlling
Protective	Moody	Mothering
Commitment	Obligatory	Score Keeping
LEO - *Concentrated Impulse – Fixed-Fire*		
Rule Oriented	Pride	Dignity
Creative	Gregarious	Need to Shine
Reputation	Fun	Conservative

Assumptive	Proper	Patriarchal
VIRGO - *Flexible Tangibility – Mutable-Earth*		
Details	Discriminatory	Flexible Practicality
Neatness	Idiosyncratic	Perfectionism
Hypochondriasis	Specific	Observant
Patternistic	Analytical	Purity
LIBRA - *Attempting Balance – Cardinal-Air*		
Balance	Mental Activity	Choice
Justice	Sharing	Tactfulness
Refinement	Social	Anti-Confronting
Diplomacy	Procrastinating	Fairness
SCORPIO - *Concentrated Feeling – Fixed-Water*		
Secrets	Privacy	Intensity
Depth	Investigative	Hidden
Detached	Unforgetting	Calculating
Hidden	Jealousy	Passion
SAGITTARIUS - *Flexible Impulse – Mutable-Fire*		
Freedom	Energy	Ideals
Unbridled	Expansive	Obtuse
Unconditional	Exploration	Altruistic
Playful	Sports	Borderless
CAPRICORN - *Generated Tangibility -Cardinal-Earth*		
Mean Justifies End	Building	Responsibility
Self-Control	Dedication	Organization
Goal Oriented	Policy	Order
Ambitious	Discipline	Seriousness
AQUARIUS - *Concentrated Thought – Fixed-Air*		
Humanitarianism	Strategy	Research
Detached	Silent Judgment	Group Oriented
Scientific Method	Unpredictable	Precision
Uniqueness	Uncompromising	Visionary

PISCES - *Immersed Feeling – Mutable-Water*		
Immersive	Empathetic	Victim
Undirected	Ungoverned	Hyper-Sensitive
Evasive	Fluid	Unconditional
Spend-Thrift	Paranoia	Impressionable

Every sign has admirable qualities that can be worked on and achieved. Every sign also has characteristics that the native needs to be made aware of and consciously diminish. Most of us understand this and see it as true. However, qualities and characteristic s that we haven't yet learned to integrate smoothly into our personality end up sticking out like a sore thumb and their expression often puts people off rather than impress them. There are two different ways we need to look at the expression and rebalancing of these characteristics. Let's look at the first look at the characteristics and then what we encounter when attempting to in rebalance them.

First, extremes of any quality or behavior may be individualizing and contribute to a specialness of identity that we might like to portray. But in the same breath we can also say that too much of a good thing *or* a bad thing is not in anyone's best interest. In the long run they end up appearing to be the dominating characteristics for anyone assessing us. Whether the characteristics are endearing or despicable, their overshadowing tends to interfere with any balance we can hope to accomplish in our lives and makes others wary and sometimes avoidant of us while fearing how we will react to *them* and affect *their* balance. No one likes a braggart. Also, no one likes one who feigns helplessness guilting us into "giving" to their "cause." But both qualities in proper balance are an acceptable part of the human condition provided they are not "overdone." Our challenge is in achieving this balance between seemingly disparate characteristics.

When we look at the Sun, most astrologers and laymen assume a list of characteristics that are pertinent and relative to recognizing the signs he falls in and their potential. What's not recognized is that those characteristics are opposed by another set that often run contrary to what's assumed and expected about the sign the Sun is found in. These *opposing* characteristics are usually promoted and exhibited in the sign *opposing* the Sun sign and they are touted as the characteristics that should be aspired toward for a person born under *that* sign.

Oddly enough, this is where we find planet earth. That is, the earth is always found in the sign opposing the Sun sign. So, if the Sun is found in Cancer, the earth's position will always be in Capricorn. This opposition is what enables the native to perceive the qualities of the sign the Sun is in. Remember, the native has chosen the Sun sign to recognize, master and integrate its qualities into their spiritual makeup in this lifetime. But the earth sign *is the perspective he is seeing those qualities from*. Please re-read the prior sentence.

When someone opposes us, the end result is almost certainly that they make us more aware of *who we are* by virtue of what we *perceive* them opposing. This opposition operates much like a mirror. This dynamic operates in the same way our projected *shadow* does (remember the action of Pluto?) It brings to light the things that need to be addressed and worked through.

Untamed and unlearned qualities are always used, initially, unskillfully when they are first discovered within us. These unrefined presentations are easy for others to see and recognize in us. However, this grossness or unskilled use also attracts their unskilled and mirrored use in its opposite extreme form. *This* is what creates the awareness of who we are through others, what we're doing and what we need to work on.

Take, for example, someone who is exceedingly frugal. The person who is frugal will tend to attract someone who wastes or throws away money. Or someone who is neurotically neat, will attract someone who is a consummate slob. This will make them aware of their extremes and, hopefully, dampen their expression. Think in terms of Felix and Oscar in the sitcom "The Odd Couple" and you'll recognize and even understand the reason for their pairing.

In the same fashion, if our earth sign is extremely frugal, we will attract a Sun sign person who wastes money and throws away resources. Yet, we may also attract someone who is *more* frugal than we are making us frustrated and painfully aware of the extreme we operate through. It's not so much that opposites attract or that "birds of a feather" attract but that the *extremes of what we do* brings us people and situations that tend to make us aware of those extremes in ourselves so we can work on changing them. Our earth sign is just that; a perspective representative of the extremes we operate under that attracts us to people and circumstances that make us aware of how we are acting in any extreme.

In this way I look at all Sun sign positions in terms of an *axis of polarities* that need to be brought into balance through exposure to the opposing extremes of the subject being dealt with. In the case of Felix and Oscar, the universe is attempting to rebalance attitudes of frugality and wastefulness of resources and neatness and "slobbery." We might attribute these polarities to the axis of Taurus and Scorpio since that axis primarily deals with possessions, resources, their use and their connections to the second and eight houses.

With this understanding in place, now let's look at what we encounter when we attempt to bring these extreme characteristics back into balance. This requires a little more understanding of the subtlety in how opposing characteristics might interact and then "level out."

Imagine that you are learning to drive a vehicle that you've never driven before. For many people, this might be the first time that you're learning to drive a "stick" or manual transmission instead of an automatic transmission. Driving a stick involves coordinating the actions between a shift lever operated by the hand and a clutch pedal operated by the left foot. What adds a little more difficulty is that you must also learn to alternate the use of the right foot on the gas and the left foot on the clutch petal. So, you begin.

You push the clutch down to the floor, put the shift in neutral and start the vehicle. Once it's running you push the clutch to the floor, shift into first gear and slowly let the clutch up while your pushing down a little on the accelerator. The vehicle lurches forward and stalls. You're told that you let the clutch up too fast. You push the clutch down, put the shift back into neutral and start the engine again.

You repeat the procedure but let the clutch up more slowly as you increase the gas with your foot a little more slowly. The vehicle gives a much smaller lurch and starts to move forward as you slowly let up the clutch, giving it a little more gas. The faster you move the less violent the lurching occurs until you're moving smoothly while in gear and let the clutch all the way up. While you're moving you repeat the procedure to change gears to move a little faster. Each time you change gears the lurching becomes less, and you begin to get the feel of how to make the shifting smoother. The fast or slow and the hard or soft of using the clutch and gas are the polarities you're working to integrate with each other. The smoother the integration, the smoother becomes the ride.

What an onlooker sees as you first start to learn to drive the vehicle is a lurching motion different from the average experienced driver. You stand out from the smooth moving traffic like a sore thumb. But as you get more experienced in driving the new vehicle, your lurching diminishes, and your driving becomes smoother. Onlookers can no longer tell you from the average driver.

The same thing happens when you are born into a sign. Using the new characteristics of the sign you exhibit a stalling or lurching motion. To the onlookers it's easy to tell that you're a beginning "driver" with the Sun sign. They can easily tell what sign you're working with due to the "lurching" motion. As you get older and more experienced working with the sign, the lurching subsides, and it becomes harder to see a difference in your driving from the other drivers. It is then that the new Sun sign qualities have been integrated into the persona.

The lurching is representative of the extremes. As the lurching subsides, Felix starts to become a little less stingy and obsessive and Oscar becomes a bit less wasteful and inattentive. The universe's way of bringing things into balance is by bringing the things that are extreme opposites or extreme equivalents together so they can begin to nullify what sticks out like a sore thumb in each other.

BALANCE & THE PENDULUM

When the process of balancing the *axis* commences, it moves through a few gyrations before it settles into a balanced state. We can liken this to our vehicle again in the act of our learning to steer it.

When we begin to learn to steer, the natural tendency is to over-correct until we get used to the wheel. When we need to correct having moved too far to the left, we will most likely correct too far to the right. When we re-correct, we may easily correct too far to the left. Steering is a process of refining our movements so we move just enough in the corrective distance so that our path becomes smooth and within the limits of what is necessary to be in line with our traffic lane. Time and experience provide us with the feel and information that we need in order to master the task.

Working with the qualities and abilities inherent in our birth sign works exactly the same way. When we first use the new qualities, we are unaware of the limits that are necessary for us to use them properly. We tend to over or under judge how we should apply them.

If our sign says we are learning the dynamics of being generous with our time and we're coming from a habit of frugality, we may initially assist or benefit others with too much of our time leaving ourselves open for abuse by others or be left with an insufficient amount time for taking care of our own issues. In realizing this, we may tighten up our "donations" and move too far back into being frugal. Until we learn the limits of our abilities and requirements of our new sign, we may oscillate back and forth a number of times before we recognize where that "sweet spot" of balance for our new qualities rest. Every *axis* of signs has this ability for the see-saw motion between them in some quality of life.

This pendulum motion between qualities and attitudes can be seen in history. With a small bit of research and observation we can generally see this action happening in our family structures. One generation may be extremely strict with their rules and traditions while the following one becomes more lenient. In turn, the next generation may return to a sense of strictness in compensating for what they observed occurring in their parents.

Any kind of refinement is a process of adjustments becoming smaller and smaller until near perfection has occurred. This is true in family dynamics, occupational skills, emotions, business, intellect and more. Everything naturally returns to a sense of balance through this pendulum process. After water has been disturbed, it sloshes back and forth until it reaches its lowest point and comes to rest. If we look at the subtleties of life, we can also see that karma works *exactly* the same way, lifetime after lifetime until we arrive at mastery through experiencing all the possible perspectives. Karma is not a "payback" but the universe's way of bringing us awareness with the opportunity for recreating balance.

With these understandings in place, let's now look at the *axes* of signs and the interaction of their opposing qualities.

ARIES-LIBRA AXIS

The most widely accepted statement made relative to Aries is "I am." That of Libra is "I relate." It's obvious to see that the focus for Aries is, essentially, about themself and for Libra, about others. This is an obvious polarity in their focus and where their attention is going to end up.

The primary quality for Aries is *independence* and the primary quality for Libra is *sharing*. On a "sliding" scale, one will be more independent and the other might be more sharing. So, there would be varying degrees of each depending on which one was more prominent in the psyche.

Most people would assume that an independence/sharing polarity would be mostly how we address relationships and contacts of intimacy. Though this may be a primary area of rapport, the independence and sharing covers a much wider area of experience. The independence polarity may be how much a person would choose to be or work alone as opposed to being or working with others. The sharing polarity could be how much a person would allow participations in issues and events by others. Both polarities would also relate to privacy issues and how free or restricted they would feel or be in the involvement of others in what they do. This could even extend into how much crowding or even the presence of others would be felt or considered. Growing up in a large family could bring lessons in sharing. Being deserted or having to live on one's own could bring on the self-staining potential in independence.

In remembering that the sign we're born underrepresents the qualities that our psyche is "ingesting" and incorporating, it will be easy to understand that if we are born under a Libra Sun that there is a likelihood of us being of a more independent nature (Earth in Aries) and learning to develop a more sharing nature. And the if we were born under an Aries Sun that there would be an equal likelihood of us possessing a more sharing nature (Earth in Libra) while learning to become more independent.

It is not uncommon to find people born under a particular Sun sign acting more like their opposing Earth sign and vice versa, especially, if the oncoming life experiences brought on by the Sun sign are or have been strongly resisted.

There is another perspective that needs to be understood. The "see-saw" effect always operates between any polarity of signs between the Sun and the Earth's positions. This will often lead an observer to mistakenly identify a person's Sun sign. The dynamic is simple. We can look back at our example of learning to steer a vehicle, only the steering corrections operate between the qualities of the polarity of signs rather than simple direction. If you remember…

When we begin to learn to steer, the natural tendency is to over-correct until we get used to the wheel. When we need to correct having moved too far toward *Libra*, we will most likely recorrect too far toward Aries. When we re-correct, we may easily recorrect too far toward Libra again. Steering our attitudes and perceptions between the signs is a process of refining our attitudes and movements so we move just enough in the corrective distance so that our path becomes smooth and within the limits of what is necessary to be in line with our preferred action: not too short and not too far in either direction. The objective is to establish a balance between seemingly extreme characteristics. Done repeatedly, we may appear to zigzag between qualities and characteristics for years or even a lifetime. Sometimes, a young person can just pop out of the gate with everything in place. When this occurs, it is likely that there may have been previous lifetimes where this was dealt with more extensively.

With this understanding we begin to realize that sometimes a Sun sign Aries might correct *too* much toward independence or a Libra Sun sign might correct *too* far toward sharing making our sign assessment difficult, if not impossible. In any of an individual's polarity of signs they could spend a lifetime zigzagging between characteristic polarities attempting to move toward a balance.

Other polarities in play between Aries and Libra have a similar flavor but may be different in detail and application. Competition and antagonism may polarize with surrender and conciliation. Disregard and ignoring may polarize with consideration and caring. The flavor overall focuses on too much attention toward what is inside us (Earth in Aries) or placing too much attention on others (Earth in Libra). We can say that the Sun in Aries promotes a very strong internal directiveness based on the *individual's* own values and experiences *(internal locus of control)* and that the Sun in Libra promotes a very strong external responsiveness based on the *outside* world's values and expectations *(external locus of control)*. Having to live in the world, we would need to learn to know when to use which depending on outside circumstances. Both would need to be brought into balance to live smoothly and seamlessly. Any extreme either way would lead the "universe" toward bringing us experiences countering those extremes.

TAURUS/SCORPIO AXIS

The most widely accepted statement made relative to Taurus is "I have." That of Scorpio is, "I feel." The main focus of this polarity are the facts verses feelings about what we have, do, are or not. Taurus is noteworthily the most materialistic sign of the zodiac and Scorpio is regarded as the most intense feeling. Both are fixed and constant about their perspectives, intentions and actions. Their concentration starts with tenacity, moves on toward stubbornness and occasionally can become obsessive. These qualities yield an onlooker's perception of depth within the two signs.

The main polarity to be balanced is between the Taurean's realization of the tangibility of life and the Scorpio's recognition that feelings must play a major role in how we address life's tangible circumstances. All that have known or encountered those born under either sign have learned of the intensity of belief and dedication on both their parts.

The perspective to be understood is that a native born with the Sun in Scorpio has the majority of its experience in the *tangible* arena of Taurus (by virtue of its Earth position) while learning to handle the elicited Scorpionic *feelings* (Sun position) encountered as a result of being involved in the tangible experience of life's circumstances.

Conversely, it is also to be understood that a native born with the Sun in Taurus has the majority of its experience in the *emotional* area (by virtue of its Earth in Scorpio) while learning to handle the *tangibly* oriented circumstances encountered (Sun position) as a result of being involved in the tangible expression of life's circumstances.

The see-saw effect, as described in the "learning to steer" experience in the Aries/Libra axis, will take Taurus and Scorpio back and forth between being tangibly oriented, then emotionally oriented and then back again. This may happen a number of times in the native's life. This pendulum effect is designed to and will, hopefully, bring balance between the two perspectives.

This see-saw effect can be best be observed in how both signs values themselves, their abilities, disabilities and the handling of their resources (I have/You have). This can be seen through the intended application and use of the abilities and resources that both of them have at their disposal to work with. Initially, Scorpio's Earth in Taurus will find the emotional content of Scorpio virtually irrational while Taurus' Earth in Scorpio will also find a tangible perspective, content and focus unintelligible and even obsessive. Hopefully, time and life experience will slowly ease this dichotomy, create a little more tolerance of opposing views and eventually master the blending of the two perspectives into a more complete understanding…in most people.

The lowest vibration of this process will exist in possessiveness. In humor we can say Taurus might say, "What's mine is mine and what's yours is mine." Scorpio might say, "What's yours may appear to be yours, but I'll make you wish you gave it to me." The next level will be more concerned with usefulness and fair distribution of resources and the highest vibration will embody synthesis and the actualization of our fullest potential with those resources.

GEMINI/SAGITTARIUS AXIS

The most widely accepted statement made relative to Gemini is "I communicate." That of Sagittarius is "I believe." Because Gemini is on the internal part of the wheel, we know that *evolved* communication issues will manifest as a concentrated communication about the diversity of what Gemini thinks and feels as perceived from the world. For the *evolved* Sagittarius on the external part of the wheel, he will manifest a pointed focus toward acting on what *he* values, perceives, and does based on what *he* intuits and feels. Gemini's issues are to learn to listen and Sagittarius to learn to act and do.

The primary lesson for *unevolved* Sun in Gemini will concern their willingness or ability to *listen to the diversity of thought and values* coming from the others they communicate with. Unevolved Geminis are often too busy talking *at* someone to listen and *recognize* the thoughts and values of others. Remember, for a Gemini, their Earth lays in Sagittarius giving them a pointed focus for *their* values and *their* expression with an unrelenting urge toward the freedom while ignoring others and to do and be what their instinct and intuition direct them toward.

The primary lesson for *unevolved* Sun in Sagittarius will concern their willingness or ability to *act* on their intuition and instincts and to become free of the confusion involved with the diversity of choices for action that the world may press them toward. Unevolved Sagittarians are usually too busy listening to others rather than having the fun and freedom of acting on what *they* feel or intuit. Remember, for a Sagittarius, their Earth lays in Gemini giving them a perspective that every option and permutation for choice must first be examined, thought about and talked about *before* action is ever taken. The primary lesson for a Sagittarius is learning to simply act on what their heart tells them is right.

The primal polarity operating in a see-saw fashion between Gemini and Sagittarius is the pendulum moving back and forth, respectively, between being able and willing to listen to and hear others versus having fun and freedom while acting on and expressing their experience without premeditation or preconceptions. Again, these perspectives may waffle back and forth during their lifetimes. It should also be understood that since these are mutable signs that these wafflings may happen certainly more frequently than the fixed signs and a bit more than the cardinal signs. These changes most often happen at the Saturn cycle change points at twenty-eight, forty-two and fifty-six years old.

CANCER/CAPRICORN AXIS

The statement most commonly heard describing Cancer is *"I Nurture"* and for Capricorn, *"I Sacrifice."* With Cancer we know the most important focus is on the preservation of home, family, and tradition. However, underlying those qualities is the *unevolved* Cancerian's relentless urge toward finding and establishing some semblance of *security* in order that their "home base" may feel safe and unthreatened. With Capricorn, we know that an all-important focus includes their social standing, image, and accomplishments. Underlying those qualities is their *unevolved* and assumed belief that they must *sacrifice* something of great value in order for that to happen.

With a Sun in Cancer, the Earth is naturally in Capricorn. In Cancer's unevolved quest for temporal *security*, she draws from the *sacrificial* quality of her Earth in Capricorn. However, the qualities of *security, nurturance* and *sacrifice* operate within a curious mix. Unevolved Cancer grows up feeling like they're an orphan within their own family and then proceeds to use the quality of *nurturance* in giving to someone whom they need or want something of. They choose to give something that's convenient and easy for them to give and doesn't mean that much to them. Cancer assumes that the giving makes the receiver feel obligated. Then, when Cancer asks for something of the receiver in return, the receiver feels obligated to give or do what is asked for. As a result, Cancer avoids being asked to give something that they might not want to do or give. Creating obligation is a trademark behavior for the immature Cancer and other water signs. What's really odd, is that karmically, Cancer Sun sign people usually end up caring for the people they sought to be taken care of by.

With Sun in Capricorn and the Earth in Cancer, the relationship between *nurturance* and *sacrifice* starts conversely and, again, in a bit twisted of a fashion. Capricorns are raised in a family environment where the family depends on the things that they are made responsible for. This teaches Capricorn that their personal *sacrifice* is necessarily both proper and expected on behalf of the people they are taught to be responsible for. They are made to feel that their participation is indispensable. They grow up assuming that taking care of others is *their* responsibility and that they must be in charge. They usually spend the first half of their lives taking care of everyone else.

At midlife (approximately forty-two) the Capricorn Sun sign native comes to believing that they've been duped into sacrificing their own satisfaction for the unappreciated service they've been giving to the family members they were trained into believing they were responsible for. They slowly begin to shut down the gravy train and live more for themselves. Generally, their see-saw effect has a much wider time span - approximately forty-two years. Occasionally, we have a few astute Capricorns recognizing the need for change much earlier on. In both cases the change usually moves them into the extreme opposite perspective, and they manifest their Earth sign Cancer – *nurturing* only for a price. This change is often one of the reasons that Capricorn Sun sign people are often seen as opportunists.

Because Cancer and Capricorn are mostly tangible signs as opposed to fire and air, their likelihood of waffling between polarities to any great degree is minimized. Even after these changes, both Cancer Sun signs and Capricorn Sun signs begin to slowly evolve and mature, ultimately achieving a balance between *nurture* and *sacrifice*. Tough love is often a result of the maturing of this polarity.

LEO/AQUARIUS AXIS

The statement most commonly heard describing Leo is *"I Will"* and for Aquarius, *"I Know."* One of the strongest factors in the life of an unevolved Leo Sun person is their belief in what is "supposed to be." This leads them to search for the highest and most dignified values that they can find. Once this set of values is found and adhered to, their *will* takes over and a tenacious drive for accomplishment and recognition of the same values follows. Following their acquisition, belief and acceptance of the rules governing what they believe is "supposed to be," they become the motive behind every one of their life pursuits and activities. The difficulty arises when they begin to *assume* that everyone else either is or should be following the same values that they hold dear. This becomes a cause of major misunderstandings between the Leo Sun sign and the people he expects should adhere to the values that *he* holds. It never dawns on him that people would feel any different than he. This assuming becomes his worst enemy.

One of the strongest factors in the unevolved Aquarius Sun makeup is not the assumption that others should know and follow what *he* feels is important but the assumption that *he knows* what is true and appropriate for others while they don't. This leads Aquarius toward looking at others as if they're bugs under a microscope. This puts other people off making them feel dehumanized, disrespected and condescended toward. Aquarius' assessment is purely mental in nature and devoid of any emotional content. This leads them toward developing an outstanding ability in practical strategy. While those assessed by a Leo Sun sign may feel, at the least, that the Leo has a heart, they feel that the Aquarius Sun sign is cold, calculating and has no compassion.

The major focus in the unevolved Leo/Aquarius axis is about the rules. Leo follows them and Aquarius makes and breaks them. Both believe that they have the right to determine what is right for others. Leo assumes others will follow and Aquarius manipulates them into doing so.

The see-saw effect is very similar in nature in that both polarities maintain an intended or perceived control over others. However, the difference is one of perspective. For the Leo Sun sign and Aquarius Earth sign, they believe that it is their necessity to either *manipulate or to tell people how* to live, behave and think. This effect produces the commonly held belief that Leo Sun signs are often to be found in middle management positions. This also accounts for the negative perspective of others feeling that they appear to be pompous, bossy and lacking compassion.

For the Aquarius Sun sign and Leo Earth sign, they *assume* that other people *don't know how* to behave and have to be *manipulated into or told to do* what the Aquarius Sun sign person believes is appropriate for them.

The final aspect of the see-saw effect is that the pendulum swings between avidly following and expecting others to follow an external set of idealistic rules or making their own rules that others should follow but not them, to which they are in charge of and selectively privy to. The quest to gain and maintain power is the largest contributing factor against the native's growth beyond self-interest.

The evolved Leo and Aquarian Sun sign persons are actively involved in the maturation and welfare of others either through creative endeavors and sharing their energy and wisdom (Leo) or through social and scientific assistance and other humanitarian avenues (Aquarius).

VIRGO/PISCES AXIS

The key words for a Virgo Sun sign are *"I Analyze"* and for the Pisces Sun Sign are *"I Empathize."* In other astrology protocols, *"I Believe"* is the motto for Pisces, but based on the Piscean tendency and ability to *empathize* everyone they come into contact with, their belief become a self-prophesied or self-fulfilling reaction. *Empathy* seems to be a much more inclusive quality to expand on.

The primary focus for a Sun in Virgo to learn is one of *discrimination*. But there are varying degrees of *discrimination*. There can be either segregation between details or, in a larger view, encompassing when or when not to serve, to whom and how.

The unevolved Virgo Sun sign will obsess over minute details. They usually miss the forest for the trees. This keeps them small minded and minutely focused. Although accuracy in detail should be strived for, getting lost in minutia only serves to "ground" the Piscean Earth sign's need for a stable and tangible base in something small, specific, and manageable in order to avoid the sea of emotion they constantly find themselves in generated through their unconscious sensitivities empathizing others' feelings and emotions. This small and specific issues almost always concern some sense of judgment or classification about the issues and actions of others. In this way it helps them to escape their own tsunami of feelings they "pick up" from others empathetically. Their Pisces Earth sign allows their empathy of others to act as an iron curtain against facing their own life circumstances. Unevolved Virgo Sun signs often find themselves obsessed with the "welfare" of others in the helping fields. Their sacrifice only serves to strengthen their iron curtain.

The primary focus for a Sun in Pisces is one of *empathy*. For the unevolved Sun in Pisces, this *empathy* happens *involuntarily*. On a conscious level, this is terrifying. With an Earth in Virgo, they are used to being able to nail themselves down to small earthly issues with details that are mostly tangible in nature. To have all the minutia to bury themselves in, an unevolved Pisces Sun need have little to do with feelings. Yet, the intensity of the *empathy* that their Pisces Sun sign provides them with creates a growing paranoia that easily rises to the surface of their consciousness. It leads them to bury themselves so deeply into the issues of others for protection that they begin to take on the characteristics of the persons they're buried in. Now, they lose themselves in the other person's identity behaving as if and believing that it is their own. Getting a handle on the recognition and taming of their involuntary *empathy* is a daunting challenge. Every sign is born with the ability to *empathize* involuntarily; however, Pisces is born with a much larger dose than most, with it being already totally "switched on" and with it closer to the edge of their subconscious creating tidal waves of interference in their daily lives. To manifest sanity, they must learn to intentionally bring it under control.

The see-saw effect of the Virgo/Pisces axis moves between extreme *discrimination* to the extent of all things becoming only black and white all the way to the other extreme of having no boundaries or discrimination whatsoever through involuntary *empathy*. This pendulum may swing wildly back and forth for an entire lifetime until the native is able to get a handle on distinguishing between what is self-generated and what is not. With a self-mastered and balanced Virgo/Pisces energy, they become the best of the world servers without diminishing themselves and while maintaining a peaceful balance of their own soul, its creativity, their responsibility, and the needs of others.

THE PRIMARY HOUSES of SELF
1 through 6

There are many rooms or "houses" in your home. Even though each "house" has its function, people are different. Each of us will use the room or "house" in a different way depending on how we live our lives. For example, your bedroom allows sleep and storage of clothing by virtue of the equipment found there. Yet, you may not have much clothing. Therefore, the closets may be relatively empty, yet you may sleep more than the average person. Others may need a wheelbarrow to move all their clothing because they have so much. Yet, they are out so much wearing all their clothing that they don't sleep much.

Your habits or tendencies for how you use your "houses" or rooms will vary depending on how you live your life. These tendencies or differing qualities are determined by what sign falls on what house. One of the qualities, for example, that the sixth house represents is your work environment. If, in a chart, we were to find Sagittarius there, would you say that your client was very attentive to the neatness of their workspace? Of course not. You know Sagittarius to be somewhat obtuse about what is just beyond their nose. They don't even NOTICE that there IS an environment let alone a neat one. On the other hand, if we found Capricorn there, the environment would be extremely neat and controlled and they would be very aware if someone or something even ENTERED their workspace. In another light, with Capricorn there, we may find them to be a bit obsessive compulsive. Each sign color operates just a little differently depending on the house it's found on.

The "houses", then, represents specific activities of life whereas the signs that fall there color how we experience those activities. The houses are a constant or a template of what circumstances we will find in that number house. The signs that fall there will change from reading to reading and client to client.

Each house has signs that "feel more comfortable" there than on other houses. For example, for a house that represents finances and self-concept you would want to find a sign that was practical, consistent and "grounded." Taurus embodies those qualities. We would feel very comfortable with the activities of that house. Whereas, if we considered Gemini, the house would be more changeable, adaptable and much more mental than practical. Gemini would hardly be a fitting representative of solid and secure finances. However, there will be times in a reading where Gemini's qualities might prove to be an advantage, especially, if we needed to be fluid and flexible and mentally oriented in the resources we used.

As we discuss each house keep in mind that the sign offered as its best representative is only that; it's best representative. Statistically you have only one chance in twelve that the best representative will fall in its "home" position. Since the "money" house resonates best to an earth energy, consider that there are two other earth signs that could fall on the second enhancing its energy in different practical ways.

The best place to get an extended list of house meanings is in the *Rulership Book* by Rex Bills. With these ideas in mind let's continue with the descriptions and best representatives of each of the houses.

FIRST HOUSE

The first house pertains to two basic meanings; the client's immediate situation and/or how the client presents themselves. In astrology the best fit for the first is Aries. Aries is a cardinal fire sign. Cardinal means generative or projective.

The house relates to the projection of self or the display of a situation. This is, also, how other people see your client. Depending on what sign falls here will tell you what kind of perspective the client has on his or her situation and how they're perceived by others. If it's water, it will be emotional. If it's earth it will be material. If it's air it will be mental and if it is fire it will be intensely idealistic and/or physical. Generally, water and earth do not work well with the first hose which is normally a fire house (Aries). However, air feeds fire. Depending on what sign falls there will tell you what observable qualities will be brought to the forefront.

SECOND HOUSE

The second house pertains to the client's resources or the resources supporting the client's immediate situation. This includes money, possessions, earning capacity, abilities, disabilities, and any aspect of life that contributes to how we value ourselves and our environment. In astrology the best fit for the sign is Taurus. Taurus is a fixed earth sign. Fixed can be taken to mean concentrative, stable, focused and immovable. Here we can find the basis for our judgments, preferences.

The signs falling on and planets falling in the second house indicate changes and developments in our resources. If a cardinal or mutable sign falls here, this may indicate a new or fluctuating focus and/or influx involving resources. If air, new ideas on how support will be applied. If water, new feelings concerning resources or perhaps we are developing our feeling as a more dependable ability (psychic). If fire, maybe we are developing inspiration or intensity. The possibilities are endless and are dependent on your experience. The second house also rules the fourth, eight and twelfth child. The sign there often reveals their most common characteristics.

Integrating the signs and planets with life issues may seem difficult at first but with continued practice your unconscious will adapt to the process and begin to link your intuition to practical applications. Be patient and a whole new language will develop. It's the same process as learning to understand your dreams by developing a language that you can understand based on your experiences and how they're symbolized. It's YOUR experience that will give meaning to the signs, house and planets. Books and teachers only add possible information. Trust your "gut" and your first impression. First impressions are always right, you know!

THIRD HOUSE

The third house pertains to communication and/or any form of exchanging information or materials. This includes speaking, listening, brothers and sisters (who do you learn peer communications skills from?), neighbors, elementary school, short distance trips, commerce, computers, newspapers, etc. The sign ruling the third house is Gemini. Gemini is a mutable air sign. Mutable is adaptable, changeable and flexible. Because the sign is mutable it can also pertain to beginnings and endings in the realm of thought and communications. This house also includes our ability to speak and listen.

Also, remember, that if the sign that represents the best fit for the house, in this case Gemini, appears in another house, it links the issues of BOTH houses together. They affect each other with equal intensity. For example, if Gemini appeared on the eighth house this would suggest that our communicative ability might be dependent on other people's resources (eight house). How? Suppose we needed feedback from someone before we were able to perform a task or service for them? From the other perspective, they would be dependent on our communicative skills for the service that they could receive. We could add other contingencies by finding the most comfortable eighth house sign, Scorpio, on a completely different house thereby involving an additional set of circumstances and qualities from a different area of life. The possibilities are endless as are the experiences. Keep an open mind for the possibilities and trust your intuition.

FOURTH HOUSE

The fourth house corresponds to our home, family, Mom, foundations, roots, physical house or condo and beginnings and endings. This includes traditions and to whatever place we retreat to for security. The sign ruling the fourth house is Cancer. Cancer is a cardinal water sign. Cardinal is generative and water relates to feelings and their corresponding emotions. Please note that there is a difference between feelings and emotion. Feelings relate to what is felt at the moment of experience. It relates ONLY to the present; not the past or future. Emotions are our stored feelings previously attached to our accumulated experiences. These are SELF GENERATED. In general, the fourth house relates to our emotional history and our self-generated reactions to our upbringing and traditions. They show the emotional patterns that we feel the most secure with.

If we were to find the Capricorn on the fourth, Mom might be a businesswoman or maybe Dad is a stay at home dad performing Mom's role. If the five of wands appears there we may come from a physically abusive or physically challenging home. If Pisces appears here maybe Mom may have been the most compassionate person ever or had an substance problem or emotional issues were blown out of proportion. Obviously, these are only a few possibilities and we require corroborations from other houses, signs and planets in order to be certain as to what the issues actually are.

The Cancer brings all its issues and qualities with it no matter what house it falls on. If we were to find it on the seventh house (relationships), we might attract a mate that would "mother" us and take care of us as a child or, perhaps, we would find relationships where we would have to provide the mothering ourselves. If poorly aspected (badly connected to other houses and planets), we might find the need to control the relationship in order to maintain our narrative and security at any cost. Remember, in this case values and outside issues might be secondary. Security and status quo may be of prime concern. All other positions must concur.

FIFTH HOUSE

The fifth house pertains to children in general, childhood, the first and fifth child, recreation, "recreational" sex, gambling, creativity, romance, "recreational" sex and any form of enjoyment or pleasurable activity. The ruling sign is Leo, which is a fixed fire sign. Fixed is concentrative, stable, focused, immovable and receptive (yes, even for a fire sign!). Fifth house relates to recreation, creativity, play, vacations, amusements, gambling and how we give love. It also relates to children and specifically the first, fifth and ninth child.

If we were to find the Leo on the tenth house of career, we might find a career in recreation, art, theatre, children' s services or other issues that connect to the fifth house issues. As a career boss, they might even treat their employees as children or be playful with them.

The sixth house corresponds to health, work environment, pets, attitude toward service, (to self and to others) and attitude toward work in general. The sign that eels the most comfortable on the sixth house is Virgo. Virgo is a mutable earth sign. Mutable is reactive, adaptable, flexible and adjustable. Earth relates to all sorts of tangible and physical issues.

The sign falling on the sixth house indicate our patterns in health, habits, service and environment. If we were to find Scorpio here, we would find an unshakable worker strategizing through the worst of circumstances with resolve while also being able to keep a secret.

Since the sixth house is a major indicator of health, the sign that falls here will reveal volumes about our client's attitude toward health, the health of others and any maladies that might be present. Pisces here might also indicate issues with addiction or sensitivity with one's feet. Or the work they do might utilize a tremendous amount of compassion. Just use your creativity and intuition and let the meanings fall together.

When Virgo appears on other houses he brings with him all the issues and colors of the sixth house. For example, on the tenth house of career could indicate a career in medical, human or veterinary service. On the eighth house (other people's resources) could indicate an accountant. On the second, having or lacking discrimination with money.

The sixth house's connection to health lends itself to a unique way of determining what parts of the body are at risk for health issues. Generally, air indicates the nervous system, respiration and any communication between bodily systems and organs. Earth represents anything structural such as bones, teeth skin, gums, cartilage and nourishment relating to sugars, minerals and salts. Fire indicates circulation, blood, lymph system, toxicity and inflammation. Water indicates overall nourishment, fluids, liquids, hydration, semen, discharge, digestion, absorption and emotional components of health. Below you will find a chart that may be helpful.

For illness two conditions must be filled; first, there must be a hereditary disposition and second, there must be an emotional trigger that focuses strain on that particular part of the body. Please remember that these are only suggestions or possibilities. These signs and houses may relate more to other issues than health, especially, if your client is taking care of their health. DON'T jump to conclusions!

There are thousands and thousands of body parts, conditions and issues that each has their own astrological and tarot references. This included list is a simple generalization.

Sign-House	Body Part
Aries – 1st house	Head, eyes, mouth, ears, face & ears
Taurus – 2nd house	Neck, throat Eustachian tubes
Gemini – 3rd house	Shoulders, limbs, upper respiratory
Cancer – 4th house	Stomach, lower respiratory
Leo – 5th house	Heart, chest, brain & spine
Virgo – 6th house	Digestive system, malnutrition
Libra – 7th house	Lower back, kidneys
Scorpio – 8th house	Sexual organs, eliminative system
Sagittarius – 9th house	Thighs, spine
Capricorn – 10th house	Bones, teeth, skin gums, knees
Aquarius – 11th house	Ankles, nervous system, shins
Pisces – 12th house	Feet, infections, misdiagnosis

THE EXTERNAL OR MIRROR HOUSES
7 through 12

Until now, all the houses have been those that relate specifically to the self. They are internal and are not readily seen except through the reflection of the client's participation in the "other than self" world. The only exception is the first house which is how others perceive the client AND how the client internally perceives those "other than self." The first house, called the *ascendant*, serves as a gateway permitting the exchange of energy in and energy out of the chart. EVERYTHING must pass through this "lens." Like the lens on a motion picture projector, it filters and tints everything that comes in or goes out through the colors and shades of the signs and planets that are deposited on and in it. Its interpretation is purely subjective. With the addition of the next six houses, we add objectivity – we add the responses of the "other than self" world to the client's actions or inactions. Now, whenever one of the first six houses is activated it prompts a counter balancing response or decision by others based on the issues presented in the opposing house or the other house on its "axis." For example, the action of the second house must include the perceptions and responses connected to the eighth house. The same is true of the first and seventh, third and ninth, etc. The opposing house serves as a mirror to the "other than self" world. As we fold the bottom of the wheel over on the top we can see why. Examine the chart below:

SUBJECTIVE ACTION	OBJECTIVE RESPONSE
First house = I am	Seventh house = You are
Second house = I have	Eighth house = You have
Third house = I communicate	Ninth house = You communicate
Fourth house = I sustain	Tenth house = You sustain
Fifth house = I create	Eleventh house = You create
Sixth house = I serve	Twelfth house = You serve

This quality of opposition creates the awareness of others through their response, which, in turn, teaches us how to operate in the world without stepping on toes. We then make value judgments that set up our patterns for relating. This works with every *PAIR* of houses. I have and you have. I say, then you say, etc. This is a simple form of the law of karma. Whatever you give you must also receive or what goes around comes around. You can either work with this knowledge and have a smooth and steadily growing awareness or ignore this and occasionally get punched in the nose. With this awareness in mind let's proceed on to the first of our mirror houses.

SEVENTH HOUSE

The seventh house corresponds to partnerships, close friends, marriages, long-term contracts and "open" enemies (a different house relates to clandestine enemies). Libra is the most comfortable on this house. Libra is a cardinal air sign. Cardinal is generative or projective and air relates to mental functioning. This includes thought, whether it is abstract or concrete and the *quality* of communication. Everything seen through this house is seen as a relationship; person-to-person, person to career, person to home, person to family, idea to idea, etc.

This is the house where we see ourselves through the eyes of others. It's house through which we compare ourselves to the world when we want to assess our influence on it. It is who we attract in a relationship and the response to what we project onto others.

If we find Aries on the house we may attract a mate who is impatient or we may be the one who is impatient with others. If we find Sagittarius on the house, we may attract someone who is overly freedom conscious. If we have Scorpio on the house, someone who is emotionally closed and secretive. If we find Capricorn on the house, we may share a career (tenth house connection) with our mate. If we find Libra on the second, our relationships may be involved with our finances or shared possessions. The combinations are endless. Each sign colors our relationships differently.

EIGHTH HOUSE

The eighth house pertains to issues of death, sex, regeneration, other people's money (remember the axis?), banks, corporations, legacies and any resources or actions that can be taken or dealt with behind the scenes. The sign that rules this house is Scorpio. Scorpio is a fixed water sign. Fixed means concentrative, focused, immovable and receptive. Water is feelings and their corresponding emotions. Please remember the difference between feelings and emotions (see fourth house).

This is the house through which we judge another's character through their values and resources (opposite the second). Any vocation tied to the eight allows the placement or guidance of other people based on their abilities and disabilities. This house is dominant in counseling or advisement careers.

This eighth house represents the client's current attitude toward sex. Scorpio is the "let's get straight to it" sex. No foreplay. No amenities. What's the bottom line? The fifth house, on the other hand, is "recreational" sex. The fifth is the house of what we consider pleasurable, playful, and less "driven." This is what we do to have fun, not just satisfy the urge.

If we find Scorpio on the second house, we find someone who is very closed about their resources, finances and how they value themselves, others and their possessions. If we find Taurus on the eighth, the client will attract someone who is very solid, stable and consistent with their finances if not stingy and stubborn. If we find Sagittarius on the eighth, our client may attract someone who has big ideas about money or can't hold on to it. The eighth house also is involved in the "mine vs. theirs" battle (remember axis) which seems to interfere with their judgment of themselves and others.

Whatever sign is found here, remember, it *must* reflect and/or coordinate with what is happening in the second. Each house should be viewed through the eyes of relationship or axis in order to establish a balanced perspective. Light needs dark to define itself and vice versa.

NINTH HOUSE

The Ninth house pertains to higher learning, philosophy, other cultures, other cuisines, religion, long distance journeys, in-laws, other people's communication (axis to the third) and spiritual values. The sign that rules the house is Sagittarius. Sagittarius is a mutable fire sign. Mutable is reactive, adaptable, flexible and adjustable. Fire is intense, physical, intuitive, idealistic and action oriented.

With Capricorn on the house we might have someone with very conventional beliefs and with Aquarius there, perhaps, very avant-garde. If we found Taurus there we may have money issues (2nd house) interfering with travel or the client may have a very materialistic view of life and its values. The possibilities are endless. Never assume a conclusion must have a specific meaning about any planet or sign positioning and let your intuition be your guide. Verbalize what you see and what it relates to. Let your client confirm or deny if you like but if your intuition is working and you've got yourself "out of the way" you will, more than likely, be on target.

The tenth house pertains to our career, Dad, authority issues (inner *and* outer), our social status in the eyes of our public, material accomplishments, and what we must chose to sacrifice in order to gain it. It also includes our mate's home, family and traditional issues (axis to fourth house). The sign that rules this house is Capricorn. Capricorn is a cardinal earth sign. Cardinal is generative or projective. Earth relates to the tangible, usable material world and any medium that will allow itself to be measured on a "sense" oriented scale (sight, sound, etc.).

The sign on the tenth house and its ruling planet and placement would speak volumes about the career our client would presently be in or prefer to be in. If we found the Capricorn on just about any other house we would find that house somehow contributing to our client's career and social standing. Obviously, we might want to find Capricorn on the second or sixth house (natural earth houses) where these kinds of activities would benefit the issues of the house (practicalities). However, we would *not* want to find it on the fifth house of recreation or the ninth house of travel and mind expansion for obvious reasons.

In this particular house (usually cardinal and active) you must also consider what is in the fourth house of home and family. Remember…axis? Capricorn and Cancer, generally, have difficulty separating family responsibilities from career responsibilities. They seem to overflow into each other in terms of mental and emotional focus. When in one environment they often think about what they've forgotten to taken care of in the other. I often advise these clients to have a two-sided pad to write down what they remembered about the other environment to get it out of their head so they can concentrate on the tasks at hand. When in the other environment they should "flip" to the other side of the pad.

This house also represents the spiritual focus of the soul at present. It gives a good insight as to what issues must be learned and handled about any given situation.

ELEVENTH HOUSE

The eleventh house corresponds to love received, wages from the career (second house from the tenth), who we consider our friends to be and our attitude towards them, our aspirations, ability toward group participation, our mate's childhood, their ability to have fun and what they find pleasurable. The ruling sign is Aquarius, which is fixed air. Fixed means concentrative, focused, immovable and receptive. Air is mental, visual and intellectual.

Aquarius is considered to be an innovative thinker. This may be so in but some cases it may only seem that way to others because Aquarius doesn't verbalize the process that led to their conclusions so, to the onlooker, it is always a surprise from left field. Hence, the assumption that the eleventh house is our house of innovation. When Aquarius falls on other houses it brings that feeling of innovativeness if only because the mental path used in that house hasn't been verbalized by the client seeming like it's out of the box of what's expected.

If we find Sagittarius on the eleventh, the client may have grandiose ideas about what their accomplishments might be or may consistently receive exorbitant pay raises. If Pisces is there, they may allow themselves to be used by others in their career or everyone in the workplace may come to them with their problems. If an earth sign appears there, our client may be too down to earth or restrictive in their aspirations to allow their dreams to manifest. If an air sign appears there, the mental qualities will lend themselves very well for planning how to use career related resources to acquire their goals. The possibilities are as endless as there are people. Be flexible and let your intuition speak.

THE TWELFTH HOUSE

The twelfth house corresponds to that which we are unaware of, self-induced patterns of our undoing, anything we feel imprisoned by, the unconscious, the sleep state, dreams, the "basement" where we "throw" the things we don't want to deal with, the unconscious factors that contribute to any illnesses that appear in the sixth house and a tremendous reservoir of empathetic, intuitive and creative artistic possibilities. It is ruled by Pisces, which is mutable, and its element is water. Mutable is reactive, adaptable, flexible, and adjustable. Water represents feelings and their corresponding emotions. Please remember the difference between feelings and emotions (see the fourth house).

This house is where we divest ourselves of all the feelings and qualities we don't want to acknowledge, let alone accept, about ourselves. Remember, pair of houses acts as an axis. This makes the sixth house the most poignant location for the exit of those unacknowledged qualities in the form of diseases and ailments whether physical, emotional or mental. This is the basis of the twelfth house representing the unseen or clandestine enemies. Whatever we repress, including undesirable qualities of ourselves, causes a vacuum in the opposing house drawing to us what is needed from the outside world to rebalance the inequities. This becomes our undoing. Whatever we fear or hate is drawn to us through some form of twisted person or circumstance exhibiting an aberrant and unnatural pattern within us such as a mental disorder or disease attempting to expose what we don't want to acknowledge or face about ourselves. What we repress in ourselves we will empathize coming from others and react to it, even if we don't recognize it.

It is the house where we feel paranoia and feelings of persecution but, also, the potential for creative genius. Through this house we can follow the energy threads from one person to another or from one abstract concept to another through the invisible web that connects us all. At times we may not be aware of this and "pick up" the thoughts and feelings of those we have had a recent rapport with. The hard part is figuring out what is actually ours and what we're picking up through our "antenna."

There are two things we can do to make this easier, or at least, recognizable. We can either meditate to discover what is "not self" or we can invest ourselves in some form of artistic, creative, expressive endeavor that utilizes and focuses this energy into a project or "mode" of attention. This way the emotional energy is grounded and we don't feel like a cork on the ocean under the influence of everyone else's emotional tides. This will also diminish the pressure leading to disease.

The sign on the twelfth house cusp will reveal those qualities we have the most difficulty integrating back into our consciousness. This is the house that everyone finds the most challenging for reintegrating back into conscious self by virtue of the fact that this is the refuse pile we throw everything into that we don't want to see or deal with. This is truly a karmic house.

The planets we find here or the ruler of the sign that appears on its cusp are the keys for unlocking our fears and self-imposed limitations. Any air sign will contribute to poor sleep and regenerative time due to the static created by a chattering mind. Additionally, fire will create too much energy to ground during sleep. The sign will tell us the qualities we have the most difficulty with.

Lastly and again, I cannot emphasize the importance of the twelfth house enough. Generally, we are a culture that represses anything that goes against the grain of our conditioning. The repository of these repressed factors is, always, the twelfth house. This makes the circumstances of this house extremely important in how our actions in daily life are filtered and manifested. Delineate this house very carefully and NEVER assume any factors are in play unless you can confirm them through the cards on the other houses.

THE VISITORS

Before we begin delineating the "meanings" of the planets, we need to consider exactly what they are and what they do. Most astrologers interpret them in terms of something that yields a type of useful energy to the client as a result of their sign position at birth. When they move through the signs we might say that they're seen as rocks passing through space and when they pass a place and time that's important to us, our birth time and place, they drop something off that we can either accept or reject; much like a truck drops off a delivery. Then, the planets continue moving on to "other deliveries" for other people, times, and places. You might say that the position of our planets at birth is a snapshot or still-life of energies that are at our disposal to use throughout our lives. The house will determine *how* what's dropped off will be of use to us and the sign will determine its *flavor, style, and tangible characteristics* of their expression and whether making it useful will be easy or not.

The natal planets (their still-life birth positions) begin affecting us the moment we take our first breath spiritually "cementing" us into beginning our composite earthly lessons and experiences. This is much like a house builder dropping off the raw materials just as construction begins. This is also why it is so important to obtain the birth time and birthplace otherwise the building materials will be dropped off at the wrong address and wrong date and the snapshot of planetary positions will be off invalidating any predictive timing.

When I speak of mundane or daily ordinary earthly matters, I speak of astrology being done from an *exoteric* perspective (essentially tangible). This is the perspective that most astrology books, especially beginning books, operate from. They will talk about earthly events, tangible occurrences and issues that will pertain to material outcomes. There is nothing wrong with this way of ascribing "meaning" to the planets, houses and signs. It is simply the most tangible and materialistic perspective available to us for interpretations. *Exoteric* interpretation will lend itself best toward scientific proofs and assessments.

The *native* (client) who operates from an *exoteric* perspective, which most people do, sees the astrologer as having the potential to tell them how they could make the best use of what they've been given in the tangible world. How many children will they have? Will they be married? Will they move? Will they stay healthy? Will they move and a whole plethora of expectantly conclusive determinations. The fact that most of these quests can only be answered potentially never occurs to the client. The assumption is that predictions are written in stone. Most people believe that worldly circumstances are ordained by fate or a deity. It's a very rare individual indeed who actually believes that their fate is solely a function of their choices.

Clients will also expect to get the jump on when the next "delivery" (progressions and transits) will occur and what it will "drop off" or "pick up." In these dimensions, each planet has its own set of *exoteric* characteristics that specify what objects they "rule" on the physical plane. I will only touch on that type of mundane information in these short pages, so, if you are interested in pursuing those specifics in more depth, you may consult *The Rulership Book* by Rex Bills. It covers the planets, houses, and the signs in terms of physical or mundane rulership.

Like us, the planets have their physical manifestations, but they are also much more. They are a dynamic life form. They are a living energy. If we are going to look at the planets and what they represent in a more *esoteric* light, we must view them as a dynamic ever-changing energy. Hence, rather than viewing them as a manifestation (static like a photograph), they should be perceived as a fluid and moving *process*. The type of meaning we will want to ascribe is as a *verb* rather than as an *object*. If we look at a planet from an *exoteric* perspective, its presence in a house will be much like ingredients added to a bowl as in preparing a meal, inanimate like sugar or salt. However, if look at it from an *esoteric* perspective (dynamic), their presence in a house is active much like a hand holding a spoon that would actively mix the ingredients in the bowl. We can understand this better if we imagine Mars fulfilling this role in a house.

The presence of Mars produces action. The spoon itself, a tool, may be represented by Mars *exoterically*. But the *esoteric* component, or the energy it brings, is the process that it applies, stirring. In another example, if we were dealing with bread, it would be put into an oven where *exoteric* Saturn would manifest the oven and pan and the *esoteric* Sun and Pluto would heat and transform it. The *esoteric* planets bring the opportunity for growth and change through energy and dynamism and change. In humans this *usually* brings increased awareness. Hence, we start to "wake up" from our reactive slumber.

For the purpose of deepening your awareness of how the planets will act under different circumstances I have included a chart that shows their corresponding names throughout history. This will assist you in examining the similarity of their application in different cultural and religious formats. As you look at the chart you will notice that prior to the Greeks and the Romans there are no names for the outer planets. Prior to these civilizations Uranus, Neptune and Pluto were unknown to the common man. Their symbolic meanings laid deep within their unconscious waiting to surface as human evolution slowly progressed enough to include them in their conscious evolutionary landscape.

	BABYLONIAN	HINDU	EGYPTIAN	GREEK	ROMAN
☉	Shamash	Ravi	Ra	Helios	Apollo (Sol)
⚲				Hephaestus	Vulcan
☽	Sin	Chandra	Chomse	Artemis	Diana (Luna)
☿	Nabu	Buddha	Thoth	Hermes	Mercurius
♀	Ishtar	Sukra	Hathoor	Aphrodite	Venus
⊕				Gaea	Earth
♂	Nergal	Kuja	Horus	Ares	Mars
♃	Marduk	Guru	Amoun	Zeus	Jupiter
♄	Ninurta	Sani	Sebek	Kronos	Saturnus
♅				Ouranus	Uranus
♆				Poseidon	Neptune
♇				Hades	Pluto

In the figure to the right is a diagram of the rulerships prior to the Greek and Roman civilizations. Please note that Mercury, Venus, Mars and Jupiter each have *dual* rulerships. Each rules an active sign (fire or air) and a receptive sign (earth or water). These are traditionally referred to as day or night rulerships respectively. Saturn rules two signs and the Sun and Moon each rule one. This diagram exemplifies what Alice Bailey refers to as the *orthodox* rulerships. The mundane *orthodox*

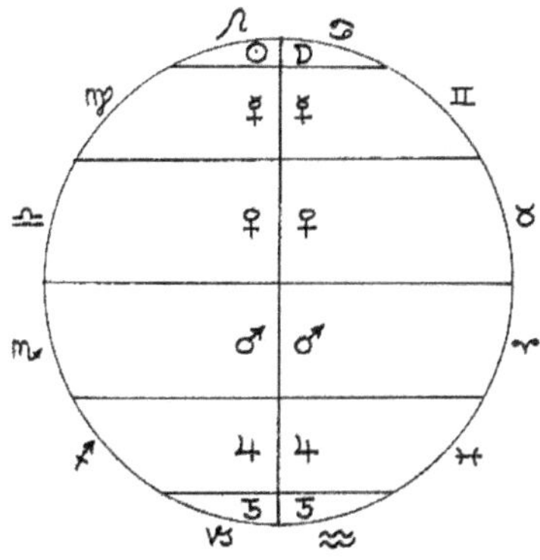

rulerships can be held as synonymous with the *exoteric* rulerships. I will use them interchangeably throughout the rest of this book.

In increasing distance away from the Sun, the order of planets in our solar system are Mercury, Venus, Earth & Moon, Mars, Jupiter and Saturn. The trans-Saturnian planets (outside the orbit of Saturn) were known to the Greeks and Romans only through their mythology. They were gods called Ouranus (Uranus), Poseidon (Neptune) and Hades (Pluto) and obviously contributed subtle effects on the primitive life of the time, were not recognized and as such were assigned only nebulous qualities devoid of any *exoteric* rulerships. After their discovery much later, observable Uranus was assigned to Aquarius, Neptune to Pisces and Pluto to Scorpio.

When delineating *exoteric* (tangible) circumstances, the simple or mundane meanings for each of the *inner* Saturnian planets should be used. After the discovery of the observable trans-Saturnian planets, *exoteric* meanings were assigned to Uranus, Neptune and Pluto in as much as they were fitting to the emerging circumstances of the era that they were discovered in. But their mundane co-rulers, Saturn, Jupiter and Mars, could also symbolize the new developments of the time. Even though Uranus was discovered in 1781 by William Herschel, the industrial revolution can still be explained with Aquarius' co-ruler Saturn. As Neptune was discovered in 1846 by Urbain Le Verrier, the worldwide explosion in exploration of the unknown could also be explained through Pisces' co-ruler Jupiter. And as Pluto was being discovered by Percival Lowell in 1930, the discovery of atomic energy could be explained by Scorpio's co-ruler Mars in the sign of hidden resource and energy. Since Uranus, Neptune and Pluto are all trans-Saturnian, I feel it's best to apply to them *trans-physical* world issues that are *esoteric* or more subtle and energetic in their nature. For the grosser, more tangible interpretations I prefer to use the inner Saturnian co-ruling planets.

On a different note, there is tremendous insight and understanding that can be gained by reading the Greek and Roman mythology behind each of the planets. Their stories and their lore will touch us on a primal level far below the threshold of our conscious mind.

As we begin to cover the action of each planet, it's important to note that Sun and Moon should be viewed and handled in a slightly different manner than the others. I will leave them until last along with the planet Vulcan of which there is considerable controversy as to the validity of its "existence" and acceptance into the astrologer's consideration for delineation. Although we astrologically call each planet by its Roman name, I have included the Greek names in the beginning so that you may remember to research their mythology in order to gain a deeper and more thorough understanding of what energies each planet brings into our daily lives.

In astrological tradition Mercury has been accepted as being the sole representative of communication. Under its purveyance are the forms of communication such as speaking, writing, and listening and all the tools that make that more easily and technically possible such as the telephone, computer, radio, television, the US mail, UPS and on and on. Aside from its traditional meanings, Mercury represents, essentially, the flow or *exchange* of energy.

Communication is nothing more than the exchange of goods and information. We can attribute the goods exchanged to the *exoteric* realm. The fact that they are tangible and static is self-explanatory. However, even though *what* is being exchanged may be tangible and may yield tangible results, the process of exchange, itself, is not. The process, or essence of Mercury's dynamic movement of energy, is *esoteric*.

The exchange of information, from the perspective of the communicator, is almost always done with a purpose and intention in mind. This intention is in line with what the communicator prefers or avoids. His intended goal is almost always to create and maintain an end result in a preferred static or tangible state. However, regardless of the purpose or intention or how it relates to what the communicator chooses, the net effect, through *dynamic* movement, will be to continually broaden the potential perspectives of understanding concerning the information and goods. That is, in spite of the communicator's wishes, the process will continue to "fill in the blanks" and increase understanding and clarity by continually adding more "facts" and information as long as communication is allowed to progress. This process of clarifying our understanding by bringing more and more into the light I call *elucidation*. *Elucidation* is my distilled keyword for the energy process of Mercury.

In looking at this from another perspective, we can say that when Mercury is natally posited or transits (moves through) a house, the issues of the house can never rest in a static state due its dynamic fluidity. This is exhibited through Mercury's natural representative metal, quicksilver. It may be contained in a container such as a thermometer, but its natural state still remains the same; fluid and having no static shape.

Mercury's energy may oscillate between polarities such as male and female, hot and cold, left and right, spirit and matter, but its motion is always in the process of exchange between its polarities. In this way Mercury is sexless. If allowed its natural motion, its action in Gemini continually broadens the perspective inclusiveness and scope of polarity and its action in Virgo constantly refines discrimination.

There are two directions that Mercury can take when coupled with the ego. (*Please note that when I refer to the ego, I am not referring to pride. In psychological terms, our ego is the structure our mind uses to interact with the rest of the world. Knowing this, let's move on.*) If the ego operates from an unstable perspective, that is, reacting to external circumstances from an insecure or fear generated motive, the native will use energy of Mercury to "erect fences" or close off the potential for undesired results. They will use the energy to *condense* (Virgo influence) the world into manageable or controllable sized pieces, so they feel more secure with the minimal abilities they perceive themselves as possessing. The more insecure they feel, the stronger the push toward minimizing Mercury's movement.

They may also preserve their security by moving in the opposite direction by *scattering* the energy (Gemini influence) so their insecurities are overlooked by others. In observable behavior both these tactics will show themselves as insensitivity, nitpicking, an inability to listen, disrupting the flow of conversation and/or circumstances and "over talking" others. Essentially, this is an attempt to collapse or scatter the focus of the energy into a physical, non-threatening, static, immoveable, and preferred state. In metaphysical terms we say this action is involutionary as opposed to evolutionary. In human terms we call this either clenching or *scattering* the focus. In halting or dispersing the movement of Mercurial energy the native believes that they are minimizing uncertainty and their risk of the exposure to others of their self-perceived insecurities.

If the ego operates from a reasonably secure perspective, which is, acting on circumstances from an *internally* generated motive of creativity, self-confidence and fun, the native will use energy of Mercury to "tear down fences" or open the potential for *allowing* growth-oriented results. They will have enough confidence in themselves for handling what comes up and to let the "chips fall where they may." In essence, they are accepting the feedback of others and life as it unfolds their own "dharma." Dharma is our own natural inclination to take us through circumstances that will produce *evolution* within us. This is achieved by going through a process of *unclenching* to allow the energy full freedom of movement. In observable behavior this will show itself as possessing ability for patience, listening, observing and teaching.

One note of caution; when observing the "tearing down of fences" we must ascertain that this action is *not* being taken to remove the defenses of a perceived threat to the *involutionary* ego. Additionally, some individuals may be *evolutionary* in some aspects of life but *involutionary* in others. We must remember that this is a process that is ongoing and must discriminate very carefully.

VENUS or Aphrodite

Traditionally, Venus has been accepted as being the representative of beauty, love and pleasure. Under her purveyance is all that we consider personally preferable. Such subjects would usually include those that we feel are beautiful, ideal, pleasurable, peaceful, tactful (Libra), artful, and pleasing to the senses (Taurus). Aside from its traditional meanings, Venus, essentially, employs the process of *decision*. In this light, that which we find *not* preferable must also be included such as ugly, disgusting, gross, displeasing, barbaric, etc.

To attribute such a word as *decision* may seem overly simplistic and insensitive to the breadth of qualities that Venus can potentially provide. Yet, in order to determine what our preferred state is, a *decision* is required. Our *decision* results from a personal choice based on our judgment or assessment between our options. That judgment can come from our personal experiences or through accepting the assessments of others of whom we trust. If from our personal experience, it can be considered an internal assessment and accepting the judgment of another can be considered an external assessment. Regardless of the origin of our motivation for the assessment, we still feel the need to separate what we feel is true from what we have decided is not. Since we have chosen something to be true, we now ascribe a *belief* that says this is so. Since belief is a factor of choice leading to a *decision*, we can now assert that *belief* is a major concept under Venus' jurisdiction.

In addition to what we find preferable, Venus' connection to the second house represents how we value, assess, or judge ourselves. The type of value we assess depends on the element found on the second house cusp. If earth, we judge ourselves tangibly or by what we have or own. If water, we judge ourselves by what we feel. If air, we judge ourselves by what we think and if fire, we judge ourselves by what we can do or intuit. Venus' position elsewhere in the chart will broaden these effects to a large extent according to the house and sign she's found in. Once we have judged our own value (internal), or let others do so (external), we can now determine in what ways we can trust ourselves and what ways we can't (won't). Some of these ways we will be able to admit to ourselves and the ways in which we are unable to do so, we will unconsciously attribute these qualities, preferable or not, to others. Hence, Venus is a prime contributor to the creation of our internal *shadow*. (The *shadow* is what we prefer to not see or acknowledge about ourselves and project onto others).

Since our trust and belief are connected to Venus, we can also say that *faith* comes under her jurisdiction also. *Faith* is what we have chosen to believe will occur. It will be where and how we invest our energy (having faith) and where we will be reticent to do so (lacking faith). The issue of what we choose to believe about ourselves and why is almost exclusively the domain of Venus. The concepts of choice and belief are the basic building blocks for the foundation of human psychology. In a later discussion on fifth ray energy, we will examine this and how Venus is connected to Concrete Science.

When Venus is posited in or transits a house, it applies the energy of *decision*. This will appear in the form of a need or a propensity. It will percolate the values concerning the house and, hopefully, bring them to the surface of our awareness that we may *prioritize* them. Hence, our assertion of what we consider important. Venus' presence in a house also provides a doorway through the circumstances of the house, that is, allowing us to recognize and work with our *shadow*.

Since Venus has a connection to others through the seventh house through its normal rulership of Libra, it is there that we can see our preferences and aversions as reflected through the people we choose as companions and open enemies. Those whom we choose as close companions usually agree with our strongest beliefs protecting our *chosen* self-identity. Those whom we treat as open enemies we perceive as threatening and feel will undermine those beliefs. By keeping this separation intact, we are able to keep ourselves distanced from the qualities we have assigned to our *shadow* thereby maintaining our current self-image free of deprecating qualities. This temporarily eliminates the risk of exposing our *shadow*.

Sometimes the minimizing of this threat is accomplished through collusion by establishing or joining a group with similar preferences. Anonymity and safety in numbers becomes an added insulator against the possible erosion of our self-concept and the exposure of our *shadow* while enhancing our more preferable qualities through mutual support and protection. Consider, also, that because a value or standard is held in esteem by a group, this poses no guarantee as to its validity. A widely held *belief* can be based on faulty premises and be completely in error, yet, be trusted as true by a large majority of people. Consider Europe's *belief* about the world based on the acceptance of the simple statements that the world is flat or that the sun rotates around the earth. In some cases, to disagree with these statements resulted in death at the hands of those who were "true believers." In this light, consider that beauty isn't the only thing in the eye of the beholder. Venus also rules the out of balance beliefs of "true believers" (chosen decisions about self and the world).

One of the hallmarks of personal growth, especially on an *esoteric* level, is the acceptance and reintegration of the *shadow* (projected undesirable qualities) back into our self-concept. There are two distinct paths of behavior available to our native: *involution* and *evolution*.

In the *involutionary* frame we are back to clenching or scattering and whatever action will maintain a preferably static image of ourselves through retaining the *shadow* in its submerged and out of the public eye and conscious awareness. This may occur on an individual and/or group level. Behaviors that are indicative of this type of focus are visible in the native who employs a "tit for tat" interaction with others, contrived excuses for behavior through assigning blame or absolving themselves of responsibility in situations that they might perceive as appearing to expose inadequacy, dishonesty, fear, or any other of a whole host of qualities that might be considered undesirable and relegated to *shadow*.

In light of the fact that no choice can be considered a choice through inaction, we can also include simple indecision and procrastination as *involutionary* in that there is an unwillingness to commit for fear of possible exposure of the *shadow* and risking a diminished self-image.

In the *evolutionary* frame we want to allow choiceless awareness. On first perusal this looks like an oxymoron statement but let's look closer to see why this applies. To most minds, choice is selecting one option and rejecting another. The problem with the current perception of choice is that through choosing it is implied that what is not chosen is to be resisted and pushed away. Please understand that whatever we choose between has coexisted in balance before we encountered the need to make a choice. Our choice does not change anything between the two options except that by moving with or toward one, we assert an inner directiveness, or *dharma*, relative to our existence. Can we move cleanly in one direction without the need to push what's not chosen away? If so, where, then, does the need to push away what we don't choose come from within us? It comes from the mind. In our mind's need to be able to identify itself as a separate entity or ego, it must establish a framework or language in which to perceive itself. Like yin and yang, that framework exists within a field of polarity. Like a rubber band, in pulling one half and pushing away the other, the mind creates a tension. That tension produced by the mind is what we *feel and accept* as our sense of self. In this way it makes the self-feel tangible. Yet, we must remember that we *are not* our mind but, that we *have* a mind. The question we must then ask is who is doing the pulling and pushing?

Let's look at an example. If we come to a fork in the road, our mind creates doubt, through comparison, about which path to traverse. As we begin to move down one fork, our mind will hold on to the concept of the other fork not chosen through the doubt created just like the rubber band. This doubt is an attachment to what we have pushed away and gives us a sense of self through the tangible tension it produces.

The more intense the feeling of tension, the stronger is the sense of self. Through the mind, then, we are just as much defined by what we don't choose as by what we do. *Any* form of comparison is a product of the mind and creates a stress and tension through maintaining a connection to both options.

The human mind builds a list of preferences extracted from its experience that delineates a proposed path. This produces a feeling of certainty and purpose. Choiceless awareness is beyond the minds influence. *If we accept doubt and uncertainty as part of life's path and simply move in the direction that the flow feels "right" (dharma) without making a judgment, there is no tension produced and we move with choiceless awareness.* There is no rubber band effect and therefore no tension. With no tension there is no self. The essence of selflessness is no attachments. This produces a sense of feeling whole. In this way, the mind's involvement has been relegated to its proper place; simply as a tool for continuing on a path.

Polarity can be exemplified by yin and yang and exists as a function of discrimination through Mercury. Yet, yin and yang need each other for definition. Black needs white to define itself and white needs black to define itself, but, independent of our minds, they have been in balance with each other throughout time. Venus is the process of bringing those polarities back into balance. The true beauty of Venus occurs at the point of natural balance. Why should we be any different?

The *esoteric* use of the energies of Venus is accomplished through *commitment* and *responsibility*. These qualities reflect our ability to acknowledge and accept our culpability and accountability for situations we've participated in. There is no room for the creation of a *shadow*. Underlying this is the acceptance of uncertainty as a fact of life and resisting the urge to "tie up the loose ends" which makes our "lower" polarity-oriented mind feel ungrounded and incomplete. This underlying acceptance is, essentially, the release of the need to crystallize a feeling of security through attempting to make life circumstances remain separate and static.

The *commitment* I speak of is sticking to a path once we have recognized it as our *dharma*. It is a path that doesn't allow the mind to react to its need for the establishment of a preferred external identity that packages our life description like a static snapshot. Instead, it remains moving. It remains unattached. It allows the world to remain unexplained. It accepts the premise that life is balanced and that we either move with it or against it; we either unravel karma or create it. It strives to reduce the suffering of tension through the nullifying of desire. The *responsibility* I speak of is the *ability to respond* or the mindfulness of remaining open and available to life and all of its mystery and uncertainty. Venus challenges us to diminish our *shadow* by being open, aware, detached, allowing and mindful in dealing with the issues active in the house she appears in.

MARS or Ares

Traditionally and simplistically, Mars has been accepted as the representative of action, force, aggression, libido, sexuality, competition, sports, combat, military, strength, assertion, ambition or any movement of energy that reacts to or counteracts an external force or inertia. That is, we observe and are motivated into action by circumstances that appear to be in resistance to our intended direction. The sign Mars appears in will determine the form that these actions will take: idealistic, physical, mental, or emotional. The key point to be aware of, especially if we are operating from an *exoteric* (tangible) perspective, is that our motivational stimulus originates from perceiving something in the tangible world that seems to externally inhibit our movement. Within the framework of maintaining our physical survival, there is nothing wrong with this perspective. However, if all our action is in *reaction* to worldly external stimuli, we will perpetually bounce from stimulus to stimulus, in order of their appearance, until our energy becomes depleted but to what end? In this, there appears to be no other focus than our worldly physical, emotional, or mental survival. Yet, of what use will Mars be when that is accomplished? If the needs for safety, comfort and pleasure have been met, what then? Is that all there is?

In another light this impetus can be taken as a mere cosmic tool, geared toward getting us up and out of our comfort zone and trotting in the direction of imagined security, comfort and pleasure. And when we arrive, we find that through the understanding of our actions we are no better off than when we started. We then wonder why we took any action at all. Mars' appearance in a house performs just that function. It makes us aware that there is more in life to aspire to than the simple survival and comfort goals associated with the house. Mars leads us to a place where we question our motivations. What are our goals beyond our simple physical comforts and security? The emptiness we arrive at, after satisfying our worldly needs, leads us toward questioning the existence of a creator and asking why we are here. The answer cannot be comprehended while we still exist in the physical plane; however, we continue asking the question even more strongly each time we arrive at the same empty place. The struggle for survival appears to be the universe's way of overcoming our tendency toward mental, emotional, and physical inertia. You might say that leads toward an enforced "devotion" toward seeking a higher meaning. There is a desire in us to arrive at something more than what we are aware of. It fosters hope; an open and accepting attitude toward life knowing we *don't* know it but wish to. This is the quality inherent in the *esoteric* side of Mars; the drive toward something larger than our physical, emotional, and mental existence. The house position will show the area of life that we need to "get moving" in order to create new growth in our perspective and understanding or our journey here.

Exoteric Mars, in its worst personification, will show itself as violent, obsessively competitive and with malicious tendencies born of early abuse and/or neglect stemming from this life or a prior one. The placements of Saturn, Uranus, Neptune, and Pluto play vital parts in unwinding this *involutionary* implosion. The road back to balance is eminently long and fraught with all manner of self-destructive beliefs that block the path toward regaining *Self-Trust* in our *dharma*.

The appearance of Mars in a house not only gives us a tangible and expanded strength for survival concerning the issues of the house he's found in, but also, shows us where we can find our individual path toward expressing our uncovering of and then devotion toward a higher cause. The rulership of Mars first occurs, *exoterically* (tangibly), where we attempt to overcome the physical plane inertia of our body, emotions and mind, and then *esoterically* (energetically) where we dig for, find, and intensify our higher motivation.

Traditional meanings for Jupiter include growth, abundance, *expansion*, excess, extremes, exaggeration, largesse, bulk, acceleration, augmentation, intensity or any state or action that will transform a situation beyond its expected limits or borders. Some of the more vague and archaic meanings include good luck, beneficence, prosperity, grace or any personally preferable state or situation. The underlying assumption, especially in this culture, becomes the belief that more is better. However, more might then be *expanded* into pomposity, audaciousness, conceit, righteousness, greed, insatiability, addiction, and all qualities that are representative of the native being unable to discriminate when enough has been reached. On a more positive note, however, these energies can be *expanded* through gregariousness, generosity, compassion, insight, learning, healing and in situations where the expansion can be interpreted as preferable, even if beyond the expected limits.

Jupiter's appearance in the houses applies an energy designed to move the issues of the house beyond their current limitations and bring wisdom in doing so. In this light Jupiter's relation to Saturn, the energy of *consolidation* is extremely important in that a strategic placement of Saturn will act as governor restricting the movement of *expansion* to any excess. This allows *expansion* to move past the ego's limits of perceived security without the risk of blowing one side of a polarized identity out of proportion. This will serve to prevent overcompensation on the ego's behalf.

Jupiter's connection to the ninth house, the house of other people's thought and communication, creates an environment of potential for learning. Hence, its connection to philosophy, or more appropriately labeled, life perspective. It makes us aware of how other people think and live and awakens us to the possibilities of a broader life perspective. This also brings various religions into focus; or makes us aware of the traditions held that include deities as a focal point outlining appropriate behavior generic to a specific culture and perpetuating a consistency in their way of life. Jupiter can then assist us in seeing beyond the traditions, whether religious or philosophical, that have become too restrictive. The key here is to teach us to develop an open mind through hearing the perspectives of others.

Jupiter's connection to the twelfth house is a little different. Here we have the potential to learn tolerance, acceptance, and patience through compassion. Traditionally the twelfth house has been representative of the unconscious, prisons, and the circumstances of our own undoing. On first look, this might seem like an ominous and scary place to visit, but, on a deeper examination this can be a place of redemption. Although the religious implications of the word are included, the meaning goes much, much further. To understand this will have to revisit our discussion of the *shadow*.

Remembering that one of the actions in forming the *shadow* is taking parts of ourselves that are felt to be inappropriate and unacceptable to us *and* others and suppressing them below the surface of our awareness. That place is here in the twelfth. In assuming that others cannot see these qualities either, we deceive ourselves as to their transparency to others through the properties of Neptune; co-ruler of Pisces and the twelfth. Essentially, we are putting parts of ourselves in "prison." In attempting to prevent their surfacing we exert a tremendous amount of energy plugging all the holes in our activities where recognition of these qualities might escape their imprisonment and hence be acknowledged…by us or others where our intended image would be blown. A "Freudian Slip" is an example of seepage overcoming the stress of suppression. The more we stuff, the more energy that is required to maintain their cloaking. Jupiter's action tends to expand these suppressed issues beyond our ability to keep them contained. Hence, we have the twelfth house's reputation for being the place of undoing.

These suppressed qualities surface in areas where we least expect. One of the most common vents for this compressed energy is the sixth house of health. Whatever is compressed in the twelfth always finds a route out through the sixth house of health, especially, if we choose to not willingly address the issues. Of course, all these areas are ones that we have not guarded since we are not aware of their potential exposure. Jupiter's placement and aspects to other planets and cusps will show us the easiest flow and place for the willing unmasking of our *shadow*.

One of the major payoffs for unmasking our *shadow* is redeeming the energy used to suppress the qualities we perceive as being undesirable. In this, Pluto plays a very strong part which we will discuss later as Pluto has a very strong rulership connection to Pisces and the twelfth house. The unmasking can occur voluntarily if we strive to be more aware of, accountable for and sympathetic to our attraction to the immediate issues of others. Or it can occur through our polarized repulsion and avoidance of others and with the help of unexpected, and sometimes explosive, circumstances involving Uranus. Either way, however, unmasking is necessary and inevitable if we are to grow in awareness and spiritual maturity.

Voluntary unmasking occurs as we actively work with the *shadow* by observing the people and circumstance we attract as mirrors of the most imminent qualities needing to emerge from the "basement" of our discarded traits. These qualities emerge much like a magician pulling an endless number of scarves from a hat which have been tied together. Our willingness to observe and accept what we receive from those we are most affected by is the first door toward developing forgiveness and understanding or ourselves. This self-forgiveness slowly evolves into a *conscious* attitude of *unconditionality* toward others and their apparent portrayal of our unwanted traits. This is where intense work is needed to overcome the instinct of the insecure ego to protect itself. It is no accident that Jupiter is the planet of love and wisdom.

One important note; *unconditionality* does not imply that we are accepting of any kind of abuse from others. Turning the other cheek does not mean offering the other cheek for assault. Turning simply implies walking away without retaliation. This reflects wisdom in choosing our battles.

SATURN or Kronos

Over many years Saturn has become maligned and misrepresented as being undesirable, to be feared, avoided, and resisted at every appearance. Nothing should be further from the truth. If we did not have bones, which are ruled by Saturn, our bodies would fall into a pool of jelly. If we did not have gravity, which is ruled by Saturn, we would never have developed life on Earth as our atmosphere and oceans would have drifted off into space. Saturn traditionally rules all things pertaining to structure which includes containers, fences, building (verb and noun), borders, gravity, weight, atoms, intellect, logic, philosophy, math and an infinite list of things relative to the physical world structure, its organization and its limits. Some of the more vague, archaic and illiterate meanings consist of malevolence, evil, restriction, punishment, illness, imprisonment, fate, karma, vengeance and a whole host of undesirable circumstances and conditions that the unevolved person would wish to escape. To put it in an absurdly simple perception, the house placement of Saturn shows us where we need to "fess up" and "grow up."

Until 1781, Saturn was the furthest known planet in our solar system. It and its rings then symbolized containment, the limits of understanding and the known physical universe.

In a wider focus we can view Saturn as relating to structure in all forms of consolidating, building, accruing, gathering, organizing, closure, sacrificing, patterns, cycles and cause and effect. In distilling his actions and effects we can derive the concept of our attempting to arrive at some form of *completion*. Essentially, all physical action moves in cycles that have a beginning and an end. In a cycle, the ending point is the return to the place of beginning. If you draw a circle, you finish when you return to where you began. When we throw a ball up in the air, it falls back to where it was launched from. If we heat something up, it eventually cools down. All polarities are cyclic in nature and seek to return toward their initial state. In physics, one of the terms used to describe this is the dynamic of entropy and is also ruled by Saturn. This movement is the operating dynamic in karma. This is where we get the saying," What goes around comes around."

In a broader sense, we humans begin our initial state, or physical existence, in the womb with all our needs taken care of. We float carefree in the womb (a container). As a fetus, we feel much like what an adult would experience in a desensitization tank. When we are born, the shock of birth and the need to survive polarizes us against the external world. Our adjustment toward coping with that world then happens in spurts or stages of growth and awareness that plateau or level out for quiet times between the spurts. These stages are loosely set in a general time schedule dictated or reflected through the transits of Saturn. This schedule itself is a cyclic pattern. In the current average lifespan, Saturn returns to its original place three times. Returning to the initial state or starting point the third time marks the occurrence of a third transformation or transition; generally physical death give or take a few years.

With the "advancing" field of medicine attempting to extend the time of our incarnation; we would expect to find that our new life expectancy extended to one hundred twelve years or to a fourth Saturn cycle of twenty-eight years each. However, unless our species evolves a "higher" Saturnian consciousness and in the light of how we have been perverting the quality our food supply and environment, I think that is a slim possibility. Medical efforts, having thus far attempted to exclude any "hint" of mystery or spirituality, have truly remained exoteric in their nature of endeavors.

The *completion* of each cycle is actually the death of the prevailing cycle of a circumstantial structure through its morphing into a new cycle that is more inclusive of what was learned in the prior one. This is where the concepts of building and consolidating come into Saturn's domain. When Darwin speaks of evolution, it is *exoteric*, as it is in terms of survival of the fittest as a species adapts and survives the changing circumstances of physical life. When Maslow and the humanistic psychologists speak of survival, it leans more toward *esoteric*, as it is in terms of the human mind adapting and changing the circumstances of emotional and mental life and moving toward a less tangible self-actualization or completion. These concepts give us the ability to understand Saturn in terms of maturity. Physical survival is a temporary event. The unevolved *exoteric* native utilizes the organizational qualities of Saturn as an undermining or blocking influence against competition while supporting its own self-interest. The evolving *esoterically* motivated native approaches maturity as, hopefully, a newly consistent condition or state of mind beyond the polarized focus of the individual ego in favor of the maturity of the larger group. Saturn's placement in a house shows us where we can access the referential (structural) qualities we need to recognize and discriminate our position in the larger, spiritually mature part of the whole.

The first step is acknowledging our response-ability and accountability to any situation we participate in as a cyclic circumstance requiring us to accept our return to where we started as a function of the temporality of our existence.

The second step is organizing and consolidating our efforts to meet that perspective with ease for ourselves and the others we participate with.

The third step is to be able and prepared to sacrifice what might be advantageous to our individual efforts in favor of what would be best for the overall group ideal and welfare. This is not to say that "the needs of the many outweigh the needs of the few." That, also, would be a polarized effort. Our intention is to expand any narrowly focused individual efforts into more of a balance between the native's needs and the needs of humanity, provided the objective of the larger group is not simply tangible survival but *esoterically* mature in nature. The sacrifice that occurs when streamlining efforts to benefit both the individual and the group contributes to Saturn's reputation for promoting the effects of conservation of energy and resources.

URANUS or Ouranus

In explaining Uranus, we must take a completely different tact. It is one of what is called the trans-Saturnian planets. Before 1781 Uranus was literally unknown. What's even more curious is that he was included in the Greek and Roman mythologies. Yet, before the Babylonian, Egyptian and Hindu civilizations he was, presumably, never perceived or mentioned. What this would tend to indicate is that his effects were being *felt* below the threshold of awareness during the Greek and Roman times yet there was a lack of conscious understanding as to how to integrate his qualities in their current cultures.

Among astrologers there is still a great deal of disagreement as to what earthly qualities should be attributed to him. The general consensus is that since he was discovered at the beginning of the industrial revolution, he should rule all things mechanical, electrical, and chemical. Hence, anything of a technical nature has also been attributed to him. Since energy and electricity are largely unseen except through their effects, the quality of surprise and the unexpected have been applied to him. But we must also remember that the laws of energy and electricity follow extremely strict universal "guidelines" as to their behavior in contrast to the expectation of the human application of them. As humans we tend to set things in motion that we feel follow *our own* common sense though often flawed in its logic. Our common sense is a product of our ego's expectations which is motivated by *exoteric*, selfish objectives that are accumulative, restrictive, and possessive. Energy and electricity have no mind. They simply exist and respond to the universe's movement which is often contrary to what our small, personal egos think is logical. Hence, we set conditions and habits in motion assuming that they will continue as planned. These personal expectations usually run contrary to natural law.

As we concentrate our efforts to accumulate an excess of resources and energy for our "security", the natural tendency for energy to continually be on the move builds an accumulated reservoir of pressure much like inflating a balloon. As the ego's ability to contain this pressure within expected limits builds beyond its capacity, the balloon "pops," returns to its original state and we are surprised. In this light I have attributed the meaning of *revolution* to Uranus. The *volution* comes from the word volition which Webster's interprets as "will" and I broaden the interpretation to include the will of God and *re* adds a direction that I interpret as "back to." So, *revolution* is the quality that returns circumstances back to the will of God or to the circumstances governed by natural law.

As humans we are largely unconscious as to natural law and hence see its reinstatement as a surprise. Qualities attributed to Uranus include, of course surprise, sudden action, the unexpected and any other motion or action that occurs outside of "normal" expected circumstances. The surprise can be favored or not. Under expected guidelines this can include explosions, shocks, quick or sudden movements or any action or reaction that's faster that our senses can follow. Understandably, lightening is also ruled by Uranus. Uranus positioned in a house brings the circumstances and energy of the house back to a simpler and more neutral state when our intended human survival pressure pushes past the limits of what nature will allow. The sign tells the coloring and flavor through which this action will be performed and the planets and houses it will gain support from through the sign's rulerships.

You will notice that I did not include things of a chemical nature in this explanation even though it was included above. It's important to note that Uranus, relative to ancient astrological tenets, is viewed as a higher vibration of Mercury which does rule alchemy. The alchemical key is numerologically symbolized through the qualities of the number five (Mercury) and its connection to evolution.

All planets work with and within the laws of karma, but Uranus portrays the actual movement of energy back to its original state demanded by karma. This movement is a kind of *reorientation* toward our path in evolution. *Esoterically* and through his action he returns us to the path of evolution, whether we submit willingly or not. The house that Uranus appears in tells us where we can break outdated habits that prevent us from moving along the path of least resistance concerning our growth and evolution.

NEPTUNE or Poseidon

Neptune is also a trans-Saturnian planet. It was discovered in 1846 while parts of the world were still unknown and being subjected to exploration. This was the beginning of the time when Charles Darwin began exploring the world and formulating the origin of species that exposes the web of nature as an intricate interweaving and diffused pattern of life. It began to show the organization of life as an interdependency of heavily integrated factors. The assumed simplicity of nature began to evaporate. Here began the first major contradiction to the widely accepted theory of creationism and the slow dissolution of blind faith in whatever religious autocrats dictated as "gospel" concerning our origins.

Traditionally, Neptune has been attributed with the qualities of deception, illusion, dependency, delusion, misdiagnosis, drugs, fog, gas, liquid, irrationality, and mental illness. The word I choose to use that best describes the action of his energy is *dissolution*. We can best describe him as having qualities that generally distort, blur and dissolve any effective borders, limits, descriptions, labeling or discrimination that leads us to perceive the physical, emotional and mental forms of *exoteric* life as having clarity.

In terms of the ego, we might consider Neptune the arch enemy of Saturn. The action of Neptune's *exoteric* form has been the mental bane of the ego. Anything that is supported or structured by the egotistical side of Saturn is dissolved by Neptune. There's one catch. Not everything is dissolved. What is created by Saturn and in line with the natural laws of the universe *will be refined* by Neptune rather than dissolved. In this way Neptune is much like an acid wash that a mason or metallurgist would use to remove the extraneous debris not pertinent to the creation being perfected. Hence, if our awareness and logic is in keeping with the laws of the universe we will be supported and augmented by Neptune's process and the "acid wash" will have little or no effect since what remains after it is necessary for the creation's composition. What remains can be considered the *esoteric* component of Neptune since it falls in line with the natural laws.

Neptune is responsible for the *dissolution* or disintegration of the personal and insecure ego. The selflessness that's usually attributed to the refined vibration of Neptune can be compared to a drop of water in the ocean. The drop is delineated enough to be distinguished as water, according to natural law, but undifferentiated enough to be able to diffuse into oblivion or the larger frame of the ocean. Throughout the known history of Taoism, the recommended path for the disciple has been the emulation of water; accepting lowly places by taking on the forms of the spaces it fills but yet retaining the quality that defines it as water. Water exemplifies the essences of humility and compassion. Herein lies the connection of Neptune to Pisces and circumstances concerning the twelfth house.

Neptune's appearance in a house tells of a need and/or desire to dissolve the structures and beliefs that have outlived their usefulness and are barriers to the development of a broader understanding and acceptance of the issues connected to the house. The process has the potential to go well beyond the simple dissolution of barriers while integrating the circumstances of the house through allowing the refining of a skill, ability, or quality toward *mastery*. Developing these skills, abilities or qualities requires the application of nurturance. Hence, Neptune occupies an *esoteric* connection through the sign of Cancer. This gives us a clear line of continuity from our beginnings as a species until this moment in our evolution.

As a small aside, the qualities inherent in contemporary magic and magicians are covered by the domain of Neptune due to its connection to the concept of illusion. The curious fact about magicians is that they don't bend the laws of nature to create illusions as much as they bend our perception of their effects.

PLUTO or Hades

Even though contemporary astronomers had demoted Pluto to something less than a planet, he still retains the qualities of a trans-Saturnian planet. Those qualities are, simply put, the *revolution* (Uranus), *dissolution* (Neptune), and *redemption* (Pluto) of egotistically applied energies and circumstances and their reintegration back into the realm of *esoteric* service on the universal path.

Pluto's discovery in 1930 coincides with occurrence of the dawning awareness of the inherent power of the atom; the smallest "stable" building block of the physical universe. In this discovery we learned that energy can neither be created nor destroyed; only exchanged with matter.

Pluto's traditional meanings include death, sex, regeneration, the underworld, the Mafia, banking, corporate enterprises, atomic energy, other people's resources and abilities, any type of circulation out of sight and/or any undercurrents of energy or unseen forces that power movement through an unknown source.

Pluto is connected to the underworld in Greek and Roman mythology. In this we can see the representation of a tremendously powerful undercurrent and if it could be harnessed, as the common man believes it can be, would be expected to avail the harnesser of unlimited power. Yet, the harnessing of this power is all but impossible due to the fact that it follows its own natural laws which almost always seem to run askew of human intention. The only way harnessing would seem possible is if we were to align our objectives with the natural direction of Pluto. When this is *not* done, which is more often the case, the results are disastrous; personally, and globally. To understand this more completely we must return again to our discussion of the *shadow*.

As we choose to distance ourselves from the unacceptable and animal parts of our nature that we feel create a poor projection of our desired superiority, we disconnect from them by driving them into our unconscious and attribute their qualities, through projection, to those we can now disapprove of. Our undesirable qualities have now been given a tangible human face and we can now believe that they are someone that we must be fearful of and/or keep our distance from. Our *shadow* is born. What we don't realize, however, is that it takes a consistent energy to keep the projection in place and in doing so we give our own internal resistance form in the external world.

We create our own opposition. Since it is nature's tendency to attempt to reunite all of its parts, we will naturally attract those who emit the qualities we wish to disavow. In attracting them we now assume that we are being pursued or persecuted. This is the essence of paranoia which is an integral quality of an *exoteric* Pluto. As we confront this person with accusations of persecution and persist in doing so, the eventual reaction from our perceived pursuer will be to retaliate out of frustration in dealing with us and thereby validate our self-fulfilling prophesy. *ALL* wars and persecution are born of this dynamic. The current metaphysical saying was, and still is, "What we resist persists." It is *our own resistance* that is powering the interplay. As long as we keep pushing our *shadow* away, it will keep "pursuing" us. This energy is now locked up and lost to us. One of the most famous and pitiful examples of this type of submerged energy is the feud between the Hatfields and the McCoys who had fought each other for generations. They eventually forgot what they were fighting about but kept on fighting out of habit. In attributing the *shadow* image of ourselves to others we cut ourselves off from the availability of the energy that's used to power it.

When we stop projecting our *shadow* on others and accept what we resisted and reintegrate it as part of our own nature, we cease feeding an energy hungry internal war. The house Pluto is in tells us where this energy is the most available to redeem. It also tells us of the place where we harbor the most resistance. Consciously working here will redeem the energy used in feeding the resistance and become available to us to use in more lucrative ventures. As a result, we feel lighter and more energized. This is the quality of *redemption* that enables the regeneration that Pluto is so well known for. This is also an *esoteric* application of Pluto's energy.

In a physical sense we can see the smelting of metals as an analogy. As a diffused mixture of elements is heated and melted, the differing weights of each element tend to stratify, showing a clear discrimination between the components of the original mixture. In doing so the integrity of each element is renewed. In this Pluto has a remarkably close relationship with Vulcan.

Pluto's presence in a house creates an intensity concerning the issues of the house. Since Pluto has such a strong connection with the *shadow*, it offers the best doorway to deal with it through the issues of the resident house with the least amount of resistance. That house is also the area of life that we can retreat to in order to regenerate ourselves most fully. Pluto is the *esoteric* connection to our unconscious. Reintegrating the *shadow* is one of the most *esoteric* tasks a human can perform making the resident house of Pluto one of the most dynamic in the native's chart clearing the way towards the potential of a disciple's life.

SUN – Apollo and Helios

The Sun is one of the most misinterpreted "planets" in the zodiac. Notwithstanding the fact that it is considered a light not a planet, it should also be understood that its presence in a sign does not imbue the native with the developed qualities of the sign but that it presents an opportunity for the native to learn and integrate those qualities. The fact that the extremes of the qualities of the sign are visible in the native who is born to it indicates the extent of their lack of development to which their use is being attempted. In a simpler fashion, we *are not* the sign we are born under we are learning to *become* it. More precisely, becoming the sign may be interpreted as integrating the qualities of the sign and in doing so, the evidence of its presence takes on a much more subtle tone to the observer and no longer personifies the extremes associated with the undeveloped sign.

Essentially, the Sun sign qualities are needed to "round out" the manifestation of the native's energy in this life and the ones to come. In a karmic sense, they may not have been integrated properly in a prior life for their application in this one or they may have been simply missing up to this point.

Traditionally, the Sun's presence in a house gives vitality. This is partially due to the power the Sun innately carries and is also due to the fact that he literally lights up the house he's found in. In doing so, more attention is garnered toward the issues of the house.

As the native responds to this influence, people of like mind and those reflective of the native's *shadow* contribute to an increasing dominance of the house. It is for these reasons that I attribute a keyword of *focus* to the quality of the Sun's presence. Hence, the house that the Sun resides in takes on a major influence in the life of the native and should be examined thoroughly to find developmental potential leading to *esoteric* growth. It is through the acceleration of issues in this house that the native will establish most of the new basic patterns their evolutionary growth. Special attention should also be given as the Sun progresses into succeeding signs as this represents a potential major lifetime shift in the *focus* of growth.

We should also follow the transit of the Sun as it moves, house by house. In addition to the emphasis of the house he resides in, his movement will establish a general yearly pattern for dealing with specific house issues at the same time each year. Becoming aware of this pattern enables the native to anticipate the sequence of surfacing *shadow* issues needing to be dealt with. The order of surfacing will follow the natural flow of our personal *dharma*. This shows the Sun's role concerning the *future* of the native's growth. In this way the Sun lights our path showing us how to "grow with the flow."

MOON – Artemis and Diana

The Moon is also one of the most misinterpreted "planets" in the zodiac, perhaps, even more that the Sun. It should, also, not be considered a planet. A key to its meaning is that it is a dead, *reflective* satellite circumscribing our physical planet, fully or partially obscuring the Sun (*focus*) at the beginning and end of each new temporal cycle. It possesses no emanating energy of its own. Although the Moon reflects the Sun's energy, it also acts as a *veil* for the effects of either Vulcan or Uranus. Which planet is *veiled* is determined by the native's level of development; Vulcan is used when working with the undeveloped or average native and Uranus is used when working with those who are highly developed.

Traditionally, the Moon represents our emotional makeup, our physical body, our mother, our hereditary genes, our learned cultural heritage and the "home" we live in. That home could be our physical domicile, our body and/or the point of reference we use to maintain our worldly stability. It is for this reason that I have chosen the word *manifestation* to represent its action. In this way it can be described as a construct resulting from the rightly applied, unapplied or misapplied energies remaining from past lives and current thought patterns. It is one of our strongest connections to our history and traditions. It is a current *manifestation* of *past* experience. In essence, it is a residue of past action that needs to be properly *applied* in this life to assist in the ease and progression of our evolutionary journey. Alice Bailey has called the Moon the *prison of the soul*.

The Moon and its corresponding south node can be considered among the densest points in our chart. The house the Moon appears in is the physical area of life that we, literally, take root in. *These* personal qualities we see seeping out through our social conditioning into our day to day life. These are the physical, emotional, and mental patterns we bring in with us from past lives. These can be seen most clearly in our earliest years before the family traditions of the current incarnation have been inculcated. What we consider to be our *instinct* is actually tapping into these primal patterns. The Moon's south node represents the behaviors that we resort to when our mental faculties fail us. Our *esoteric* work with the Moon consists of transforming our *instinctual* behavior first to *intellect* (Mercury), then to *intuition* (Uranus). Hence, there is the reference of Uranus being veiled by the Moon. Vulcan serves prior function as we shall see later. The action of the Moon and Mercury are connected together through the root center chakra.

For a better understanding of what needs to be accomplished in the native's life it would behoove the astrologer to substitute first Vulcan, then Uranus for the Moon. In applying their energies to the issues, what the Moon has dominance over will reveal a substantial amount of insight to guide the native's evolution.

As a vehicle for karmic processing, the action needing to be taken can be compared to the sculptor who sees the essence of the sculpture imprisoned within the granite and endeavors to set it free through strategically chiseling away one small piece of the Moon at a time. This will become much more evident as I explain the action of Vulcan.

VULCAN – Hephaestus

When we speak of the purging fires, Vulcan takes the forefront. However, solid confirmation about the actual existence of Vulcan is yet to be established. Over many years, dating from the early 1800's, what appeared to be Vulcan has been observed many times over. But verification and coordinated sightings seem to be elusive. His orbit is said to be within the corona of the Sun and never more than 8 degrees away. But remember the Romans and Greeks never really saw Uranus, Neptune or Pluto. We may yet confirm solid sightings of Vulcan in the near future, but with that being said, his symbolism and esoteric actions still play a dynamic role in our evolving into an accountable and self-directing entity.

In the physical world, Vulcan is a blacksmith. He forges the purest and strongest of tools through a process of two steps: first he smelts the composite down to the raw materials and then, once stratified and separated, he uses heat and pressure to forge incomparably strong tools. Stratifying and then separating the resulting materials into purity allows us to see the characteristics and usefulness of each of the elements. Different elements lend themselves toward different functions. Vulcan does the same thing with human qualities and abilities.

When we throw what we don't like about ourselves into the twelfth house creating the *shadow*, we lock up much of our human potential for growth and use a tremendous amount of energy keeping those unwanted qualities below our consciousness. Anytime we encounter overflow by being reminded of them we project what doesn't fit our preferred image on others. The stress we feel is our resistance to those qualities coming back at us through the dynamic "what goes around comes around" accountability wielded by Saturn. The job of clearing then falls to Pluto and Vulcan with the help of the other outer planets.

With Vulcan, the outer planets work in tandem. Uranus breaks the tension. Neptune dissolves the attachments and adhesions. Pluto bubbles the remains to the surface of our awareness and redeems the energy. Vulcan burns away our egoic safeguards and fashions the remaining elements into a vehicle for our spirit. Or in other words, the sign and house of Uranus shows us the greatest point of tension. Neptune shows where we deceive ourselves the most. Pluto shows where we need to apply our work and effort and Vulcan fashions tools for us to clear away any obstructions preventing us from full acceptance of our Sun and his directional path. (As a construction analogy - Vulcan widens the road for the Sun).

Vulcan may not be used or accepted by the majority of astrologers, but his action *IS* always apparent, and his effects soon become visible whenever we meet our resistance to ourselves in the people Saturn attracts to us. Vulcan follows the Sun much like the secret police follow the president. This scenario plays out in *every* one of our life experiences.

CONCEPTS

Now that we have the landscape and players under our belt, it would be prudent to learn to understand some of the dynamic concepts that will be employed when we begin to delineate our charts.

As with any kind of discrimination, there is always a yes or a no, up and a down, hot and cold, black and white, etc. These distinctly polarized perspectives make it easy to distinguish between different states and experiences when using Venus and Mercury for discriminating our preferences. This is what most people use to keep a conscious reference about where they stand in life relative to their values and everyone else. The less secure we feel, the more we need to have a perception of these clear differences in place. The western world thrives on polarity for its judgments and assessments of value. When we get into the grey areas, there is more of a challenge in determining where we stand in relation to everyone else. The more materialistic we become, the more these stark comparisons become necessary.

Let's look at some analogous compliments. When we talk about travel, we usually speak of our *departures* and *arrivals*, but very rarely do we speak of the time we spend between. When we talk about projects, we more often talk about the *starting* of them and then about their *completion*. We may speak of difficulty or endurance during the journey or project, but mostly we speak of *beginnings* and *endings*. They represent the clearest perception of what we've been through. Our mind needs these "blacks" and "whites" as reference points in order to be able to describe our experience to others and for us to have a clear memory and opinion about what we've experienced.

In astrology, the *beginning* and *ending* points of events are necessary, useful and often arbitrary but the "grey" areas and time between speak of harder to describe concepts of intensity, proximity, effectiveness and influence. Assessing these "grey" areas is the only way in which we can become aware of our *progress* in our journeys and projects. *Progress* is not a switch being turned on or off, but an increasing or decreasing influence felt or perceived relative to that journey or project.

Our perception of this increasing or decreasing influence is acquired over time and with constant exposure to the gradually changing distances between our black and white on and off points of reference. Refinement of discrimination and skill only come through attaching and remembering our perception about the multitude of experiential points between these gross polarities. This process of refinement comes under the heading of the trans-Saturnian planets, especially, Neptune. The more we release our dependency, or co-dependency, on black and white for meaning in our life, the more attuned we can become to the variations between them and the better we can assess any change in the degree of influence. Growing toward this skill, its understanding, and our perception of it is at the core or our evolution as a human.

INVOLUTION – EVOLUTION

When we move toward *increasing* our focus on polarizing, we become more materialistic and lean more toward *involution*. This brings us deeper into matter and our materialistic incarnation. Focusing on matter allows us to hide from ourselves. When this is the case we move more ardently into the egotistical side of human nature, where we tend to become more protective and impassioned about our preferred individuality, possessions, and earthly security. The increased pressure around us tends to increase life's tangibility and our belief in our being able to control our circumstances thereby ensuring that that the *shadow* of our denied and unwanted parts of ourselves that we have relegated to others will remain submerged and boxed in by our polarized judgments. Our insecurity always drives us toward *involution*.

When we move more toward *decreasing* our focus on polarizing our circumstances and allowing the grey areas of life have more prominence, we produce less pressure and less resistance while allowing the natural laws to run their course and contribute to our awareness and our evolution toward the higher and wider-minded

Enhancing Self Stagnant - Out of Phase Involution		Enhancing the Group Flowing - In Phase Evolution
Dwell in the Past or Future - Me-ism	**SUN & EARTH** Focus & Experience	Be Here & Now Magnetic
Abuse the Body – Inertia Fluctuating Emotions Easily Led Indiscriminate	**MOON** Manifestation	Emotional Stability Create Health & Provide Example to Others
Take Over & Win at any Cost - Weapons	**VULCAN** Purgation & Forging	Unification Tools
Insensitivity Disruption	**MERCURY** Elucidation	Listen – Observe – Teach
Tit for Tat Excuses & Blame	**VENUS** Decision	Commitment Responsibility
Competitiveness Violence	**MARS** Motivation & Mobilization	Devotion to Greater Cause
Excessive Growth of Separative Influences	**JUPITER** Expansion	Growth of Empathy to the Unity of Truth
Undermining & Blocking	**SATURN** Completion	Task Oriented & Working Together
Rigid Individualism	**URANUS** Revolution	Creative Adaptation
Delusion of Self & Others	**NEPTUNE** Fusion	Clear Vision Mastery
Manipulation & Destructiveness	**PLUTO** Unconscious	Transformation & Regeneration

Each of the planets may be used toward more of an *involutionary* or *evolutionary* portrayal in our behavior.

being that our Sun is pointing the way toward. Hence, following our dharma leads us toward *evolution* and the dissolution of our personal insecurity as protected by our ego.

I've arranged the chart in an either/or listing so you can clearly see the extreme that each of the perspectives and attitudes can take us. Please understand that to solely adopt the *evolutionary* perspective over the *involutionary* one or vice versa will create a polarization in itself. There are many people in the metaphysical field who will swear that they are "spiritually" minded and deny physical involvement simply to avoid have to deal with many of the incarnational factors that we have come here to work on. The deviousness and resourcefulness of the rational egotistical mind is unsurpassed by any other human function except that of the heart which *knows* what dharma is leading us toward. Restraint may be one of its characteristics, but prevention of exposure is often not. Let that sink in.

The depth of our potential growth lies within our ability to learn to trust our hearts and intuition over egotistical rationalization. The heart is the balance point between the lower chakras and the upper chakras attempting to allow a balanced integration between our participation in the intuitive or "spirit" world and the tangible physical world. This is not to say that the mind (Mercury) is a bad agent, but that it simply is a *tool* at the disposal of our heart (Sun & Jupiter) that should be used to facilitate acts that will balance the actions of our inner growth with the needs and wants of the physical world. Realize that there are times where we need to act in a way that *appears* to be manipulative, deceptive, restrictive or violent if only to make certain that the physical world doesn't totally overpower our heart and intuition. These qualities don't always embody malice but sometimes becomes encouragement for others, especially children, to choose the "higher" or more accountable path.

A simple example showing how these twos force balance each other but appear to be callous might be what is colloquially known as "tough love." Sometimes a child needs to live through the circumstance of their own doing that may be harmful to them. Yet, if we as parents rescue them at every turn, they will never have the opportunity to work through the adversity themselves to develop their independence and self-sufficiency. We may feel like bad parents for not assisting them but know deep in our hearts that if they don't work it through on their own, they may never develop the strength to make hard choice or for the understanding of our actions.

CYCLES & PHASES

The Sun, Moon and Saturn hold the most obvious and widely used keys for cyclic timing in an astrological chart. The Sun cycle is three hundred sixty-five days, the Moon is twenty-eight days, and Saturn is twenty-eight years. All three planets are strongly synchronized, each with a different tangible earthly cycle. All the other planets follow this cycle; however, the Sun, the Moon, and Saturn exhibit these cycles most poignantly and obviously. The action of other planets can be seen if a cyclic template is applied to them also, but most astrologers only utilize them in terms of their return to the native's birthdate position.

Remembering that everything in the physical universe moves in cycles and patterns, we have a crystal-clear understanding of the "steps" through which the natural energy moves through matter. This is the most obvious in the observing the Moon phases. The cycle can also be seen most vividly in observing the Sun's progression through the seasons.

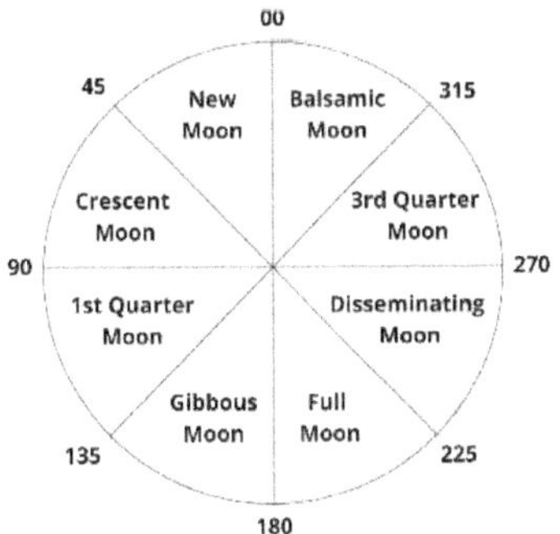

The first observation of this cycle was observed by the ancients when they began to observe their crop response to the Moon phases and the yearly Sun cycle. They realized that seeding and transplanting did better in the first half of the yearly and lunar phases than the second half. They also found that visible and above ground fruits and vegetables became fully mature and could be harvested *after* the full Moon and the summer solstice. Root crops are best if planted *after* the full Moon and harvested *during* the new Moon. Fisherman also realized that fish went through their reproductive cycle by the patterns of the Moon and that the tides had a tremendous influence on what fish were available for their catch and when. Through time and using the tides and phases for their fishing and planting, they began to notice that their emotions and life circumstances also coincided with these tides and phases as well but on a much more subtle level.

Based on these discoveries, humans began to plan and execute specific activities during the select phases of the Moon and even during the larger Sun phases throughout the year. The first four Sun phases, including two during winter and two during spring, became times for planning, building and refining projects. The last four phases, including two during summer and two during fall, became times for the completion of projects, the ability to see them in their fullest form with the awareness of how to adapt them to become more effective and for refining them to "fit" into the subsequent cycles that were to follow.

Each phase is forty-five degrees each. The yearly Sun phases start at zero degrees of Capricorn and changes at every zero-degree point of the cardinal signs and every fifteenth degree point of the fixed signs. Planets follow the phases also but relative to us start from their natal position. To find the change points for every birth planet other than the Sun, sequentially add forty-five degrees to the natal position of the planet (eight times) until the planetary return is arrived at. A chart for these forty-five degree change points can be found in the appendix of this book.

The listing that follows is a cosmic theoretical blueprint for the types of action that begins to occur most easily when the Sun or any other planet starts each new phase.

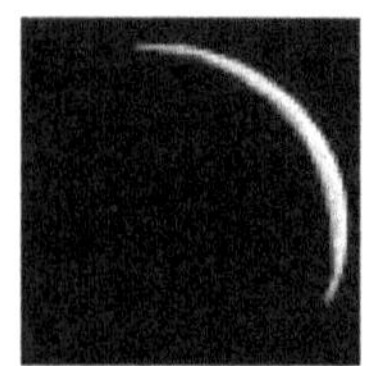 **EMERGENCE** - New Moon & winter solstice - the keyword for this phase is the unknown. This is the beginning of a totally new experience and will be entirely subjective. The impulse to new action comes *only* from within. It is powered by impulse, emotion, and intuition. Any action we take must come from our inner guidance or instinct. As the seed is totally encased in darkness of earth with no perception of what surrounds it, so are we as we conceive a new idea or project. To sense or "see" this vision we must be internally focused with no disturbance from the external world. There are no external signposts to guide us in this uncharted territory. In a personal sense we may feel more alone during this cycle than any other, yet, it includes more freedom than of any of the other phases as it is the most unmanifest

as of yet. The requirement here is of concentration, focus and a sense of withdrawing within to "allow" the vision to penetrate our awareness fully. It requires a purity of innocence that can be found in the tarot deck as represented by the Fool.

ASSERTION - Crescent Moon – the keywords for this phase are planning, commitment and value. It is here that we set up a framework that will perpetuate the values and format needed to transform our new impulse into a reality. Creating an organized plan will create a standard to help us stay focused and to overcome any obstacles to our new vision. This phase requires that we have faith in our ability to handle whatever may come as a result of pursuing our vision. As we assert ourselves, we will appear challenging to any other "system" that is accepted and in play with others. This is also the time that we are the most vulnerable to subversion and selling out to others in order to feel a sense of belonging and being accepted. If we are to succeed, we must follow our personal values and stand our ground. The requirement here is one of commitment and meditation.

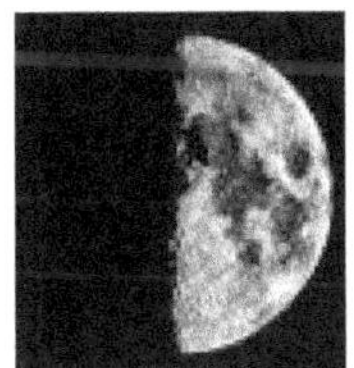

ACTION - 1st Quarter Moon & spring equinox – the keywords here are raw manifestation and growth. We may not have all the details but instinctively we know what must be done to flesh out the framework needed for our vision. This is the first physical representation of our vision and is the most physically forceful of all the phases. Tremendous energy feeds a laser focused drive almost to the point of ruthlessness. Anything standing in the way risks obliteration. There is almost a warrior mentality that focuses on purging the old and forging the new in its most basic form with lightning action. The requirement here is of accelerated physical growth, focus and vigorous exercise.

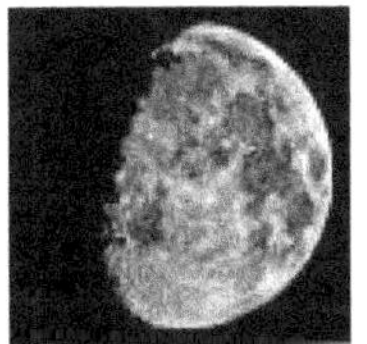

EXPRESSION - Gibbous Moon – the keywords here are refinement and personal signature. This is where the manifested vision takes on detailed characteristics specific to its author so there are no mistakes as to whose vision it is. In this way the vision finds its most individual expression. This is the last opportunity to "improve" upon it. It is here that its "fate" is sealed. This phase corresponds to the artist within all of us. It also colors and classifies our expression in the eyes of our social structure and leads toward being labeled and associated with specific group characteristics. This builds family. Taken to an extreme an exaggeration of this expression could lead to an egotistical unorthodoxy. The requirement here is of developing breath control and overcoming instincts.

FULFILLMENT - Full Moon & summer solstice – the keywords here are visible and revealed. The Moon in this position is literally opposite the Sun. The opposition, in astrological terms, is symbolic of relationships. As with an honest relationship everything is clear, visible, and obvious. What was intuited is now confirmed. Having completed our vision, we now face a crisis in perspective. It is much like a college student who finally graduates. He must now cease applying energy to his completed four-year goal and the familiar "nest" it supplied and apply his energy and what he has learned to the "outside" world. It is the same with our vision. We must disengage from our creative momentum and let our creation join the world and accept the world's judgment of it. It is past the time for the availability to make any more improvements. This will, most likely, bring a sense of loss, emptiness and disorientation since our tendency is to cling to our creation as it has defined our identity in creative terms for the term of its building. The requirement here is for introspection, acceptance and a deep letting go.

SYNTHESIS - Disseminating Moon – The keywords here are humility, adaptation, and usefulness. Not everyone is going to be able to use or appreciate our creation. So, what can we do to make it more accessible, enjoyable, and useful to others? The more homogeneous we make it the less character it will retain. But is that really important? At this point, to integrate our creation into the flow of our natural social structure would give the best complement as to its usefulness. This action would also connect with the nurturing part of our natures. It requires us to listen and accept the feedback of what is needed. This is the test of our receptivity since our response will be the gauge by which we are assessed as to how well we allow our project's synthesizing back into the social milieu. The requirement here is of blending, education and, most emphatically, the elimination of egotistical pride as related to our project.

 **REORIENTATION** - 3rd Quarter Moon & fall equinox – The keywords here are adjustment, revamping and tailoring. We are aware of the parts of our social group that our creation fits well with, but we are, also, painfully aware of where it does not. We must be careful to allow the needed new focus, gauged toward a new and different future, to take precedence over our, now past, creation. We must not insist that its character remain intact as a reflection of our ego even if it has *not* outlived its usefulness. This is a deeper and more compassionate form of letting go. We cannot insist on preservation for posterity. There is a gearing up for the future where our sacrifices will pave the way. We know, instinctively, of the new cycle that is coming and must address it in a clean and clear manner. Here we may inspire others to transcend the limitations of the dying present cycle. The requirement here is reorganizing and cooperation.

 **RELEASE** - Balsamic Moon – The keywords here are foresight, preparation, and purgation. Of all the phases this is the most intangibly received and the most tangibly directed. It is a total anticipation of the new cycle by clearing all obstacles to its intuited structure. There is a sense of "destiny" almost as if one were led by a "higher power." It feels as if we are the vehicle through which something higher is taking place. We accept the passing of relationships, circumstances and security with the confidence that something of more import and usefulness will take their place. There is a sense of never-ending preparing. There is an unseen vision waiting to be born in an aspect of transition. The requirement is of purification, preparation and allowing the inner self to direct us.

THE MAJOR ASPECTS

When we talk about planetary aspects, we are primarily talking about their relationship to each other and how they tend to temper each other's expression. Some aid. Some augment. Some inhibit and some synthesize. The effects are determined not only by the angle but by the planets themselves. The angle tells us of the type of interchange to be expected and the planets describe what types of energies are brought into contact with each other.

No planet is ever out of aspect with every other. The effects may range from being monumental all the way toward infinitesimal. When the major aspects are out of acceptable or effectual *orb* (range of potential effect), there are always minor aspects offering more subtle and indistinct influences. These minor aspects may only be felt or dealt with after the major aspects have been recognized, handled, and refined as to their effects.

Traditionally, aspects have been lumped into being *benifics* or *malefics*. That is, they can be either beneficial or harmful. When we group things in a black or white frame, we are left with no possibility for the expression of subtleties. This may give added clarity to our discrimination between them but give little understanding about any possible transition between them. Aspects must not be assessed in terms of an end result but from a perspective for their potential.

In keeping with conventional astrology, orbs have been a subject of debate as to the proximity of their effectiveness. The closer an aspect is to the exactness of its stated positioning; the more effect the aspect will produce according to the characteristics that it is said to bring with it. As it moves away, its effect diminishes correspondingly.

Relative to the effectiveness of an aspects, planets moving *toward* an aspect have more intensity than an aspect that has *passed* being exact. That is, an aspect that is approaching at any degree number will be stronger than a separating aspect of the same degree number. So, approaching aspects of five degrees are stronger and more effectual than separating five-degree aspects. This is due to the fact that an approaching aspect creates a compression of force between the receiving planet and the approaching planet. Separating aspects release that pressure.

So, let's talk about the most basic aspects first. These are aspects that, regardless of a person's sensitivities or insensitivities, will be felt by almost everyone. These might be considered the grosser or stronger aspects than any other. After speaking about these I will show where and how the transitions take place into the more subtle aspects that lie between the basic ones.

CONJUNCTION - *00 Degrees – 1 Vibration*

This is probably the most basic and obvious of the grosser aspects. This is where two or more planets essentially attempt to occupy the same space. The key word that might exemplify its process will be *synthesis*. That is, the universe's attempt to combine two types of energy creating one or attempting to moderate the effects of one over the other. Remember, any aspect won't be there simply by chance. It will be the attempt of our "higher natures" to mitigate energies that may be out of balance or over-emphasized, back into alignment or to produce a type of energy that might be specifically necessary for completing this lifetime's birth path challenges. Whatever the circumstance, the aspect may almost take on a life of its own in driving our motivations and actions.

If we look at an approaching conjunction between Mercury and Mars, we can see that most of the time Mercury will be applying to Mars as Mercury usually moves faster. In simple terms, this may be our spirit's attempt to bring thinking in as a predominant force overlooking and guiding our actions. This may be obvious to us in observing the struggles of someone who ordinarily acts before thinking while encountering a transit or progression of Mercury to Mars.

However, a planet that normally moves slower may not always be the recipient of a normally faster planet's compression. For example, if Mercury is close to being at station either before or after a retrograde with a Mars approaching a conjunction, Mars' normal speed will be faster than Mercury's at station speed. This would make Mars the applying force while Mercury would be become the recipient. This influence would then bring a press toward action (Mars) over thought (Mercury). We might see this aspect occur in a person with Mercury natally at station tending them toward over-thinking without ever taking action. The pressing Mars conjunction would contribute toward rebalancing the thought/action relationship. In these circumstances we might even see an approaching Pluto applying to a normally fast planet like Mercury, Venus or Mars if they have gone into station.

A conjunction doesn't always end up *synthesizing* the energies of the two or more planets coming into conjunction. In some cases, there may actually be a *synthesis* like combing the energies of Mercury and Venus. This might be similar to dropping salt into water and creating a saline solution. But may also involve planets like Mars and Saturn which might be equivalent to trying to mix oil and water. We might be able to shake them and mix them up into a suspension, but their natural tendency would be to eventually stratify and separate. In this case our client might be learning when, where and how to separate action from abstinence. The lesson would be a lesson in learning when we can *synthesize* and when we cannot.

OPPOSITION – *180 Degrees – 2 Vibration*

The best example of an opposition is seeing ourselves in a mirror. Its primary influence acts as an instrument of *awareness*. Depending on our eyesight and the cleanliness of the glass, it is capable of giving us the best feedback that we can get from any activity. If anything can be objective, a mirror can. Since it is inanimate, it offers no predisposition, bias or partisanship. However, when our reflection comes back from a person, it's a bit like looking into a funhouse mirror. Each person offers their own spin on what they feed back to us. Looking into the mirror at ourselves can also offer a spin on what *we* see based on *our* insecurities, rationalizations, perspectives and preferred self-images.

A key distinction about the *opposition* is that it makes us aware of what issues and qualities are being *separated*. *Separation* and *reflection* are the vehicles for all growing *awareness*. When two or more planets come into *opposition*, the activities they each bring to the chart are emphasized in terms of the planets that they oppose. For example, if the Moon is opposing Mars, the action that is being taken activates or makes apparent the native's feelings and emotions. Those feelings become more obvious and intense in their awareness. Conversely, when Mars opposes the Moon, feelings are brought forward concerning the actions that are or are not being taken. The orb that these two planets are found in determines the intensity of effect that these two planets have on each other. The signs will tell us the flavor the planets express. The energy exchange is reciprocal. The larger the separation, the less the effect. The closer to exact the aspect is, the stronger and more of an influence it will have.

One of the tangent effects of *oppositions*, especially if a person has a few of them, is that it tends to make people a bit more contentious. This can be by transit or progression for a period of time or natally throughout their entire lives. The separative influence makes the native much more aware of differences between themselves, circumstances, and other people. However, the *opposition* with the planets of another person may also trigger awareness and/or contentious responses. The dynamic of an *opposition* will always behave the same way but differ in who or what are being aspected.

SQUARE – *90 Degrees – 4 Vibration*

The *square* is probably one of the most growth-oriented aspects due to the fact that it, essentially, forces actions or decisions to be made between the squaring planets. Arcane astrologers have traditionally cited a *square* as "bad" or malefic aspects. Its keyword can be considered as *challenge*. The effect is as if the planets are working at cross purposes to each other. The two houses involved show in what areas of life the stress will manifest in.

The best analogy I can offer for a *square* is a four-way traffic intersection. Crossing the intersection must be done with caution. It's fairly easy to migrate past the opposing traffic on the other side of the intersection. But the traffic coming from the right and the left offer a bit more challenge. If we are paying attention and we are careful, we'll find that timing will be our best ally. That is, if we allow the cross traffic to move first or they allow us, we will have navigated successfully across the intersection. If we don't, we will either broadside someone or end up being broadsided ourselves. A square is not only an aspect of *challenge* but an aspect of *timing*. That is, we can avoid a collision simply by applying a sense of timing in dealing with "cross traffic."

The closer the orb, the more intense the collision might be. In we only pay attention to the traffic behind us (the past) or the traffic directly in front of us (the future), we risk being blindsided by current influences we "never see coming." When dealing with *squares*, awareness and well-timed patience are our best friends.

The effects of traffic and collisions has always fascinated me. Broadsides and T-Bones are most certainly aspects needing more patience and attention in life navigation. But Head-on and rear end collisions are a different animal. Head-on collisions often speak of people who have uncontrolled direction in their lives. Rear ended collisions speak of people who either push to hard and fast or those who refuse to move. Sideswipes are usually people who have little or no concept about proximity and their distance from others. These collisions offer interesting insights and food for thought as to how we perceive and approach karma.

TRINE - *120 Degrees – 3 Vibration*

The best keyword symbolizing a *trine* is easy flow. When planets connect through a *trine*, the energy exchange is fluid. They usually occur in the same element thus allowing their similarity to feed their ease of movement. A conduit opens between them and the movement occurs almost automatically. These connections can serve as vents if they are connected to planets involved in a *square*.

Conventional and arcane astrologers cite *trines* as "good" or fortunate. Where an ease of flow is needed or desired, this is eminently so. But easy flow is not always a "good" thing. If the connection between two or more planets involves an addiction or compulsive behavior, they can create or intensify especially harmful circumstances. Then the "malefic" squares that may be connected to them, if the native is fortunate enough to have them, may then serve as positive redirects working at cross purposes to the addictive influence thereby serving as a "benefic" aspect exemplifying their usefulness in avoiding a slippage into involuntary harmful behavior.

Although orbs are important, most astrologers tend to over-emphasize the presence of *trines* as compensation for the difficulties and *challenges* they believe are created by *squares*. They will often stretch the orbs of effectiveness in a client's chart to ease the perception of difficulty created simply by the presence of *squares*. But again, orbs are not hard and fast numbers but will indicate the degree of an aspect's effectiveness in a chart. We must also remember that this effectiveness has a great deal to do with the native's sensitivity to the aspecting energies. Someone who is perceptually dense and somewhat insensitive will require a closer orb simply to create enough intensity to get their attention to focus on an issue. Others may sense the change long before the average person.

SEXTILES – *60 Degrees – 6 Vibration*

A *sextile* has been traditionally regarded as an aspect of *production*. In light of the fact that a *sextile* exists half-way between a *square* and a *trine*, we can say that the *midpoint* between them contains some aspects of both. Any *midpoint* between two planets can be considered a sensitive point in the chart. *Transits* and *progressions* through a *midpoint* will create effects that often elude the astrologer's awareness of where they might have come from. A *sextile* can be regarded more as a *midpoint* than a specific aspect but since they are easily found at sixty degrees, they have gained popularity as a traditional aspect.

Sextiles usually occur between elements that complement each other. Fire feeds into air, earth feeds into water and vice versa for both. In this they tend to transform each other a bit. It usually takes a little bit of effort on our part to facilitate the transformation but in general, it creates new avenues of expression in us. *Sextiles* can operate as gentle motivators with the promise of *production* and reward for our work and attention.

Sometimes planets in *sextile* aspect each other but from antagonistic signs such as Aries to early Pisces or Aries to late Taurus. In this case there is a bit more of a *challenge* to synthesize the energies but still with the promise of some semblance of *production*. We may also find *sextiles* as a sort of training in refining and discriminating our sensitivities as the are a little more subtle as compared to *square, trine, opposition,* or *conjunction*.

The *midpoint* between planets involved in a *trine* will manifest at the sextile (the inside sixty-degree point) from either end point between *trining* planets. Any *transit* or *progression* to this point will have a strong effect on how the *trine* manifests.

INCONJUNCTION or QUINCUNX– *150 Degrees*

The key word for *inconjunction* is *undercurrent*. Although this is considered a minor aspect due to the subtleties and sensitivities involved, many astrologers include it in their lineup. Any planets can find themselves in a *quincunx*, but its primary influence usually remains *below* the threshold of our awareness for most people. Let's look at a real-world example at the havoc a *quincunx* can produce.

Imagine that you've just gone shopping. You're carrying a pile of boxes just barely balancing them until you get to the car. Then you get a pebble stuck in your shoe. You're so busy keeping the boxes balanced and in your arms that you're unable to do anything. Some of you may be so focused on the boxes that you don't even realize that there is a pebble in your shoe completely throwing you off balance while you're trying to compensate.

Inconjuncts have often been quoted as aspects affecting our health but in very subtle ways. They tend to create an underlying stress due to the subliminal interference that they often create in our well-being. This stress is cumulative and often goes unchecked until a physical malady manifests. Its story is reminiscent of the frog being cooked in a pot of water on the stove. The frog is fine but doesn't realize that the temperature is slowly creeping up. At some point the heat becomes intolerable but at that point it's too late for the frog to do anything to reverse the damage that has already been done.

These two examples might seem implausible but demonstrate the insidiousness contained in the effects produced by the *quincunx*. The more *inconjucts* a person has in their chart, the more likely they will be plagued with often undiagnosable maladies. The more they have, the more likely they will encounter declining health. That deterioration first begins in the mental sphere, progresses through the emotional disposition and eventually arrives as a physical malady if nothing is done. The key to dealing with an *inconjunction* is to remove and rebalance the effects of *squares, trines, conjunctions* and *oppositions* to the point where our sensitivities are no longer overshadowed by their grosser effects and then uncloaking and refining our perception of the more subtle effects.

It's unfortunate that these aspects create such hard to find and diagnose difficulties. They might also be called aspects of *infiltration.* At best, they can be symbolic of a simple irritation. At their worst, they can become a tacit deterioration similar to the dissolving and evaporative qualities contained within *Neptune.*

WAXING & WANING ASPECTS

HOW DO THEY WORK?

Most experienced astrologers agree that approaching aspects are always more powerful in their effects than those that are separating. But there is another perspective in judging aspects that is ignored if not all together missed. Aspects may also be waxing or waning. The same pattern of waxing and waning that is applied to the Moon's phases and her effects may also be applied to the relationships the planets have in their aspects to each other. For example, if a planet is in a waxing phase to another planet, its effects will manifest differently than if it is in a waning phase. Let me explain.

If we have Mercury at four degrees of Aries and Jupiter at five degrees of Cancer, we can all agree that Mercury is in an approaching *square* to Jupiter. But this is only one dimension involved in the *square*. But what if Mercury was at four degrees of Libra with Jupiter still at five degrees of Cancer. Is this really the same aspect? In the first example Mercury is approaching an aspect with Jupiter but its positioning is *before* Jupiter in the zodiac. In the second example he is in a zodiacal positioning *after* Jupiter. Should these two aspects be judged in the same way? I think not. Let's move on to a comparison.

Suppose we are looking at the Moon and her phases. Let's assume that there is a new Moon at five degrees of Aries. Seven days later the Moon goes into her third phase at five degrees of Cancer. Traditionally we would say that the Moon is *waxing* in her fist quarter phase. Based on the Moon's phases we have covered previously, we can say that the Moon's manifestation will be directed into *building* and initiating *action*. We also can say that the Moon is approximately ninety degrees *ahead* of her new Moon position. Fast forward fourteen more days. Now the Moon is twenty-one days from her new Moon position at five degrees of Capricorn. This puts her *waning* in her seventh phase ninety degrees *behind* her previous new Moon position. Traditionally we would say that she is in her third quarter phase. Her manifestation here will be directed toward *reorienting* her action in preparation for the upcoming new Moon. In seven more days she will begin a new Moon and a new cycle. Let's now return to our Mercury/Jupiter square.

We know in our Moon phases that we must have a starting point to reference our phases against. With the Moon, we know that position is the new Moon. But when we deal with planets, there is more often no new Moon unless we're dealing with the Moon's aspect to another planet aspect. In the case of other planets, the slower planet will represent the new Moon position. In our prior examples, this will be Jupiter. Since Mercury is the faster planet, *his* action will be what is *applying* to the "new Moon" position of Jupiter.

In our first example we had Mercury at four degrees of Aries and Jupiter at five degrees of Cancer. In relation to the zodiac, Mercury is *behind* Jupiter. In relation to Jupiter serving as a "new Moon" position, Mercury is also *behind* Jupiter. That puts Mercury in the third quarter phase relative to Jupiter. That means that Mercury will be directing his energies toward *reorientation* (waning seventh phase) in his application to Jupiter.

Now, let's look at our second example with Jupiter at five degrees of Capricorn and Mercury at four degrees of Aries. In relation to the zodiac, Mercury is now *ahead* of Jupiter. In relation to Jupiter serving as a "new Moon" position, Mercury is also *ahead* of Jupiter. That puts Mercury in the first quarter phase relative to Jupiter. That means that Mercury will be directing his energies toward *building* and *new action* (waxing third phase) in his application to Jupiter.

Seeing and understanding the phasal relationship gives us a much better understanding and discrimination as to how the energy will work between any two planets than just seeing it in a commonly perceived *square*. It is important to remember that *the slower planet acts as the "new Moon" for the phasal relationship between any two planets*.

All of the aspects except for the *conjunction* and the *opposition* will work in the same fashion. This is because *conjunctions* and *oppositions* do not have positions in different phases on either side of the axis between *waxing* and *waning*. They have applying and separating *orb* differences but not phases.

Now, let's take a look at the remaining major aspects to see how their phasal relationship will make a difference in their interpretation.

WAXING & WANING TRINES – *120 Degrees*

A *waxing trine* will land in the first quarter phase as does the *square*. Remember that each phase is forty-five degrees and that the third phase or first quarter begins at ninety degrees and extends to one-hundred thirty-five degrees. The faster planet will produce the action and contribute to physical manifestations relative to the slower planet that it aspects.

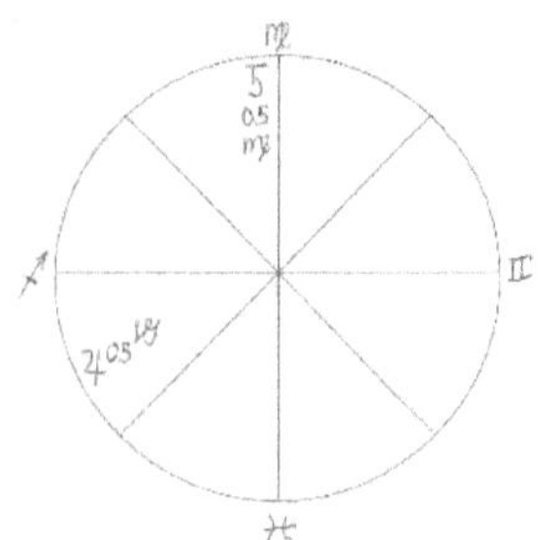

For example, if Jupiter in Capricorn is in *trine* to Saturn in Virgo, we would assume that Jupiter is *ahead* of Saturn and in its first quarter or third phase relative to Saturn. We are assuming that Jupiter is the faster planet and that it would apply action and new beginnings toward Saturn who is acting as the "new Moon" position. Jupiter would be considered as being in an *opening trine* to Saturn. That is, Saturn would receive expanded energy and *action* from Jupiter making Saturn work harder in regulating and structuring what it receives. The issues of the house that Jupiter is in would then be connected and brought to the house and issues that Saturn is in.

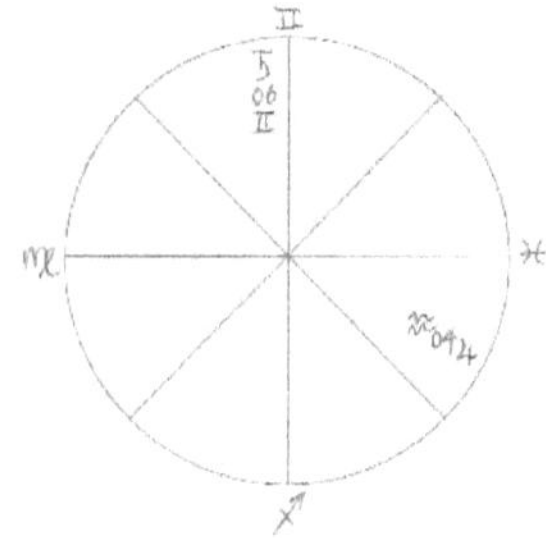

Conversely, a *waning trine* will land in the *disseminating* Moon phase. With Jupiter in Aquarius and Saturn in Gemini, Jupiter would be in the *disseminating* phase *behind* Saturn also in the *waning* part of the relationship. Saturn, still acting as the "new Moon" position because it is slower, would serve as the reference point. Jupiter would be considered as being in a *closing trine* to Saturn. Jupiter will now be *synthesizing* its energy and effects relative to the position of Saturn. Again, the issues of the house that Jupiter is in would then be connected and brought to the house and issues that Saturn is in.

WAXING & WANING SEXTILES – *60 Degrees*

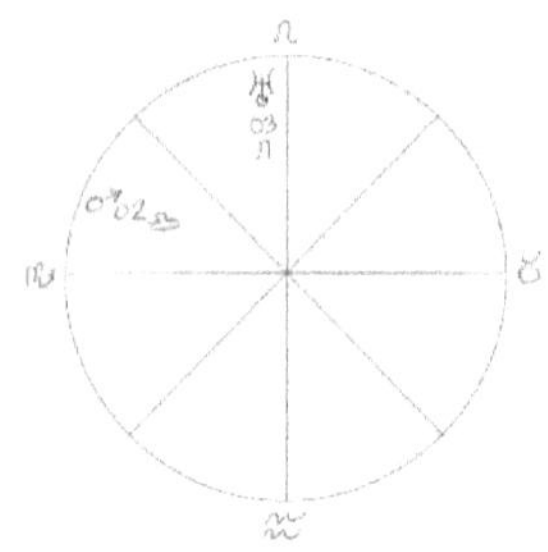

A *waxing sextile* will land in the *waxing crescent* Moon phase. With Mars at two degrees of Libra and Uranus at three degrees of Leo, Mars would be in the second or *crescent* phase *ahead* of Uranus. Uranus, acting as the "new Moon" position because it is slower, would serve as the reference point. Mars is in an *opening sextile*. His action would then be in process of asserting his action in relation to Uranus. The issues of the house that Mars is in would then be connected and brought to the house and issues that Uranus is in.

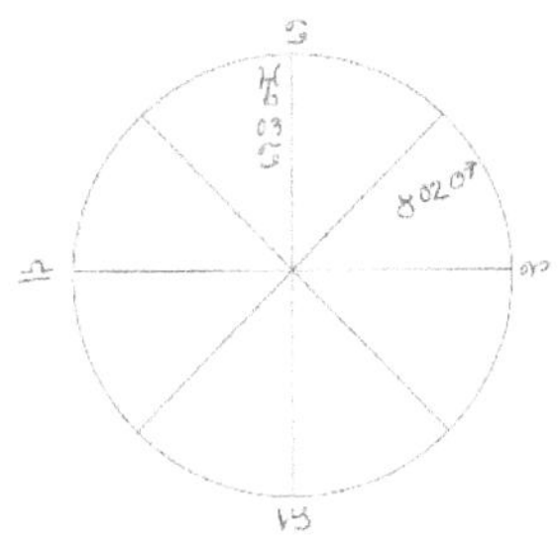

Conversely, a *waning sextile* will land in the *waning* third quarter phase. With Mars at two degrees of Taurus and Uranus at three degrees of Cancer, Mars would be in the *third quarter* phase *behind* Uranus. Uranus, still acting as the "new Moon" position because it is slower, would serve as the reference point. Mars is in a *closing sextile*. His *action* would then be in process of *reorienting* his action in relation to Uranus. Again, the issues of the house that Mars is in would then be connected and brought to the house and issues that Uranus is in.

WAXING & WANING INCONJUNCTIONS or QUINCUNXES – *135 Degrees*

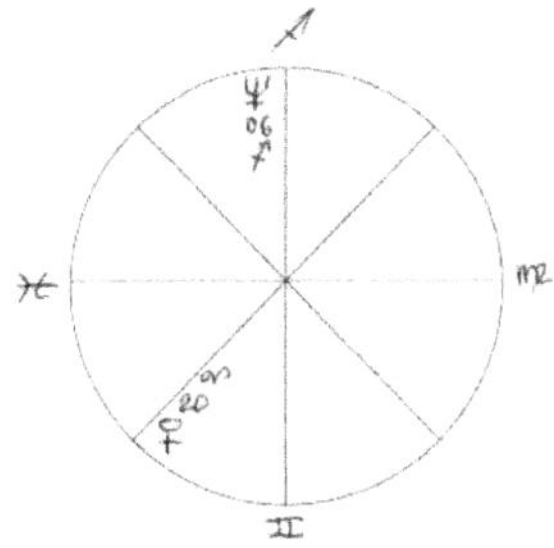

A *waxing inconjunction* or *quincunx* will aspect from the third Moon *expression* or *waxing gibbous* phase. With Venus at twenty degrees of Aries and Neptune at six degrees of Sagittarius, Venus would be *ahead* of Neptune. Neptune, acting as the "new Moon" position because it is slower, would serve as the reference point. Venus is in an *opening inconjunction* or *quincunx* to Neptune. Her decision-making process would be refining the *expression* of her values and choices in deference to Neptune's qualities and projections. The issues of the house that Venus is in would then be connected and brought to the house and issues that Neptune is in.

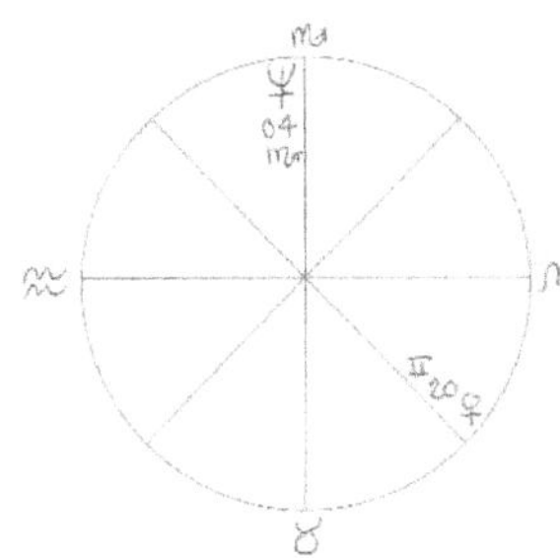

A *waning inconjunction* or *quincunx* will aspect from the *disseminating* or fifth Moon phase. With Venus at twenty degrees of Gemini and Neptune at four degrees of Scorpio, Venus would be *behind* Neptune. Neptune, still acting as the "new Moon" position because it is slower, would serve as the reference point. Venus is in a *closing inconjunction* or *quincunx* to Neptune. Her decision-making process would be *synthesizing* her choices in deference to Neptune's qualities and projections. Again, the issues of the house that Venus is in would then be connected and brought to the house and issues that Neptune is in.

THE MINOR ASPECTS

The minor aspects are a completely different kettle of fish from the majors. The major aspects are dynamic, powerful and "in your face." The minor aspects are quite the opposite. They are much more subtle, subliminal, and permeating in their influence.

Before we can even recognize their effects on us, we must first soften and tone down the loud voices of the major aspects before we can even hear or feel the minors. This is much like being in a room where everyone is talking loudly yet some people are in the corner whispering. The whispers cannot be heard until the loud voices have been quelled or diminished. Or, if you're standing in traffic, it is unlikely that you will ever hear the wind until the traffic dies down. Let's take a look at their possible influence.

SEMI-SQUARE & SESQUIQUADRATE – *45 & 135 Degrees – 8 Vibration*

I have put these two aspects together in that their active energies are relatively the same in their "feel." However, there may be effective differences in *how* they are applied relative to the phase that they are found in.

Semi-squares and *sesquiquatrates* are also aspects of *challenge* but with less intensity behind them due to the fact that the angular vector as compared to the ninety-degree *square* is a bit softer. We can compare this with our traffic intersection where an approaching collision in the form of a *semi-square* or *sesquiquadrate* might deflect off at an angle de-intensifying the collision more than it would be with a hard *square*. The same principles of *opening* and *closing* aspects apply here but of a lower intensity in their effect.

Semi-sextile would act a bit like a *sextile* but with much less energy. A *semi-sextile* is a building of energy in the *waxing* phase (*emergence*) and the releasing of prior efforts and energies while moving toward a new cycle in the *waning* phase (*release*). It would also take on some of the characteristics of an *inconjunction* or *quincunx* but to a lesser degree and awareness on the part of the native.

A *quintile* is an aspect bringing individual expression to the planets it touches. It also gives a perceptual perspective to the native about his or her existence. A *quintile* brings talents to the surface of consciousness. A *waxing quintile* brings these energies to the native's awareness while the *waning quintile* brings an understanding of where and how to release them.

A *novile* is an aspect or circumstance that seems inevitable and destined. It pulls us toward what we need to nurture within ourselves. It's almost like we have loose end characteristics and abilities that need to be pulled in and integrated into the framework of our psyche. A *waxing novile* makes us aware of the necessity of doing so. The *waning novile* tells us when we have either arrived or need to move beyond its focus.

A *septile* is indicative of an issue that cannot be solved with using rational thinking but where intuition must be utilized. It opens the logical mind to the influence of a native's intuitive sense and facilitates the translation of that "information" into words that will paint a picture and create a feeling of what needs to be known, acknowledged and, hopefully, understood. A *waxing septile* lets us know of intuition that needs to be followed. A *waning septile* lets us know if we were successful or not.

Minor aspects are primarily aspects of refinement. They sharpen the edges of whatever "structure" you're perceiving. They refine the lines, clarify the colors and pinpoint the sounds. But our awareness of them is much more vague and seemingly elusive.

What must also be understood and at the risk of repeating myself, please understand that *no planet is ever out of aspect with another*. They operate as a continuous tightly knit matrix influencing each other in not only obvious effects that most of us can see and feel but in much more subtle influences overshadowed by the more dominant aspects and our insensitivity to them. Our existence is an organic and spiritual mixture of events and reactions that is unceasing until we leave our bodies. Our task is to become as conscious of what is going on as we are able. While our chart reflects that perpetual and uninterrupted flow of energy, our task as astrologers remains to be able to see and explain as much of that as we can to our clients *and* ourselves.

The list that follows emphasizes the aspectual continuity that follows throughout the zodiac from any given point acting as a reference point. In addition to the continuity, it shows the difference in the potential of effects for the opening (*waxing*) aspects as opposed to the corresponding closing (*waning*) aspects. This should provide enough of an understanding in the range of effects to illustrate the differing energies that are available to us and how they might be applied.

WAXING OR SOWING CYCLE

The first half of the cycle is completely focused on the APPLICATION of energy and the *building* of a creation that reflects the inner self whether it be enlightened or deluded. All efforts and experiences are directed to this end whether the native is aware of the goal or not. Remember, applying or separating *orbs* should not be confused with opening or closing *phases*.

00-30 Deg.- Separating from *conjunction* & applying to *semi-sextile* - The awareness of a difference. Initial emergence.

30-40 Deg. - Separating from *semi-sextile* & applying to *novile* - Establishing the parameters of the difference by creating new forms, completely subjective.

40-45 Deg. – Separating from *novile* & applying to *semi-square* - How do the parameters of difference apply to self? Struggling with what to build upon and what to eliminate.

45-51 25' Deg. Separating from *semi-square* & applying to *septile* - Establishing guidelines for behavior.

51 25'-60 Deg. Separating from *septile* & applying to *sextile*. - Refining behaviors to deal with the unpredictable variations and contingencies of life.

60-72 Deg. Separating from *sextile* & applying to *quintile* - Preparing the groundwork for action.

72-90 Deg. Separating from *quintile* & applying to *square* - creative overcoming of obstacles to groundwork.

90-120 Deg. Separating from *square* & applying to *trine* - Committed to a course of action.

120-135 Deg. Separating from *trine* & applying to *sesquiquadrate* - The momentum has been built. The task is to now regulate the flow of inertia. –

135-150 Deg. Separating from *sesquiquadrate* & applying to *inconjunct* - comfortable with the flow we have a tendency to lay back and add changes that tend to personalize our creation.

150-180 Deg. Separating from *inconjunct* & applying to *opposition* - with the awareness that the completion of our creation is imminent we begin to feel a sense of urgency with adding the final adjustments before it's too late.

WANING OR REAPING CYCLE

The second half of the cycle is completely focused on the *WITHDRAWL* of energy and the *application of the attempted creation* whether complete or not to the native's needs and growth while providing the best reflection of the native s attitude in order that he may recognize and adjust himself toward the upcoming new cycle. Remember, applying or separating *orbs* should not be confused with opening or closing *phases*.

180-150 Deg. Separating from *opposition* & applying to *inconjunct* - with the ability to add changes past we feel a resulting mixture of fulfillment and emptiness. Fulfillment with a creation well done yet with the emptiness from the need to refocus ourselves in a new direction. If the creation was not produced according to our satisfaction, there may be a tendency to hold on.

150-135 Deg. Separating from *inconjunct* & applying to *sesquiquadrate* - by terminating the application of energy we become aware of others' regard for our creation and their feelings for it; positive AND negative. We must now release our egotistical attachment to it. Again, if the response is not to our satisfaction, we may attempt to force the recognition.

135-120 Deg. Separating from *sesquiquadrate* & applying to *trine* - we now find the need to adjust our creation that it may provide energy and vitality to others. We instruct on its best application.

120-90 Deg. Separating from *trine* & applying to *square* - in aiding others to receive the optimum benefits we adjust the flow of momentum and direction of the synthesis through organization.

90-72 Deg. Separating from *square* & applying to *quintile* - we now become aware of what aspects of our creation produce obstructions for ourselves and others. We also learn to control our reaction.

72-60 Deg. Separating from *quintile* & applying to *sextile* - we creatively adapt the flow of change through selectively weeding obstructions to the best use of our creation by others.

60-51 25' Deg. Separating from *sextile* & applying to *septile* - awareness of the groups needs and goals and adjusting the flow of adaptation to enhance them.

51 25'-45 Deg. Separating from *septile* & applying to *semi-square* - going with the flow for group benefit by listening to inner guidance even though it may disagree with our logic.

45-40 Deg. Separating from *semi-square* & applying to *novile* - preparing the groundwork for what appears to be the inevitable new cycle.

40-30 Deg. Separating from *novile* and applying to *semi-sextile* - awareness of what must be released from \ the self in order to allow the new cycle.

30-00 Deg. Separating from *semi-sextile* & applying to *conjunction* - intuitive awareness of the imminence of change. All that could be shed is gone and the focus is on the buildup of energy for future application.

Any planet, including the Moon can be *void of course*. When conventional astrologers talk about *void of course*, they almost always refer to the Moon. The most common interpretation is that when the Moon is *void of course* all new endeavors, major decisions, and our perception of "reality" are somehow "off" or unsuccessful. From an earthly or tangible perspective, this may be true. But there are positive and constructive options to *void of course* Moon in that external influences and pressures on the Moon are at a minimum and that it is an ideal time to listen to ourselves internally with respect to our deepest sense of who we are and what our lessons may entail. It is one of the best times during which our inner-self and intuition are much more accessible to our conscious mind because the noise created by major aspects with the Moon are at a minimum.

Technically, the definition of *void of course* Moon is the period starting from where she has surpassed the latest degree of any planet in the chart to the next new sign in the zodiac. For example, if the Moon is at twenty-seven degrees of Virgo and the largest degree of any other planet in the chart is twenty-six degrees, she will remain in *void of course* until she moves into Libra. Note that *void of course* Moon is only *void of course* because the potential for making any *MAJOR* aspects to any other planets has passed until she moves into a new sign. This time period which is empty of external noise enables a more potent availability of our intuition. Additionally, it is in the Moon's *void of course* that the influences produced by her *approaching minor aspects* to other planets can also be felt or heard. An analogy would be when the whispering in a room can be heard after all the loud voices in the room have subsided. This is when our intuition and more subtle influences can be felt and heard most clearly.

There are other dimensions which must be examined in terms of a *void of course* Moon. These are the differences between a transiting *void of course* Moon and progressed *void of course Moon*. In a transiting *void of course* Moon, her influence may be limited to hours or perhaps days depending on the latest degree planet other than the Moon. Her influences in transit are primarily effectual from the external. In a progressed *void of course* Moon the absent influence of major aspects may stretch to months or even years again depending on the latest degrees of other planets. Her influence in progression is primarily from the internal. Both of these influences apply a temporary effect on the relationship of the Moon with other planets. What is more poignant than both is when the Moon is *void of course* natally.

A natal *void of course* Moon creates an almost permanent disconnect in terms of her applying or receiving pressure and influence from or to any other planet in the natal chart. She is essentially free floating and not dependent on worldly cues for the information she receives. Her sign and house will show through what areas of life and how her intuitive exchange will be felt from the world. This intuitive nature will permeate the native's existence as being a prerequisite for making any decisions, assertions or taking any action. The native will also seem precognitive as there is an uncanny ability to witness and fully perceive the actions of others and "know" their eventual outcome without any tangible evidence. If the native is patient and attentive, they can become prophetic. This "knowing" or empathic receptivity is often *involuntary* and may make them intensely sensitive to people and their surroundings while leading them toward requiring more alone time than the average person in order to restore their mental balance and regenerate their energy.

Natal planets also can be *void of course* but only in the static birth chart. The latest degree planet in the birth chart has no major aspect applying to any other planet and will, obviously, not move into the next sign. This gives the planet's use of energy a freedom from the gross applying and material influence coming from any other planet. There may be applications felt through minor aspects but, generally, these influences will be much more subtle and intuitive enabling the native to work with them in a sensitive and detached manner. The planet *void of course* will be working more with the planet's refinement issues and the native's inner balance than in responding to the harsher more tangible circumstances provided by the external tangible world. The subtler effects will be used and felt from below the threshold of the usual material world's perusal and recognition.

For example, if Saturn is in the latest degree of a sign and therefore, *void of course,* his usual infliction of barriers, restrictions on physical bodies, structures, and circumstances would be tempered and perceived less intensely than they were to be in an applying major aspect. What Saturn would attempt to bring to the consciousness of the native would be his subtler effects such as the perception of Saturn's finer characteristics of awareness in terms of recognizing patterns and the karmic implications involved in the total cause and effect cycle.

NODES & DECLINATIONS

When we look at the planets going through the signs, they appear to follow a circular path around the earth. But this circular path does not move around us in an even fashion like our equator or lines of latitude do. Because our earth tilts on its axis at about 23 ½ degrees, the Sun, Moon, and planets appear to vary their movement both above and below the equator. They follow what is called the *ecliptic*.

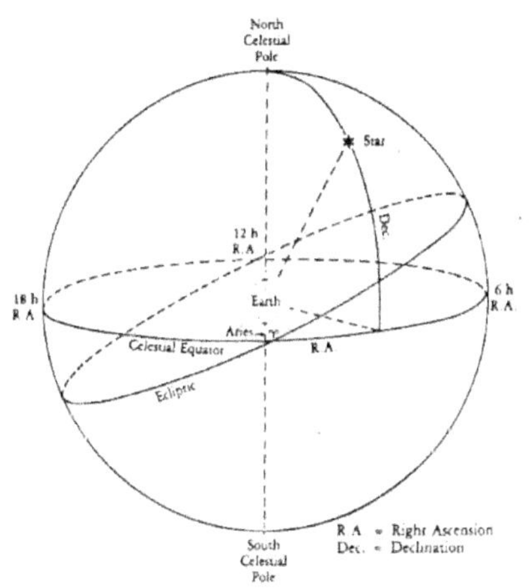

This leaves us having to create a system of measurement that lets us assess what the different effects the Sun, Moon, and planets may have on us because of this variance. Let's start with some basic *astronomical* information and terms.

If we start with the *Earth's equator* and extend it outward toward space in an imaginary plane, this will be what astronomer's call the *celestial equator*. With this reference in place, astronomers can create a scale of measurements in degrees that can reference every height or depth of objects in the sky back to this extended plane. This height or depth they call *declination*. This is shown in the diagram as a northern *declination* of the star's distance above the *celestial equator*.

With your comprehension of *declination*, let's take a look at the Moon and see how it applies to her. In this chart and the next you see a circle called the *ecliptic*. This is the direct line between the Earth and the Sun and then expanded in a plane around the Earth. Notice that at one part of the Moon's orbit around the Earth moves *above* the *ecliptic* and on the other half of the orbit moves *below* it. If her orbit is moving in a *clockwise* direction, you will notice that the Moon crosses the *ecliptic* and moves from being above it to being below it. This point that she crosses on the *ecliptic* is the Moon's south *node*. That's because from this point she is headed south or below the ecliptic. She from a northern *declination* (above the *ecliptic*) to a southern *declination* (below the *ecliptic*). On the opposite side of the Earth, she moves up toward where she crosses the *ecliptic* from a southern *declination* to a

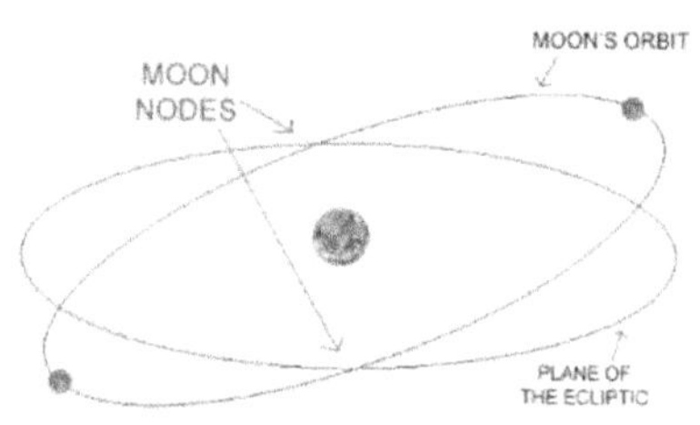

northern *declination*. This point of crossing is said to be the Moon's north *node*. These two changes of *declination* have a very strong influence on our karmic lessons and the behaviors that we must aspire toward (north node) but often fall back on when things get tough (south node). It's also important to note that the yearly cycle of the transiting nodes extends to 18.6 years with the opposition or reversing of the natal to transiting nodes occurring at approximately 9.3 years.

The nodes are, essentially, only theoretical points but pack a wallop in depicting the perspectives and attitudes we tend to bring in this life. If you look at the south nodal symbol, you'll see that it resembles a container or vase. This makes it easy to remember that this is the coffer holding our past life characteristics that have yet to be properly injected into our tangible current life experience and behavior. The south node also describes the behaviors and beliefs we fall back on when we fall into tough situations and have no idea about how to handle ourselves.

The north node also looks like a container or vase but upside down. It looks like it is pouring out what it contains on the world. These are the behaviors and beliefs that we must bring forward into our consciousness while balancing out past life issues that might be ungrounded or ineffectual in our new current life lessons and experiences. Most astrologers will quote the south node issues as harmful or as inhibiting in our new life path. But these karmic residues are not always bad or harmful. We may also bring in positive and constructive habits that simply need to be adjusted to fit current life circumstances. Remember, karma brings both "good" and "bad" patterns from past lives to this life. The nodes represent past *accumulated* but, yet unapplied experience that needs to be fit into the current life lessons. The house placements of the Sun and the nodes generally show *where* and *how* these experiences must be synthesized. Aspecting planets and sign rulerships will give added clarity and focus on the refinement of their applications.

NODAL DISCRIMINATION

I will take a different tack in defining the meanings of the nodes and how they should be applied. Rather than giving you a list of characteristics that seem to emanate from their placements, as conventional astrologers might describe, I will instead make recommendations for you as the astrologer to give as behavior changes and adaptations for your clients to consider in order to better follow their necessary path for growth and peace of mind.

You will find as you read on through my suggested counseling for your client that the nodal influences may show themselves through more than just the nodes themselves. For example, a chart might bring the qualities to be worked on with a south node in Aries to the forefront through the Moon's placement in Aries or the south node's appearance in the first house, or the Moon's placement in the first. All these placements will bring similar characteristics and issues into your client's worldly experiences but through different avenues. We can look at the chart as a puzzle to be integrated by the universe in bringing forward all the qualities that need to be synthesized in contributing to a soul's lessons to be learned. In this perspective we can see the necessity for having many ways for applying the same influence. With this in mind, let's move on to examining the issues your client may need to deal with through these varied placements.

ARIES OR 1ST HOUSE

(Includes = Moon in Aries – Moon in 1ˢᵗ – S. Node in Aries – S. Node in 1ˢᵗ)

- Learn to cooperate
- Follow the middle path
- Share the results of your pioneering and exploration

- Learn to de-intensify competition in favor of sharing
- Take time to listen
- Slow down
- To dwell in the future robs the present
- Be here now
- Allow a sense of fairness permeate all you do
- Think before acting
- Narcissism is a turn-off to others
- Allow others to experience and make their own successes and failures
- You don't have to follow others' advice but at least listen
- Learn to give rather than appease
- You are NOT alone. Realize you are part of the universe
- Learn humility…laugh at yourself
- Inspire and encourage confidence and courage in others

TAURUS OR 2ND HOUSE

(Includes = Moon in Taurus – Moon in 2nd – S. Node in Taurus – S. Node in 2n)

- Learn to let go
- You must either give everything away or lose it to realize you don't need it as an identity
- Watch others that you may learn how not to waste time
- Allow yourself to be taught
- Ease yourself into giving up "creature comforts"
- Renounce feelings of ownership
- We are imprisoned by what we control
- Reassess what is of value
- Allow your value system to evolve
- Learn to burn bridges
- Learn your own patterns of desire and subject them to discipline
- Employ self-control and moderation in all things

- Rid yourself of decadence and over-sensuality
- SOME change is good and necessary
- Eliminate possessiveness and jealousy
- Learn to find contentment in more than materialism
- Ownership is only valid where there is usefulness

GEMINI OR 3RD HOUSE

(Includes = Moon in Gemini – Moon in 3rd – S. Node in Gemini – S. Node in 3rd)

- Eliminate your fear of commitment - it is only a fear of being stuck or losing options
- Learn to focus your diversity on a larger goal
- Develop mental concentration – eliminate your tendency to be easily distracted
- You must find your own truth – it is hidden in the threads of your own experience
- Eliminate the perpetuation of trivia and gossip – Just because you divert attention away from meaningful issues does NOT mean you won't have to deal with them
- Learn what is "real" and natural in nature – Find the common tie
- You know that promising to do everything for everyone is not possible – Consider commitment carefully *before* making a decision
- Use your diversity of ability as a common tie to everyone
- Develop a commitment to higher goals and an allegiance to those who follow the same
- Allow others to interpret what you say THEIR way
- Keep your nose out of other people's business
- Get to the point – Some people don't need to know your reasoning -They will apply their own validation – Let them
- Accept the fact that there is more to know than we can learn in one lifetime – It's okay to say "I don't know"

- Learn the proper use of words – They're not weapons but tools

---

CANCER OR 4ᵀᴴ HOUSE

(Includes = Moon in Cancer – Moon in 4ᵗʰ – S. Node in Cancer – S. Node in 4ᵗʰ)

- The only security there is, is knowing there is none
- Eliminate obsessive behavior that "clutches" the past and outmoded traditions and psychic nostalgia that blocks emotional maturity and accountability – Fault and blame are not the issue – independent accomplishment is
- The "should haves" don't change what is
- Learn to say goodbye
- Accept SOME rejection – everyone else does
- Identify with the cosmic family – THAT is your spiritual destiny
- Be accountable and responsible for your own deeds – no one MADE you do it
- Overcome emotional over-reaction in order to divert away from issue you feel insecure dealing with
- Stop using others as an excuse for your own inadequacy
- Learn to grow old gracefully
- Dwelling in the past robs the present and ignores the future
- Dump the fretting and insecurity – Just do it
- Learn to feed others what you feel deprived of – Who better to know what others may need?
- Untangle yourself from your family by "nurturing" them only as much as your conscience demands – "Over-feeding" only serves to strengthen emotional "strings" of obligation and perpetuates dependency
- Cut the apron stings
- Separate family and profession
- Achieve self-dignity – Allegiances formed for honors must also share blame

(Includes = Moon in Leo – Moon in 5th – S. Node in Leo – S. Node in 5th)

- Learn to speak up – If you don't inform others of your desires, they will never know who you are or how you want to be treated
- Drop your expectations and learn to expect the unexpected – You will never be disappointed
- Eliminate your need for dominance and elitism – It is fueled by the fear of inadequacy
- Ditch the masks, personas, and the need to be Don Quixote – The honest response of others is worth more than any conjured worth
- In mediocrity no one has any expectations for you to worry about living up to
- Humility is the father of leadership – It inspires faith
- Develop universal brotherhood
- Eliminate personal achievement for glory – A job well done is its own reward
- Allow yourself to lean on others – It lets them know you're human and therefore lovable
- Consider the source and motivation in others' slights, insults, infringements, and criticisms – To take them personally is extremely egotistical and they probably didn't even notice that it was you who was in there way anyway
- Learn to appreciate beauty without tampering or accepting the credit
- Eliminate false humility and self-pity
- Count your blessings
- View life from a more dispassionate and detached perspective
- Join club and learn to be part of the group not the main focus
- Learn to become the "water-bearer"

(Includes = Moon in Virgo – Moon in 6th – S. Node in Virgo – S. Node in 6th)

- The truth does not come packaged – Eliminate rigidity and the refusal to accept anything unless it is on your terms – The truth is beyond the structure and your senses
- The physical is only a tool – let go
- The world is comprised of "greys" – Making everything black and white is only your need to compartmentalize life due to your fear of inadequacy in dealing with it
- Overcome your fear of living in a contaminated world – Everything is as it should be
- Learn faith in yourself so you can have it in others
- See yourself as being part of an imperfect world – No one is any more or less perfect
- Open your heart and learn compassion
- Refuse to pass judgment
- Learn to float – Go with the flow
- Don't let your attitude toward the job be affected by the work conditions
- NO JOB is beneath you – EVERYONE must serve SOMEONE
- That which you criticize outside yourself reflects what your struggle within yourself
- Discriminate between important values and transitory details
- Develop group consciousness – the needs of the many must BALANCE with the needs of the few
- Transcend past life physical limitations
- Your physical state is a factor of your purity and state of mind

LIBRA OR 7TH HOUSE

(Includes = Moon in Libra – Moon in 7th – S. Node in Libra – S. Node in 7th)

- You can't have it both ways – No one will respect you until you have the courage of your convictions
- Take independent action based on YOUR intuition, inspiration, and ideals
- Not everyone has manners – Don't expect them to – As a result, you must stick up for yourself
- You must learn to let your heart rule over your head
- Examine life yourself – You must learn to be less gullible
- Learn to be more independent and accountable – Relationships are for SHARING not placing blame
- Co-dependency is the worst kind of jail
- Don't live life through others – Challenge yourself…explore, pioneer, and discover
- Stop trying to save people – You attempt to make them obligated to you only because you're afraid of receiving the same rejection you grew up with
- Do not judge yourself by the opinions of others – They don't have to live your life…you do
- Assume leadership gracefully – They asked your because they thought you could handle it or they're afraid to do it themselves
- Your choice of marriage partner is EXTREMELY important – Choose and equal NOT a parent or a child

---

SCORPIO OR 8ᵀᴴ HOUSE

(Includes = Moon in Scorpio – Moon in 8ᵗʰ – S. Node in Scorpio – S. Node in 8ᵗʰ)

- Build your own new values based on your experience
- Learn to have prosperity consciousness – It's ok to have – No one will take it away from you
- Learn to be up front – People can't give you what you want unless you tell ask them for it – You are too paranoid about being manipulated by your desires
- Learn peace and moderation – Everything doesn't have to be an emergency

- Learn to determine values based on you own experience NOT the desires of others
- Accept support from others without looking for an ulterior motive
- Transmute your sex drive – dominance will not protect you
- Distinguish between want and need
- Generate stability NOT obsession
- Learn to conserve energy – have patience
- Eliminate intrigue - It's only a need to hide your perceived inadequacies
- Eliminate traps proving others' worthlessness – You are NOT superior
- Use your examination of others' values to define your own NOT judge yourself
- Learn to cherish conscience derived values and respect others' by not testing them
- Avoid "claim jumping" sue to fear of inability and unworthiness
- Enjoy sex and share – Don't barter – Avoid withholding or feeding others' addictions for control
- Learn to be accountable
- You can never know someone loves you and believe it until you stop trying to manipulate them to get it

SAGITTARIUS OR 9TH HOUSE

(Includes = Moon in Sagittarius – Moon in 9th – S. Node in Sagittarius – S. Node in 9th)

- You must learn the etiquette of listening and the value of communication
- Talk about difficult situations without running away
- Both sides must be considered – Not everyone shares your opinion
- Rise above being opinionated, bigotry and prejudice
- Take the time to do your work thoroughly – Shortcuts miss needed experience and details
- Develop an awareness of others – Respect their rights and privacy

- Cultivate social graces – They may not be necessary for you but others may find them very important to feel comfortable in dealing with new situations
- Walk a mile in THEIR shoes
- Put your previous knowledge to work – Don't charm others to take our responsibilities
- Make conscious your battle between animal and social
- You must risk your freedom to interact with others
- Yield to formal education in order to develop the skills to communicate your wisdom – You must learn THEIR language to teach them
- Teaching will fulfill your need for movement

CAPRICORN OR 10TH HOUSE

(Includes = Moon in Capricorn – Moon in 10th – S. Node in Capricorn – S. Node in 10th)

- Learn humility – False humility is self-sabotaging
- Nourish and encourage others and learn to accept it yourself
- Let go of attention getting devices and the need to display superiority – Achievement is its own reward – True recognition comes from within and is not dependent on the approval of others
- Learn to tolerate failure in yourself – Everyone is fallible including you
- Accept criticism – Don't take it personally – No one knows what you've had to go through to get where you are…nor do they care
- Learn to share your opportunities
- Let go of your need to manage and control others – It only comes from your fear of not measuring up yourself
- Apologize when it is apparent that you are wrong – Others can do it, so can you
- Eliminate your expectation of respect – Respect is earned not automatic
- Cherish what you have – Don't throw it away for the sake of what you MIGHT gain

- Learn to delegate – Then nurture and encourage those who have done the work even though the result may not be perfect
- Learn to COMBINE tradition with new and practical ways - Allow others to contribute THEIR way even if it doesn't fit your idea of what is proper
- Examine your roots – they hold the key to your fear of inadequacy
- Eliminate parental defiance – Accept that they can only love you in the way that they are capable of NOT according to your expectations or values
- "God grant you the strength to change what you can, accept what you cannot and the wisdom to know the difference

AQUARIUS OR 11ᵀᴴ HOUSE

(Includes = Moon in Aquarius – Moon in 11ᵗʰ – S. Node in Aquarius – S. Node in 11ᵗʰ)

- Learn to develop through independence
- Isolation is only necessary to contemplate and gather strength
- Overcome self-doubt – Allow others to know your wishes and values – They cannot give you what you want unless you tell them
- Leadership is accomplished through example NOT strategy
- Learn self-discipline
- Independence encourages creativity, resourcefulness, and originality
- You are special by virtue of HOW you contribute not BECAUSE you contribute
- Surrender your direction to the service of humanity
- Mediocrity is not oblivion – It is belonging
- Learn to tolerate self-pitying people – They are a reflection of what you hide behind your mask
- Identify with accomplishments NOT status
- Find goals that serve everyone INCLUDING yourself
- Develop a practicality and vitality in creative adaptation
- Stop wasting energy on daydreaming and strategizing – It blocks the potential for the here and now

- Make a connection between thought and occurrence – Thoughts are things
- Be careful what you wish for – You WILL get it but not in the way or at the time you wish
- The wish to serve others will bring others to serve you – There is no need to manipulate service to you
- Risk failure – Acting on only a sure thing does not increase faith in yourself
- When someone doesn't follow your values or live up to your expectations, you must let them know WHY you are leaving – Have the courage of your conviction – You can't escape rejection
- Life is not a chess game – To be loved you must let others know who you are

PISCES OR 12ᵀᴴ HOUSE

(Includes = Moon in Pisces – Moon in 12ᵗʰ – S. Node in Pisces – S. Node in 12ᵗʰ)

- Overcome superstition
- Eliminate the use of pity as a manipulative tool
- Discriminate your own feelings from those you absorb from others
- Eliminate escapism through food and substance abuse
- Learn not to overcommit through guilt or fear of exposure – You are not responsible for other people's work or lessons – Don't interfere
- Allow others to learn their own lessons – Don't use "helping" as an excuse to make others obligated to you to justify your worth
- Learn to say no
- Apply an "on/off" switch to empathy – Just because you were born with the *ability* to be a "psychic sponge" doesn't mean that you must always be in "sponge" mode – Learn to detach – You're allowed to have personal space
- Eliminate co-dependency and martyrdom as components of your identity
- Don't used poor health or poor circumstances as a way to manipulate for energy and attention – It will only make others resent and avoid you
- Learn to deal with issues directly – Use the front door

- Ask for help if you need it – Don't hint or manipulate through helplessness – It abuses the compassion of others
- Strive for purification of yourself and tolerate, with gentleness, weakness in others
- Pay attention to details and take care of your own health and environment – If you're not happy and healthy, you are useless to others
- Never doubt the purity of your heart – Have FAITH in yourself
- Eliminate procrastination, worry and "what ifs" – Release your felling of paranoia and persecution – If you don't, they will surely materialize
- Learn to organize and clean up your own loose ends before you attempt to "help" others
- Become accountable for your own actions – No one "made" you do it
- You are not responsible for others' feelings and lessons – only for being of service by PROVIDING OPPORTUNITIES NOT doing it for them – If they absolutely must hurt themselves, you must let them.

TANGENT SUBJECTS

UNDERSTANDING & DISCRIMINATING DECLINATIONS

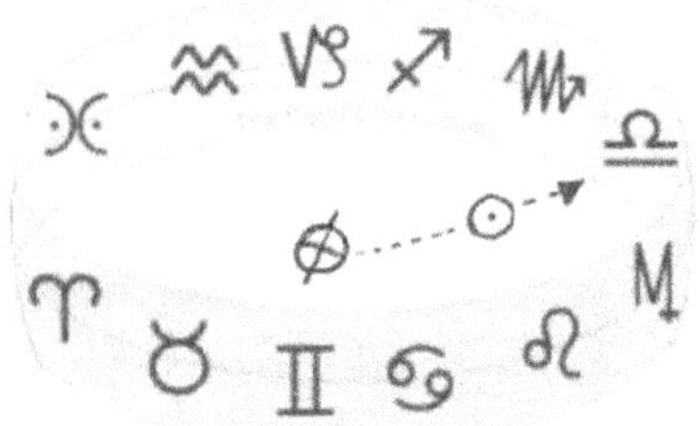

Planetary positions exist in two dimensions. First, they are determined by sign. The signs lie in a circular band that surround the Sun, the earth, and our solar system. These planets lie within the band of signs and are essentially in a horizon-oriented plane measurement depicting the locations of the signs by what we call *longitude*. These are the north/south *longitudinal* lines that surround the earth, north to south pole, and measure, in degrees, their distance east or west of Greenwich in terms of a twenty-four-hour clock. Each sign rises on the eastern visible horizon as the rising sign and, approximately twelve hours later, sets on the western visible horizon and twelve more hours later reappear on the eastern visible horizon again.

They exist in an east/west framework comprising 360 degrees around the earth. (The Sun is shown in Libra).

The second dimension exists in an up or down measurement relative to the Earth's *celestial equator*. This measure is called *latitude* and is comprised of the horizontal lines measuring the distance north or south of the *celestial equator*. This distance above or below the *celestial equator* is called either a northern or southern *declination* and is also measured in degrees.

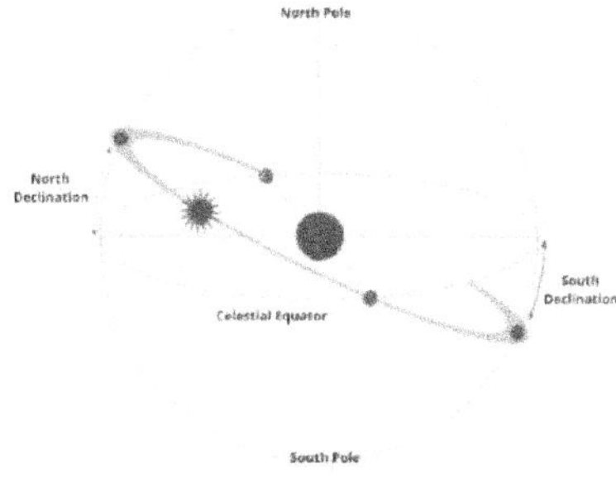

When we look at the *longitudinal* measurement through the signs it's easy to see *conjunctions, oppositions, squares* and more. This is what almost all astrologers use to determine the relationships (aspects) between the planets. But this second dimension, *declinations*, is rarely used. Although it only encompasses *conjunctions* and *oppositions*, it is an invaluable hidden asset to assess the relationships between planets but instead in an altitude dimension above or below the Earth's equator.

Aspects through the zodiac encompass mostly tangible and recognizable issues that can be contested in our day to day lives. The *declinations* are different. They operate on a different plane which is more internal than outwardly recognizable. Generally, planets in a southern *declination*, much like the Moon's south node, are symbolic of qualities, perspectives, issues, or habits that need to either be properly re-integrated within our psyches or altogether dropped. Their current quality of use "evolutionarily" lags behind the application of how other planets on or above the *celestial equator* function. They essentially need to be "updated" much like a computer program might need to update their drivers to be compatible with other contemporary programs. Planes in a northern *declination*, again like the Moon's nodes, are symbolic of qualities, perspectives, issues, or habits that need to be aspired toward or worked toward incorporating into the native's psyche. We might compare this to adding a *new* computer program to our hard drive repertoire to broaden our awareness and effectiveness.

What gets interesting is when planets occupy the same degree of *latitude* above and below the *celestial equator*. When they are both in the same degree of northern *latitude*, they operate like a *conjunction*. When one is north and the other is south at the same degree, they operate like an *opposition*. Remembering our aspects, *conjunctions* bring attempted *synthesis* and *oppositions* bring attempted *awareness*. In the *conjunction*, the closer the orb, the more intense the attempted *synthesis*. In the *opposition*, the further away from each other the planets are, the more intense the *awareness* potential.

For example, if we had Uranus at fifteen degrees north and the Moon at fourteen degrees thirty-five minutes north, we would have a north *latitude conjunction*. The implication would be that the native must work to align their emotional content with their intuition rather than simply following and directing their emotions intellectually. If the same *conjunction* were in a southern *latitude*, the directive would be to somehow drop or reprogram how the Moon and Uranus interact.

If the Uranus was at fifteen degrees north and the Moon was at fourteen degrees thirty-five minutes *south*, they would reflect an *opposition* and it would present a need for the native to become more aware how their intuitions and emotions interact in order to better sort out the relationship between them.

Declinations offer an additional dimension for astrologers to recognize the depth of the matrix of potential and variations that an astrological chart can provide us with. The range of possibilities is endless, and its potential for variations is capable of displaying the individuality inherent in every human on the face of the Earth.

RETROGRADES & THE PLANETS

A retrograde is where a planet is *perceived* as moving backwards. Notice I said *perceived*. The planet doesn't actually move backward but from our perspective in the solar system, it appears that way. Since it is from our perspective, the influences also occur from our perspective. From the other planets and their perspectives, they may still appear direct.

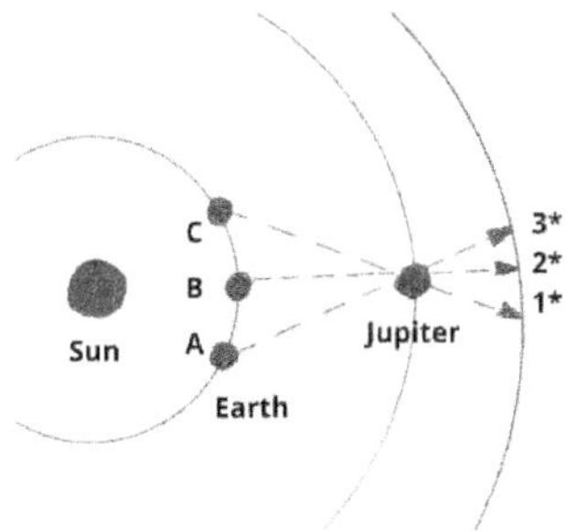

In the following diagram we have the Sun in the center with Earth and Jupiter orbiting around him. *Retrogrades* are, essentially, a function of planets moving at different speeds in their orbit. Jupiter takes much more time than Earth to complete his orbit around the Sun as he has a much further distance to travel. When Earth moves in her orbit, she will pass him twelve times since it takes one year for Earth to complete her orbit while it takes Jupiter twelve years to complete his. In the diagram we see Earth passing Jupiter moving from point A to point C. If we look at Jupiter's orbit while this is happening, we can see that from Earth's perspective, Jupiter *appears* to be traveling backward. What we can say about the resulting energy is that the appearance of any planet moving *retrograde precludes* the perception of the *increasing* effects it might create during its forward motion.

There are a couple of things that need to be addressed concerning *retrogrades*. First, as Earth overtakes a soon to be *retrograde* planet, it first appears to slow down its progression through the sign. As she passes, the movement appears to stop. This is called being *at station*. This is the point at which whatever the *retrograding* planet is bringing in in terms of effect is the most powerful. This happens at the beginning of the *retrograde* and again at the end. The beginning is the most powerful and the end brings an easing of any tension that might have been created.

Second, the general consequence of a *retrograde* is a slowing of the planet's energy moving forward in its progression of effects. This slowing eases any pressure for change that the planet may have been creating in its forward motion and enables "breathing room" for the native to retrace the most recent changes that have been brought about by the planet. In a transit or progression, the effect is temporary, and we can see and feel the ebb and flow of those effects. In a natal chart, the intensity and "reverse" direction is a stable perspective that is used by the native for their entire life. That is, whatever energies the *retrograde* planet brings to the chart will remain in a retrospective pattern. This will create a resistance or even a consistent operating pattern where the native always hesitates or holds back when issues with that planet come to the fore.

For example, if Mars were to be *retrograde*, it would be difficult to motivate the native to move or create action where the average person would be inclined to act. Or if Jupiter were *retrograde*, the native might find it difficult to move past any values or barriers thereby allowing Saturn to have the dominant effect over any expansion or contraction requirements concerning action.

It's also important to note that any planets *outside* the orbit of Earth would only appear *retrograde* once per year where the planets *inside* her orbit may do so multiple times. The farther the outside orbit, the longer the *retrograde* would last.

Additionally, when a transiting planet returns to its birthplace and the natal chart shows that the natal planet is *retrograde*, its approach will create tremendous pressure conflicting with the native's propensity to maintain a retrograde perspective. This effect will last through all of the planet's transitory cycles and peak every time it passes its birth position and hard angles to it. Typically, *retrogrades* offer a karmic opportunity to "reset" the characteristic presentations of some planets that might seem to be off or need to be properly reset.

It's also important to note that the *retrogrades* of the outer planets exist in a much larger sampling of the natal general population due to the fact that they last for longer periods of time. This would make the *retrograde* characteristics of those outer planets more common and seen more often. In these cases, the natives that have them would be more common, widely understood and accepted as they would embody, typically, generational issues in their presentation.

PLANETS IN MUTUAL RECEPTION

Planets can be in *mutual reception* based on sign rulership, house rulership or by sign/ house rulership. Most easy to see is, first, when ruling planets are in each other's sign. That is, the ruler of one sign exchanges positions with the ruler of another sign. For example, if Mars is in Cancer and the Moon is in Aries, they are said to be in *mutual reception* by sign/sign rulership combination.

The second example is in *mutual reception* through house rulership. If the Sun is in the third house and Mercury is in the fifth house, they are again in *mutual reception* by house/house rulership combination.

The third example is a little more difficult to find. If Mercury is in Aries and Mars is either in the third or sixth house, they are again in *mutual reception* but by sign/house rulership combination.

The major significance of this type of relationship is that their actions are often contingent on each other's actions, perspectives, and motivations. So, Mars in Cancer will be unable to act without being influenced by the Moon in Aries and vice versa. From a karmic perspective, the signs and planets are "forced" into a synthesis of energies. They must be included in each other's circumstances. If the circumstances for a synthesis of energies is not available, then there, at the least, must evolve an awareness and consideration of their interaction on the part of the native. This could be due to the fact that they were too inseparable or that they precluded each other's activities in past lives.

Planets can be found in *mutual reception* in the birth chart. They may also move into *mutual reception* through transit or progression. In transit, they would most likely reflect in external or visible circumstances. In progression, they would more affect inner development and growth.

FINAL DISPOSITORS

Psychologically, there are patterns that we follow when we deal with issues, events, values and circumstances. These follow a sequence of processes that are determined by rulership. The rulerships are connected through a "chain of command." They sequentially bring together qualities of endeavor including our motivations, values, preferences, relationships, emotions, planning, history and a whole host of other perceptual factors. Since each chart is an expression of individual qualities, the "chain of command" toward the *final dispositor* will also reflect our individuality. Please understand that this "lineage" reflects the flow of energy as it moves through our psyche and motivates us onto action, inertia and/or stasis.

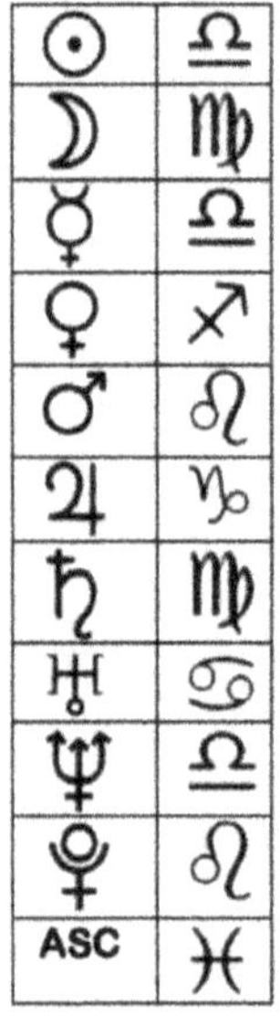

Let's begin by starting with a list of a native's planetary positions.

When we begin our "chain of command," we usually start with the Sun. Since the Sun is in Libra, we look to its ruler, Venus. Venus is in Sagittarius. So now we move to its ruler, Jupiter. Jupiter is in Capricorn. Since Capricorn is ruled by Saturn, we move to his placement in Virgo. Virgo is ruled by Mercury and he is in Libra. Libra is ruled, again, by Venus. This constructs a cycle of flow for the energy.

Leftover we have Uranus in Cancer leading to the Moon in Virgo that leads to back to Mercury in the loop. We also have Neptune in Libra, again leading to Venus and Mars and Pluto leading to the Sun all feeding the loop. Lastly, we have the ascendant in Pisces feeding into Jupiter. We now have a primary pattern for the energy flow.

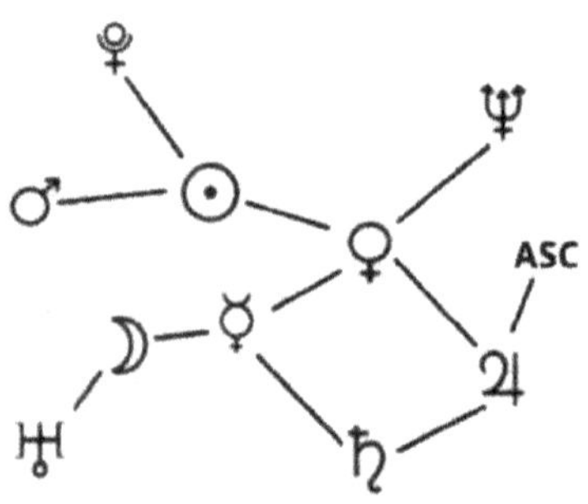

This pattern of energy regulates our participation in the physical world. Since it is tangible and is mostly what we can see the consequences of, we call this an *exoteric* pattern. We call it *exoteric* because it exemplifies the external shell of our energy pattern much like a lobster retains an exoskeleton. The rulerships are strictly the older day/night representatives that handle what is mostly in the visible world. There are other rulerships patterns that I will present later in this book called *esoteric* and *hierarchical*. The *esoteric* focuses on our personal and internal growth and the *hierarchical* focuses on the White Brotherhood and the evolution of our civilization.

We can see that there is a dominant loop in the cycle of energy between Venus, Jupiter, Saturn and Mercury. We can see that the other planets simply feed the loop from a tangential perspective. The dominant flow of energy resides within these four planets and how they interact. I would now like to take us back to the keywords used for these four planets to give us an understanding what part each planet plays in the process as the energy moves through the loop.

Since the Sun is in Libra, his ruling planet is Venus. Fortunately, Venus is in the loop, so she is a primary player involved in the energy circulation. The keyword for Venus is *decision*. So, in her *decisions* and *choices* she will assess and decide the *values* behind the issues at hand. After Venus processes what has been received from the Sun, she passes on the task to Jupiter who addresses the *expansive* aspects of the focus. He will determine what parameters need to be broadened, encouraged to grow, and will generally apply enough energy to enliven the experience to a larger and more recognizable form embodying the native's perceived limits the issue's current potential. Then the issue is sent to the organizational department of Saturn to bring about its *completion* through streamlining the energy and materials used to power the issue. We might say that Saturn will put it through an "efficiency detector" which will address its conservation of energy. This will also address the required responsibilities and accountabilities concerning the issue. When *completed*, the issue will be moved on to Mercury. Mercury will determine how the issue will be communicated with and distributed to others in an *exchange* of ideas and clarifications. Once all the permutations have been discovered, the issue will move again to Venus to refine the process even more if needed.

Relative to the signs the planets are in; Venus will determine the highest values at hand (Sagittarius), Jupiter will construct and organize the *expansion* and examine the responsibilities and sacrifices needed (Capricorn), Saturn will consolidate and specify the details (Virgo) and Mercury will balance the communication and the *exchange* of energies connected to the issue (Libra).

Neptune's connection to Venus will offer refinement of the values examined. The ascendant in Pisces will add additional refinement, compassion, and sensitivity to Jupiter's deliberation. Uranus will offer intuition concerning nurturance (Cancer) to the Moon's discrimination of service (Virgo) before it passes on to Mercury for distribution. Mars and Pluto will offer energy and depth to the Sun's perception of the equilibrium present or not in the relationships brought to consciousness (Libra). For more depth, look at each of the twelve factors attributed to each of the signs from the *Sign Qualities* section of this book. This will broaden our scope in how the energy applied to the issues might be processed and/or manipulated through the "chain of command." We can also look at the houses that each planet resides in to know what specific life issues will be brought to the interplay of energies at each planetary juncture.

Each *final dispositor* map is a unique matrix of energy interplay utilizing and integrating the planets, rulerships, signs, and houses. On top of that, the aspects and declinations offer an additional dimension to broaden the perspective covered to produce a "4D" hologram through space and time.

In our next *final dispositor* map we not only have a path of energy travel, but we have a "singleton" planet that has no visible *exoteric* path to connect its energies to the workings of the other planets. In a positive perspective, this allows, or maybe even forces, the native to create detachment for the full expression of the planet's qualities. Perhaps, in prior live the native integrated the "singleton" too deeply into the matrix of the other planets for its full expression and needs extraction from the karmic mix. Now, as a "singleton," it has plenty of room to express itself without any interference. On the negative side, if the native is either reluctant or unable to grow into dealing with the detached planet in a positive way, it may result in their inability to utilize the energy of that "singleton" making that quality in them act almost like a schizophrenic or split personality. Let's take a look at our next candidate for analysis.

☉	♋
☽	♎
☿	♊
♀	♋
♂	♎
♃	♈
♄	♋
♅	♉
♆	♓
♇	♉
ASC	♈

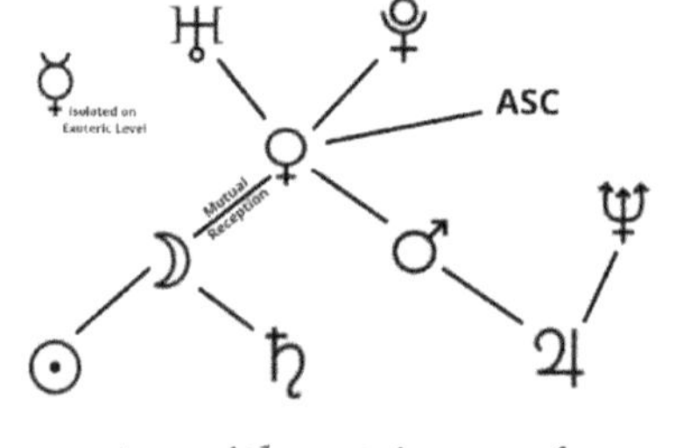

Our native was born on July 10th, 1856. Let us again start with the Sun in Cancer. Cancer is ruled by the Moon who is in Libra. Libra is ruled by Venus who is in Cancer which feeds back into the Moon. This is a *mutual reception*. In this case the Moon *cannot* operate without input from Venus and Venus *cannot* operate without input from the Moon. We can also see that both Uranus and Pluto are in Taurus which feeds into a Venus rulership. This gives tremendous unconscious power through them toward Venus. We must also be aware that Pluto was, as of yet, undiscovered until 1930. So, his influence manifests as a tremendous undercurrent for the power and regeneration of Venus' decisions and values. Pluto is also a representative of the collective unconscious. This makes the native uniquely in tune with the unconscious energy of his generation. With the native's ascendant also in Taurus, this makes them uniquely receptive to their environment and milieu through Pluto's position in Taurus in the first house.

The last leg of the energy matrix starts with Neptune in Pisces feeding into its rulership by Jupiter in Aries. Jupiter feeds into Mars. With Mars in Libra, he feeds into Venus and with the ascendant in Taurus, it also feeds into its ruler, Venus. The matrix is complete with the exception of the "singleton" planet Mercury in Gemini. Since Mercury is in its own rulership, Gemini and Virgo and with no other planet in either sign extending a tie of energy, it stands alone with no other *exoteric* connections through rulership. What further isolates Mercury is the fact that it is also *void of course*. (latest degree in the chart with no approaching aspects). The only connection available is through separating trines from Moon and Mars in Libra.
The lone Mercury "singleton" is just one example of the potential available visibility for the astrologer through the *final dispositor*. It shows the individual's uniqueness through a different perception and projection of the unique energy and its imaginable path. This is the chart of Nicola Tesla. His example shows the tremendous potential available to us if we work with configurations that might, at first blush, appear to be a "deformity" but, in the final analysis, a blessing in disguise. Make no mistake. Following through and allowing this type of energy to steer our will is a challenge in itself. Even though he was a recluse, genius and social "oddball," his legacy to the world must draw the thanks of his sleeping generation for the miracles he has brought to us. It takes tremendous courage to follow and forge this kind of path.

PLANETARY PICTURES

Combinations of aspects contain stories in themselves. We have all been aware at some time or another of a peculiar distribution of planets through the signs creating artistic patterns or even discordant pictures. It occasionally evokes feeling in us that trigger our intuition about the native who possesses them. But the pictures themselves are not as important as the energy patterns that are generated through their configuration. Kites or six-pointed stars are pleasant to look at but really don't enable any specific energy patterns other than an overall balance.

The most common pattern is what is called a *splay*. This is where the planets are distributed relatively evenly throughout the chart. This pattern is indicative of a person who is relatively balanced in their investment of energy into different life endeavors. On the positive side, this may be a person who is comfortable in their own skin and handles themselves well in just about any area of life. On the negative side, this may also indicate a person who is unable to focus on any one life issue due to feeling interfered with by all the planets being scattered other areas of life overlapping life issues which have been permitted to demand equal attention. It takes a solidly grounded mind and perception to handle a *splay* well. This is the chart of psychologist Carl Jung.

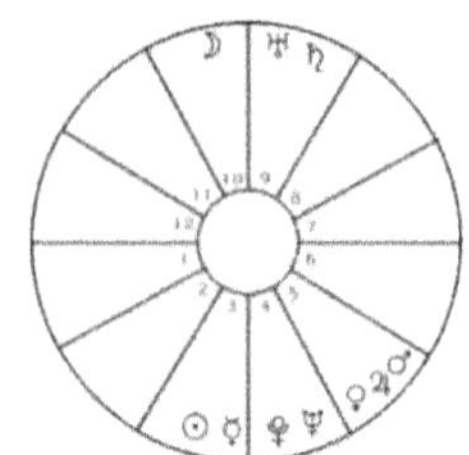

The *see-saw* is a little bit different. The *see-saw* effect is comprised of several *oppositions*. If we think back to our definition of aspects, we remember that an *opposition* is significant of *awareness*. This is the chart of Jiddu Krisnamurti 20th century Indian philosopher. His wisdom and awareness have guided millions. With a *see-saw* pattern we will either have an abundant wisdom or be in a dire need or the same or may even waffle between the two depending on the area of life we're dealing with.

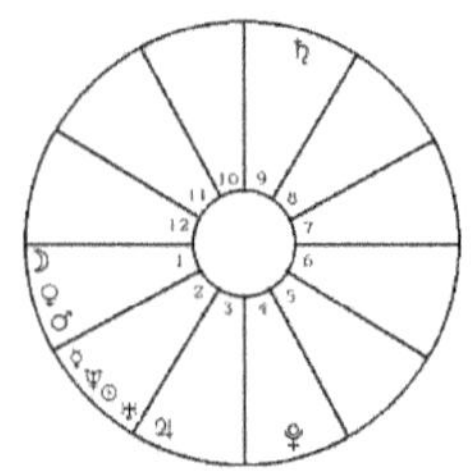

The *bucket* is the pattern of the specialist. The house that the *stellium* or main group of planets reside in will determine the area of life that receives the most concentration. In this case, the first through the fourth. The *handle* or the *singleton* planet(s) will become one of the most important factors in the release or production of the specialty concentrated on. This is the chart of the author Lewis Carroll. With his Moon and ascendant in Sagittarius Jupiter is a dominant planet in his life direction. Jupiter is in the third house which signals the point of concentration for his specialty.

In Carroll's most famous book, *Alice in Wonderland*, the unconscious workings of humans are exemplified through Pluto's placement in the fourth house of *foundation* with Saturn (physical reality) being far away from the *stellium* in the ninth house of beliefs.

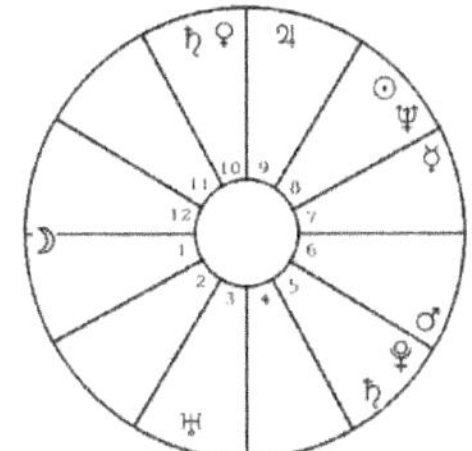

The *finger of god* is perhaps a bit more common in charts. It's comprised of two or more mirrored *inconjucts* with the concentrations of energy at the narrow point and at the *midpoint* of the open end. This is a pattern that seems to compel us to act or focus using specific planets or houses in our chart and the point between the planets in *inconjunction*. Remembering that the *inconjunct* operates on a subliminal or below the threshold of awareness, we can see that the Mercury and Mars are in a *sextile* to each other. But they both form an *inconjunct* to the Moon. This means that the relationships between the Moon and Mars and between the Moon and Mercury will operate below our threshold of awareness. So, when it comes to discriminating feelings (Moon) with Mercury (thinking), it may be very difficult to make a conscious connection between them. It may also feel like our thoughts and feelings have never been connected. When it comes to the connection between Moon and Mars, it will again be hard to perceive their connection if there is any but, since most of us operate on impulse rather than conscious intention, we might not even notice the actions we take until we have already completed them.

When we looked at the *inconjunct* in prior pages we learned that diminishing the grosser vibrations around us makes us more able to sense the subtleties that the *inconjunct* presents to us. The *finger of god* is a concentration of energy "encouraging" us to pay more conscious attention to the issues the pattern includes.

Generally, in a birth chart we adopt patterns over time and experience that allows us to handle the issues when we feel them come up. The urgency becomes accelerated when a transit or progression contacts the point planet (Moon in this case) or the midpoint between the two planets in the open end (Mars and Mercury). With a *transit*, the shift may begin and end quickly. When a *progression* hits the *midpoint*, it could last for years. Remember also that the *midpoint transit* or *progression* opposes the point planet (Moon). We may also find a planet natally in this position which would make it pivotal in determining how the energy might be used, especially, since the inconjunct brings only subtle and apparently buried awareness.

In this example the tangent planets may offer influences on the pattern's effects. If Neptune is in the same sign as Mercury, it may bring confusion or a potential for refinement. If Pluto is in the same sign as Mars, it may offer the intensity of obsession or potential for regeneration and the courage to examine and confront our subliminal issues.

AN ALTERNATE LANDSCAPE

BEYOND FLAT EARTH

Up until this point our focus has been on the mostly tangible known world with a peppering of influences that we might consider come from someplace a little less tangible than the world we currently live in. Our understanding about where those influences might come from or where they might direct us are hazy at best. But, nevertheless, they are there, we do acknowledge them but infrequently and are still confused as to what they might be telling us about our lives, our "purpose," if there is one, and what to "do" with them. The politically correct assumption is that they are some mysterious life journeys laid out by a mythological deity with a whole system of rewards and punishments dependent on our behavior on this earth. Although there is a sprinkling truth in this assumption, we must look more deeply into connecting the dots between the morsels of truth that we intermittently receive above and beyond our survival and our immediate physical, emotional, and mental gratification in our attempting to "know" and control how the universal matrix operates. Since we haven't left this world and come back yet with any earth-shattering knowledge or directives about our "purpose" here, it's up to us to reach into the deepest part of ourselves, free of our earthly egos and attachments, to find the path our intuition is leading us toward and why.

Astrology beyond the "flat earth" variety of cause and effect is divided into three basic levels: *exoteric*, *esoteric*, and *hierarchical*. *Exoteric* we know as being tangible, deals with the physical, emotional, and mental worlds and is primarily based on our tangible and "predictable" existence. It works with proofs, evidence and experience that mostly is verifiable by others.

The *hierarchical* is, for most people, totally foreign to our lives here except for the tiny sliver of a doorway that we might intentionally leave open through religion due to the fear that there *might* exist something more than our tangible world. The level of awareness required for our perception "there" is so far beyond our earthly consciousness that we haven't any inkling of what it is, let alone, how it works. We might say that its premise holds a tiny similarity in that it *does* represent a "master plan" for the universe as we've been told about our "creator." Probably the biggest stumbling block to our coming to any understanding or recognition of it is our need to maintain our possessive sense of self precluding any perception or attitude of selflessness which is one of the main prerequisites for its comprehension. Attempting any conveyance of understanding about the *hierarchical* level would be pointless except to say that we are simply evolving into being vehicles for its manifestation.

AT THE CROSSROADS: A NECESSARY CHOICE

Our spirit is much like a homing pigeon. We have a *knowing* within us that directs us in our daily and long-distance activities. When we are absorbed with survival and the capacity toward attempting to identify ourselves, we may not be aware of the inner compass that is gently directing us. We may only have a vague feeling that something is off if we move in a direction contrary to that urge and similarly have a feeling of ease if we move in alignment with it. Recognizing and accepting the directiveness of this inner source is our beginning for creating the bridge between the tangible world and the world of "intelligent energy."

Over the centuries man has tried to identify the source of this directing force by applying the cause of its application to a source outside ourselves. Since we cannot know the ultimate "goal" of this directing source, it would only seem natural to apply its generation to something separate from and greater than ourselves. Since our human mind can only either identify *with* or *separate* from "things" as a function of achieving a knowledge of our bearings and where we stand relative to that "goal," it would seem only natural to attribute what we *don't* know to something outside ourselves. The most obvious example of this perspective is the evolution of superstition and religion. Once these come into play, it is then only a small step further for man's descent into asserting his animal instincts for survival over each other through their manipulation. But herein lies the challenge for the *aspirant* to see and work toward something less temporal than worldly gain and prominence.

When I refer to an *aspirant*, I'm referring to someone who has seen enough of the world to know that there is something more than our simple survival and need for dominance over our environment and our competitors for its space. In this understanding we intuitively know that the religion and superstitions that men have created to explain the unknown are feeble attempts to gain personal security and freedom from the fear that the world is not under our complete control. It isn't and never was. We simply need to "let go." And those who attempt to control it merely becomes slaves to their own perceived insecurity buried in their own learned belief system. And rather than easing a conscience that demands that we answer for our shortcomings to a personified god to whom we have credited as conquering our own failings, we can begin to sense a world that is not so temporally bound. It is responsive to our efforts to align with it if we simply detach from our cravings and perpetual urge to control what we see and feel. But for many, accepting the world as it is is much harder than it sounds. And the fear of be overwhelmed by the unknown is more than many can bear.

Regardless of how we use our mind to play tricks on ourselves or others, this inner urge of the homing pigeon continues to persist in its intrusive influence and the knowledge that there is certainly something more to the universe that we are part of. All we have to do is listen. Its essence is intuitive and is the major key toward achieving discipleship and eventual initiation. But on top of simply listening, we must also concurrently work on moving past our need to control that which we sense or intuit and simply listen and accept what comes to us. Those of us who are deeply invested in controlling and holding on to our present belief system on how the universe works will have the most difficulty in letting go. The closer we get to letting our intuition direct our attention and actions, the more we will be able to build the bridge between the physical world and the *hierarchical* world dedicated toward the unhampered manifestation of universal law. This bridge is called the *antahkarana*.

Acknowledging the potential for the *antahkarana* present in all of us is a necessary perception for us to align with in order to understand and promote universal law. In describing the *antahkarana* I hesitate using the word *lesson* as it appears to infer a specific path that *must* be traveled. Again, this is an assumption naming an externally dominating force requiring our acceptance and acquiescence. A better word we might substitute for *lesson* might be an awareness of our part in the scheme of things. This reflects more the fact that we have the option for choice in all that we do regardless of the implications that some choices may seem to be inevitable. It often seems to be silent within us over lifetimes until this path is recognized and undertaken. And even then, it may be started and forgotten several times before it becomes a "permanent" endeavor growing in our psyche.

The focal point of this next section is to enlighten us about the characteristics connected to the *esoteric* level of awareness and how astrology gives us a language to actively approach our personal to impersonal evolution. The simplest explanation would be that the *esoteric* level leads us to the *antahkarana* beginning a larger awareness of and moving us toward the selflessness that allows us to consciously be part of and contribute to the "master plan" embodied by the *hierarchical* level. I look at the *esoteric* level as being our "spiritual workshop" for our evolution. Mind you, the evolution I speak of is not about the abdication of our physical selves, as many New Age thinkers have assumed, but its recruitment into the service of the egoless universe *incorporating* the physical and maintaining a balance between the physical and energy worlds.

AN UPGRADE IN RULERSHIPS

Since we're moving beyond a strictly earthly representation by the planets and the signs, it's only fitting that the rulerships for the *esoteric* and *hierarchical planes* should also be different. These new rulerships, and much more, comes from the work of Alice Bailey, a turn of the twentieth century writer. Alice was a housewife who took automatic dictation in channel from "Tibetan" or Master Djwal Kuhl. Her work in *esoteric* astrology is the primary source for *all* the later work that appeared on the subject thereafter. Although there were many other authors who penned work on spiritual evolution and its teaching, Alice and Master Kuhl were the only ones of the Theosophical Society who addressed astrology. However, her channeled work encompassed much more than just astrology and is only a "capstone" for the tremendous volume of work accomplished by Blavatsky and many others in the organization concerning world service and spiritual development.

The "new" rulerships all encompass different perspectives in how the energy of each planet is expressed and manifested. The first and most poignant difference is the concept of personal detachment which is necessary to "see" beyond the scope of earthly survival and personal preference. In terms of evolution of spirit, our perception of possession, separateness, and personal preference have been the most prominent roadblocks to our comprehension of ourselves as a cohesive species. This is not to say that we shouldn't have them, but that they should be shifted into being in balance with a wider view of our intrinsic connection to others through being compassionate and initiating personal accountability for the welfare of the spiritual growth of others. By the same token, this does not promote the abdication of selfhood in favor of others' preferences and "needs" but bringing to our consciousness the inevitable awareness and understanding that what we do to and for others we ultimately do to ourselves. In this light we can better comprehend our "new" rulerships and how they might be interpreted.

In the diagram you will see the *exoteric* rulerships paired with the *esoteric* rulerships. You will notice that two of the rulerships, Scorpio and Capricorn, appear to be the same. This brings to the forefront the fact that every planet has many levels of awareness and manifestation. In the same way that the element water can be expressed through solid, liquid, and gas, it is analogous to the potential for the planets to also express themselves in different forms at different levels.

You will also notice that there are two new rulerships that were not mention before: Vulcan ruling Taurus and Earth ruling Sagittarius. They both only connect to *esoteric* and *hierarchical* levels

	EX	ES
♈	♂	☿
♉	♀	Vulcan
♊	☿	♀
♋	☽	♆
♌	☉	♅
♍	☿	☽
♎	♀	♅
♏	♂	♂
♐	♃	⊕
♑	♄	♄
♒	♄	♃
♓	♃	♇

In looking at the new rulerships we must understand that our perception of their potential must be well broadened beyond our *exoteric* viewpoint on how they operate even in the physical world. For those of us who totally place our beliefs in only tangible and evidential proofs, this will be a very difficult transition. For those of us who have at least some acceptance that there *is* something more than what we can perceive while we are primarily *participants* in the larger world scenario and trust that we can *never* be in total control over what surrounds us, it will be significantly easier.

ESOTERIC MERCURY

Exoterically, we know Mercury rules Gemini and Virgo. We also know that Mercury's primary influence is one of *exchange, duality* and *discrimination*. It's easy for us to understand when Mercury discriminates between mental diversity (before, during and after) and physical diversity (hot verses cold). Both the mental and physical perceptually reside on the tangible or materialistic plane since they both are akin to and often follow the linearity of common sense and logic. Since *esoteric* Mercury rules the fire imbued Aries rather than the mental or physical planes of Gemini and Virgo, the Aries *esoteric* rulership works primarily with our *intuitive* function. Here, *there is no before, during or after*. It's all happening at the same time. This is a decidedly different use of the energy. The *exoteric* use of air and earth energies works primarily in the physical while Mercury's *esoteric* use of fire energy works on *both* through acting as a bridge between the tangible and intangible.

Mercury in Aries works on the *non-linear* comprehension of what comes through our *intuition*. On a baser and more common level, this kind of action can be seen as the result of impulse, instinct so some sort of intangible perception. We may prefer to drive down a different street or decide to participate in an event simply because we feel that it would be better for us. We may decide to not to participate due to a vague feeling that it might not turn out favorably for us. We also may just *know* that the phone is going to ring and who it will be without prior warning or knowledge. Most people consider *this* to be our *intuition*. Some of us may even call it psychic or prophetic. In today's work, very little past the intangible is considered to be even close to rational or practical. But *intuition* can work on a much broader scale than what most people are familiar or even comfortable with. Some occurrences of *intuition* come with a whole symphony of parts and movements all being perceived in a split second. Most of the few people who are cognizant of it call it a flash or burst of light that overwhelms the senses one moment and the next it is gone. Those who reside on the *exoteric* **and** *esoteric* know of it and some have even learned to use it. They call it a vision or *intuitive* flash. Those who reside *only* on the *exoteric* level call it a daydream or irrational.

Intuition comes through in flashes that bring a full "picture" into our perception all at once often including a full array of sights, smells, tastes, sounds, tactile sensations, and sounds normally perceived only on the physical dimension. Beethoven described it as receiving a symphony in its totality in an instant. Everything fits together like a matrix or multi-level puzzle all at once. In this way *intuition* works in a "now" time frame without any linearity. The challenge is to render it into to a linearly understood framework capable of being manifested and conveyed to others. Like a dream, many of us lose it before we get to that point. It takes a repeated and concentrated effort to make its workings familiar enough for us to construct the bridge between both tangible and intangible formats. This is one of the reasons that Mercury's meanings include fluidity and "genderlessness."

ESOTERIC VENUS

Exoterically, we know Venus rules Taurus and Libra. Mercury may rule the senses and how we perceive them but Venus rules our choices and preference between them. What we value or not (Taurus) and whom we prefer to have in our company or not (Libra) is the domain of Venus in a tangible or *exoteric* dimension. In this light Venus works toward decisions, priorities and commitments between tangible applications and polarities. *Esoterically,* Venus rules Gemini and works instead toward *choiceless awareness.* This is the state of seeing polarities as a whole while they contribute to the definition of each other through their opposition. In doing this we see the polarities as a whole or in in terms of halves and partitions yet not having or expressing any choice or preference for either. Venus in Gemini encourages us to eliminate any form of bias which jades our perception and understanding of polarized qualities, concepts or circumstances thereby inducing us *not* to choose between the polarized options. The aim is to induce inclusion in the whole and to seeing all its parts in terms of a unified entity.

Exoteric Venus encourages us to select preferences in discriminating our priorities which effectively lays out our life path. These will be circumstances that move us through our *dharma* and most feasible growth processes. Toward becoming a maturing soul our objective is to slowly move away from polarizing our choices while allowing others to take sides without our reacting to them. The moment we choose a polarity we plunge back into the *exoteric* world with both feet. Venus in Gemini asks us to back away from polarizing ourselves and to allow the world to unfold without our personal resistance. Our polarization is the basis on which our ego is founded upon. It differentiates us from others through our choices and preferences and sets us apart from the world with an identity which adds to the overall polarization load of the planet. This makes the world more of a divided place allowing for continued prejudice, superiority, bigotry and a whole host of identity-based separations. Being an individual and exemplifying a specific character is one thing but needing to blow our own horn and oppose others to validate it is something very different. The line between the two is thin and our conscience has domain.

ESOTERIC MARS

Exoteric Mars rules Aries and Scorpio. On this plane Mars rules all forms of action. In Aries Mars acts out in the open and in Scorpio Mars acts from either behind the scenes or incites others to act in his proxy. From Aries the actions emanate from impulse or intuition (cardinal fire). From Scorpio the action is set in motion through feelings and emotions (fixed water). *Exoteric* Mars brings the native movement, power, and kinetic potential. His actions enable survival, identity projection and egoic power. He enables the action that we take to stand out in the world. *Esoterically*, Mars has only one rulership which is still in Scorpio. Even though Mars embodies an *exoteric* perspective in Scorpio, a change in depth of perception and focus will also allow his *esoteric* portrayal. The primary difference between *exoteric* and *esoteric* is that in *exoteric* Mars' application of energy the movement is directed *outward*. In an *esoteric* application, his movement is directed *inward*.

The inward movement of Mars is in answer to the requirements for the bridge to be painstakingly constructed between our *exoteric* and *hierarchical* being. The *hierarchical* plane is a much broader awareness encompassing the lesser planes in which we are systemically less aware of the totality of our combined physical and spiritual existences. For us to begin to become aware of, bridge and use the energies that connect the three planes, we must follow a process of dropping our egotistical attachments and emotional patterns that prevent us from being more aware. That requires us to go through a process of "soul searching" while questioning the motives for our actions and the expected outcomes that we assume must result. Mars in Scorpio allows for just such a penetration that assists us in evolving us from the scorpion to the eagle and eventually toward the phoenix. This is one of the reasons that Scorpio is considered to be the sign of death, sex and regeneration – all of which require the surrender of our egotistical attachments in the process. Be aware that we are only speaking of the attachments we have that nurture and emphasize our self-perception and how we believe the public perceives us. This not the elimination of the ego but a reframing of it with diminished personal earthly concerns. A strong ego, devoid of egotism, is comprised of self-knowledge, honesty and dedication and is still necessary for us to accomplish our evolution.

Once we have begun to successfully assess and understand our own motives it is then that we can "see through" the rationalizations that others have for not using their abilities and actualizing themselves. This opens the door for us to provide them the direction and encouragement that effective therapists are able to provide clients toward their emotional rebalancing and spiritual realization.

ESOTERIC JUPITER

Exoteric Jupiter rules Sagittarius and Pisces. His modus operando is that he expands and exaggerates anything he comes in contact with. In Sagittarius he is outwardly directed and broadens our perception, awareness, and exploration of wisdom, culture, religion, philosophy and encourages our ability to *listen* to others and learn how and why they live, work, and play differently (ninth house fire). In Pisces he moves us toward becoming receptive and inwardly directed. The expansion takes the form of reaching out, both consciously and involuntarily, in sensing what others feel around us and comparing or confusing the feelings of others with our own. Empathy is innate in all of us. However, recognition of it, let alone mastering the use of it, is absent from most people's awareness and emotional repertoire, especially, for those who base their reality primarily in their physical senses and tangible reference points.

Esoteric Jupiter rules Aquarius. It brings with it the recognition of how things are connected together much like an interactive spiderweb. It provides the capacity to perceive the organizational and cyclic structure of the physical and emotional world. The most tangible example of this is physical science and the recognition of the consequences of the application and use of energy. Seeing this gives the native a choice; arrange the world in terms of personal control or present knowledge of the world to others with opportunities to comprehend their existence and their part in this matrix. That is, expand one's influence over the world or present insights and opportunities for others to perceive and move past their personal issues and concerns. The root value to be adhered to and acknowledged is personal accountability while understanding and accepting that each of us are small parts of a much larger whole that is attempting to move us toward group cohesiveness and awareness. Examples of the most personally invested individuals would be Joseph Stalin and Genghis Khan. The least personally invested would be Mohandas Gandhi and Albert Einstein. Our current day movements in westerns society indicate a strong current toward the Khan and Stalinist use of the prevailing world energy and circumstances.

On a personal level *esoteric* Jupiter is encouraging us to vacate the strategy that puts our environment under our dominance and control in favor of allowing others to determine their own fate in dealing with the world at large. Allowing others to choose their fate is a hallmark of self-love and strength of character. The need for control and dominances is a veil for hiding our believed unworthiness from ourselves and others. Most who feel this are unaware of these feelings as they have structured their existence to obscure their perceived powerlessness in attaining the love, respect and expression that they believed they were denied as a child. *Esoteric*

Jupiter exaggerates these feelings and impulses to the point that they will surface in our consciousness thereby allowing us recognize and hopefully eliminate them. This brings transparency into group dynamics and allows a stronger participation in our group evolution.

ESOTERIC SATURN

Exoteric Saturn rules Capricorn and Aquarius. Saturn in Capricorn relates to our structural, organizational and cyclic characteristics in our physical environment (earth). The building of our career and social status (acquired respect or flaunted authority) comes as a factor of the effort and materials we put toward any goal regarded as requiring a personal sacrifice. Saturn in Aquarius relates to our ability and strategy in handling our group participation, our positioning within that group and the social and career goals we aspire toward (air). These ultimately depend on our formed opinion of and rapport with those same or opposing groups. The groups we identify with or avoid also determine much of the social and humanitarian values, goals and perspectives we set and hold. Saturn in Aquarius may often result in a judgmental attitude toward people and groups we deem inferior or that have betrayed the values we hold but never spoke of. In the extreme of this occurrence, those who are perceived as betraying the assessor are often "excommunicated" without any knowledge or understanding as to why.

Esoteric Saturn also rules Capricorn. Like Mars, Saturn rules the same sign *esoterically* as it does *exoterically*. The primary difference is again one of perspective for his interaction. In his *exoteric* rulership the concept of sacrifice is actualized through the letting go of one option or potential in order to actualize or acquire something of a more personally advantageous return. The recognized cycles and patterns that fulfill his action are directed toward personal gain. The main focus is personal acquisition whether that be status, authority, restriction, control or any other symbol of Saturn's structuring effect in the physical and emotional world. In the *esoteric* rulership Saturn learns when in the cycle to "step aside" and permit others to take the advantage. The stepping aside is not so much a function of choosing who should receive the "benefit" but that the recognition of a larger and more evolutionary path is actualized providing for the structuring of the world toward creating more awareness for more than just one person or group. The stepping aside is a sacrifice made by the individual who has grown aware of a larger scheme of things and allows the cyclic pattern to advance our spiritual growth and evolution rather than promoting worldly domination or survival for one person or group. This resonates with the choiceless awareness of Venus in Gemini. The borders and thrust blocks representative of Saturn are used for opening doors for those who are ready for initiation rather than corralling and restricting them for domination. In this light the true meaning of Saturn as a teacher can come to mind. In Taoism, *The Way* is gained through daily loss.

ESOTERIC URANUS

With our assessment of *esoteric* Uranus, we begin our delineation of what were previously the "intangibles." Planetary rulerships have been primarily explained and exemplified through the conditions permeating our physical world. Even though religion has been used over the centuries to explain the unseen forces, the planets from the Sun through Saturn have been used to explain only what stimulates the five senses. With the discovery of Uranus in 1781, a new and as yet unknown manifestation began to accrue meaning based on the times, their ensuing circumstances and consequent discoveries. His domain of rulership grew in application as the times and circumstances changed. The most poignant representations of the Uranian influence at the time are the American revolution (1776-1789), the Industrial revolution (1760-1840), and French revolution 1789-1799). The obvious key Uranian concept we need to focus on is the idea and concept of revolution. In explaining the meaning of my keyword *revolution* for him, it will do a lot to explain the mechanisms and energy movements that seem to be so akin to Uranus' accepted meanings. You may begin by rereading my prior description of Uranus and his similarity to the "popping balloon" relative to his "use" and redirection of energy.

For those of us who may be distracted and absorbed by worldly matters, Uranus serves as a sometimes-startling reminder of how far off course we may have gone in following our assumptions about life, our participation in it and how much control we actually have. The *exoteric* person lives within the boundaries of Saturn.

Dione Fortune described Saturn as a sentry representing the "ring pass not" for our existence in our then tangibly structured and perceived world. It can be no surprise to us that Chyron straddles both the orbit of Saturn (tangible world) and Uranus (the energetic world) as a vehicle for healing and teaching between the two planes. Whatever sign and house Uranus appears us will tell us the area of life containing life patterns and personal traditions that might need to be diminished or even shattered for us to be able to stay aligned with our chosen life path.

Esoteric Uranus' effect is always geared toward returning all activities and energies back into the auspices of natural law and the cycles that support it. The place where we may recognize this is through our intuition. Remember, Uranus acts as a more subtle vibration of Mercury. We may not be able to see the exact logic behind the process but we can certainly intuit or feel the overall flow of where the energy needs to go. We can also say that Uranus and personal ego are at constant odds with each other. The more we invest in personal ego, the more maddening and frustrating the actions of Uranus will seem to us. There is an order to the universe and most humans are unable to fathom it with their mind. To perceive the meaning and work of Uranus, intuition is a necessary capacity to develop. And even then we won't see the whole story. Perception itself is polarized.

ESOTERIC NEPTUNE

Esoteric Neptune can be approached on two fronts. First, he dissolves anything that he comes in contact with. Second, once the grosser and more distracting influences have been neutralized or at the least minimized, his influence becomes one of refinement. Let's take a look at the dissolving influence first.

Since Neptune *esoterically* rules Cancer, we can quickly see that this speaks volumes about our ideas concerning security and anything that pertains to patterns that make us feel grounded. We must first ask what is it specifically that makes us feel secure or grounded? It is primarily any consistent structure, physical or otherwise, that gives us a continuous reference toward our position in the physical, emotional or mental world. That could be a physical barrier, emotional support or even the linearity of time. Remember, all physical, emotional and mental constructs respond within the structure of time and distance. If time and distance are both absent in our perception, we have no way of judging or gauging where we stand in the tangible world. This can be eminently unnerving for our earthly oriented psyches. Our perception and feeling of security comes from that consistent referencing to patterns and structures that we have become familiar with. Anything that is ruled by Cancer such as home, family and traditions all contribute to that sense of security and familiarity. If those signposts are remove, we totally lose our bearings.

This is exactly what Neptune's *esoteric* rulership of Cancer does. Why is this necessary? For us to grow beyond the psychological borders of our limited perception and anchoring in the physical world. If we are to move on in consciousness and awareness, we have to dissolve the ever-changing borders and preconceptions of how we perceive our position in the world. Neptune turns the ground below us into shifting sand where we must more and more depend on our inner balance rather than cues from the outside tangible world. In this way Neptune and Saturn work antithetically to each other much like matter and antimatter. I also find it curious that Saturn rules Capricorn *exoterically* (personal gain) and *esoterically* (personal sacrifice) from the opposite side of the zodiac from Cancer. This only serves to verify their "polarity" in types of perception and conception in the choices we must make to enhance our consciousness yet, while maintaining a footing in both worlds. As an evolving human we endlessly hang suspended between the two realities which are constantly changing in their relationship to each other due to the constant change and flow of life requirements. We must perpetually recreate and maintain the balance between the two so we may be aware and work in both worlds. Neptune's placement of sign and house shows the most poignant areas of life where this kind of growing awareness must occur. His placement also indicates the areas of life where mastery and refinement are the most necessary and possible for human growth to continue.

Now our second front, sensitivity, is also the domain of Neptune. Whether we are hyper, hypo or dead as a stone, it is the main factor that will determine whether we master and refine our skills or remain ignorant of our abilities. Stop and remember for a moment, when the noise and the din subsided in a noisy and chaotic environment, it was then that we began to see and sense subtle differences in our surroundings that we'd never seen before. The same is true for our inner environment. When we stop the mental and emotional chatter and cut our preoccupying attachments, our finer and more precise recognitions become more apparent. Neptune's affects, in this respect, are much like the minor aspects. We don't feel or recognize them until the harder aspects have been quelled or neutralized.

These refinements enabled may apply to any skill. They can range from tangible world carpentry to the most sophisticated emotional energy manipulation. The key is in allowing our perception to have free and unhampered domain over the subtle adjustments that must be made for us to approach the perfection of their application. Simply put, we must let our feeling and intuition, not our emotion, direct us. In this respect mental interference becomes a hinderance. Those who feel it but don't understand it often tell us "don't overthink it." Remember, emotion is a result of past pattering, our feelings and the mental judgments we have attached to them. These attachments act as an interference. They must be dropped for Neptune to do his finest work. Neptune's house and sign will tell us which areas of life the dissolving and refinement should provide the greatest opportunities for growth.

ESOTERIC PLUTO

Pluto *esoterically* rules Pisces. In this he connects to the *collective unconscious* of our species. This serves as a tremendous reservoir of energy and innate knowledge contributing to our ability to incarnate into these bodies. The unique trans-Saturn evolutionary trio is now complete. Uranus shatters unnatural or energy wasting patterns, Neptune dissolves the components holding them together and Pluto will now forge them into a new reality from the remaining elements.

Strength comes from simplicity. Although we don't think of simplicity when it comes to Pluto, we can say that what Pluto does is unify all the components of the physical world into a powerfully pointed focus for whatever the material and energy is used for. Since energy has no mind, it will go wherever it is directed. If directed as a result of ego or obsession as Pluto is often characterized, it will faithfully fulfill our personal directive. If directed toward a way that is more in line with what universal law specifies, then it will fulfill spiritual and evolutionary objectives as well.

Pluto's action is that of a blacksmith. First it smelts the "substances" to where they stratify on different levels. For example, if they smelt something metallic, it would be melted to the point where it would stratify different layers of the ingredients the same way oil would sit on top of water. They could then be taken separately and used for different applications. Even if the "substances" are intangible like gas, they would also stratify. This relationship exists between all the planes. Physical energies are denser than emotional. Emotions would stratify as a lighter energy. Feelings would stratify on a level lighter still because emotional attachments are heavier than simple feelings. Up the ladder in density, simple feelings would be lighter than emotions, thought will be more subtle than feeling and intuition will be lighter or less dense than thought. When we talk about the "purging fires of Pluto," we're talking about this smelting process.

Our pain is caused through resistance by our holding on to something that provides us a believed security. Pluto separates "substances" or beliefs according to their spiritual density. If we have any significantly attached energies, we end up being burned in the process. Regardless of our chosen beliefs Pluto will first stratify everything according to its density. Then the resulting components will be recombined in a way more in alignment with universal energy than our perception of them and forged into tools. These tools could be forged in steel alloy, or, depending on the "substances," tangible or not, fortitude, perseverance and courage. The house and sign that Pluto are found in will tell us where our greatest opportunities for spiritual consolidation and regeneration may originate through.

Lastly, the hardest physical substance known to man is diamond. The strongest energy is our unshakable will. Pluto is responsible for the forging of the hardest substances and the strongest energies. Is it any wonder that when the atomic bomb was invented that it was attributed to Plutonic rulership?

ESOTERIC EARTH

On first glance you might think that Earth does not have an *exoteric* rulership. But if you look at a picture of a chart, you will see the circle with not only the twelve houses but with four angles. These four angles in the form of a cross inside the circular chart actually symbolizes the Earth. Earth's *exoteric* rulership is all twelve signs. Her *esoteric* rulership is in Sagittarius and resonates in the sign opposite our Sun sign.

Earth in *esoteric* rulership brings our attention to the world as it is perceived by others. In this we must learn to listen and observe how and by what "standards" and methods others believe and live their lives. This perspective is designed to pull us out of self-absorption and into awareness of the larger world and our part in it. This is made obvious by its usual position in the zodiac *opposite* of where the Sun is positioned at birth, meaning that it takes us out of the focus that the *exoteric* Sun has put us in *after* we have dealt with our earthly survival requirements and *exoteric* lessons. This opens the door to a broader awareness.

The sign and house Earth is in will hopefully bring balance between the emphasized lessons and intended experience brought by the sign and house that the natal Sun is in through offering opportunities to gain awareness from the opposing sign and house. As the polarities balance out, we will have the potential to slowly gain the ability to see that this polarity *esoterically* is an overall whole and gain of awareness beyond tangible world similarities and differences.

ESOTERIC VULCAN

Exoteric Vulcan has no basis in the tangible world. This is no surprise as Vulcan has only been sighted three times and those sightings are unverified. Vulcan lives within the corona of the Sun. He is never more than eight degrees away. He serves as a purgator and operates like a Rotor-Router for the Sun's path so the native's lessons may proceed without being interfered with, misinterpreted or eclipsed by any outside force. He literally burns away any superfluous information and impediments. Since Taurus is the densest sign in the zodiac, it makes sense that he is its *esoteric* ruler.

Unlike the trans-Saturnian trio, Vulcan does all the work himself. He shatters, dissolves, smelts, and stratifies earthly matter, emotions, thought and attitudes and forges them into the tools necessary for our spiritual development. He is the Black-Smith of the universe. Vulcan is ruthless. Mercy and compassion have no place in his domain. Supporting the *hierarchical* agenda is his only objective. Nothing can stand in his way. Like *Star Trek* says about the Borg, "Resistance is futile. You will be absorbed." Vulcan's directive is simple; fulfill universal law. Nothing and no one will stand in is way. We can go willingly or we can go dragging our feet…but we *will* go.

Although he has no rulership in the material world his footprint in the tangible world is easy to see. He clears the way for us and each other to move past our personal and group limitations regardless of the security we think we may have or think we have provided. His is one of the strongest representatives of what our will is capable of once our goal has been set and our dedication has been confirmed. His spirit is indomitable. In literature, his energy can be felt through the poem written by William Ernest Henley called *Invictus*.

ESOTERIC SUN & MOON

I have left the Sun and Moon for last as the process for them is a bit different from the others. The Sun rules Leo *exoterically, esoterically* and *hierarchically* and the Moon *esoterically* rules Virgo. Although the Sun lights up the sign and house that he is in, there is little more that can be said about his obvious influence. That is, shedding light on the sign and house that he is in and bringing the native's attention to those areas for the development of their awareness. The Moon brings to the sign and house she is in past influences and patterns that need to be dealt with, properly placed and used. But there is another influence involving both the Sun and the Moon that needs to be understood. They both "veil" another planet bringing our awareness to the sign's *esoteric* planetary rulership that they are found in as a doorway for our evolutionary growth. For example, if the Sun were to be found in

Cancer, the veiled rulership would be Neptune who *esoterically* rules Cancer. A main issue that would be brought to light would be the need for detachment (Neptune). If the Moon were found in Libra, the veiled rulership would be Uranus who *esoterically* rules Libra. An issue being brought to awareness here would be our evolving from mental perception toward an intuitive knowing (Uranus).

THE SEVEN RAYS

Now that we've set some new preliminaries for interpretation and the perspective that they are designed to promote, it's time to observe a new framework for our use and understanding in astrology. The first concept to consider is an analogy with the *Seven Rays* by using a prism.

We are told by science that white light contains all the colors in the visible spectrum. This becomes evident when we shine white light through a prism. When we do this, all the colors are dispersed on the opposite side but at different angles. This spreads the colors out so we may see them. The dispersion occurs because each color vibrates at a different frequency. Because they vibrate at different frequencies, each color has a different wavelength and is bent at a slightly different angle through the prism. As a result, we can see a spread of the different colors. We can see this same principle operating in nature as the Sun's light shines through a wet atmosphere after a rain and creates a rainbow on the horizon.

As there are seven major colors in the visible spectrum, there are seven major influences emanating in the universe called the *Seven Rays.* For the larger majority of individuals, these energies are not seen in the visible spectrum but are witnessed by a very few as we might see the aura that surrounds every living thing. These energies are the building blocks for everything perceivable *and* not in the universe. However, since they are universal energies, the laws they follow, as does everything else in the universe, are the same as those of visible light but on a monumentally grander scale.

As with the earth's atmosphere acting as a refractory prismal agent, so also is the human body since we are composed of approximately seventy-three percent water depending on specific body parts. As the *Seven Rays* focus through us, the density and refractory qualities of our light refracting bodies channel these energies into varied forms and expressions accounting for the myriad of each individual's similarities and differences in their expression.

Each of the *Seven Rays* have a particular set of qualities dominating their expression. They are arranged in a set of three with the third one offering four more variations. This is very much like the three primary colors combined and producing more. Each of the *Seven Rays* are represented by a triangle of three zodiacal signs and their representatives. Let's take a look at a simplified version of each.

RAY ONE

The *First Ray* is an energy that embodies all aspects of *will and power*. This is not the will or power that we might perceive a human exhibiting over the environment or each other but that of universal energy literally powering the universe in a "framework" well beyond our comprehension or expectation. It is the power and ability to create with thought. This energy is primarily unexpressed in our world now due to the fact that its use and expression would create utter chaos as a result of our inability to maintain control of our thoughts and emotions.

Can you imagine what kind of world would occur if everyone's desires and whims instantly materialized within the blink of an eye? However, we do all have a small inkling of the capability we might have by having seen the accomplishments of a selected few people with indominable wills. As humans, we see this the most in handicap people who are essentially single minded and therefore, tremendously strong. The quality behind this is unity with a laser focus. We've also all seen the power of a unified and focused group of people working in concert. This is evident in an elite military special ops group or in mob rule. Both are driven by purpose but with an absent egotistical focus. The military group is focused intention and the mob is a destructive tsunami of overwhelming and irresistible emotion. Our innate empathy makes the mob's "success" possible. Both can be an irresistible force.

We know that when egotism becomes a component in relationships or in a group, our focus becomes split and the force behind it is diminished. Intention and purpose are powerful motivators and fuels. The planets associated with the *First Ray* are Vulcan and Pluto. The triangle of signs are Aries, Leo and Capricorn. The aspect most closely related to the *First Ray* is the *conjunction*. Read back to my descriptions of the Vulcan and Plutonian energies and the three signs and you'll see the connections and parallels with *First Ray* energies. The chakra associated with the *First Ray* is the crown center and the master representing its qualities is master Morya. Its human representative would be the *Warrior*. The symbol is the *baton*.

RAY TWO

The *Second Ray* is an energy that embodies all aspects of *love and wisdom*. The love depicted by the *Second Ray* is not the possessive or conditional love exhibited by us humans. It is something much broader and beyond our comprehension. It is the energy of attraction in a way that all matter seeks to pull together. It is a binding force in the universe. On a physical level its best representative might be gravity. Gravity has no preconditions or prerequisites before it creates attraction. It simply pulls everything and everyone together including us.

The wisdom of the *Second Ray* is a little more difficult to describe. For most people, wisdom has been equated to knowledge. But knowledge does not necessarily embody knowing and doing. This knowing embodies and inner knowing of the spirit. The Chinese say the wise man knows without going out of his doors. He knows without doing, without seeing, without feeling, without hearing. This knowing is centered in our heart. We come into this life with it innately intact. It comes mixed with empathy and intuition.

The awareness of the spirit is much more prolific and profound than our human awareness. We have built this inner knowing over many lifetimes of experience through trial and error. Our inner individuality is colored and compounded by many lifetimes of experience and its accumulation. The biggest challenge for us in this lifetime is knowing when to act on it and when to "let nature take its course."

The best human example of this is when we administer "tough love" in letting a child make their own mistakes and both of us to feel the pain or joy in their doing so. As adult to adult, this is reflecting in our love for another by allowing them to be themselves and do what *they* feel is right and necessary.

To evolve on the *Second Ray*, we must learn to allow this occur in ourselves. Self-love is necessary for us to truly love another. In today's western culture, this choice and accepting its consequences is an almost impossible thing for the average person to do. The insecure and possessive human is virtually unable to allow another to say, do or be anything that might in anyway contradict their need for the self-validation, self-approval and self-respect as a valued and loved person. These qualities embody the possessive and conditional love that we almost always perceive in the average person.

The planets associated with the *Second Ray* are Jupiter and the Sun. The triangle of signs are Gemini, Virgo and Pisces. The aspect most closely related to the *Second Ray* is the *opposition*. Read back to my descriptions of the Jupiter and Solar energies and the three signs and you'll see the connections and parallels with *Second Ray* energies. The chakra associated with the *Second Ray* is the heart center and the masters representing its qualities are master Kuthumi and master Djwal Kuhl. Its human representatives would be the *sage* and the *teacher*. The symbol is the *crossed pens*.

RAY THREE

The *Third Ray* is an energy that embodies all aspects of *active intelligence*. When we speak of intelligence, we normally think of personal thought, memory or something that relates to process or mathematical strategy. The intelligence of the *Third Ray* pertains mostly to the organization of the universe which is also reflected through the workings of the human mind as a network or matrix. For humans, it is totally abstract. It is also multi-leveled and interwoven much the same way that a spiderweb would be interconnected.

The keywords for the *Third Ray* are understanding and philosophy. The concept of understanding, personal and universal, can be perceived in a wide frame of comprehension including physical attributes, emotional qualities, and sequential thought and how they interrelate and cross dimensions. The *Third Ray* also envelops the study of philosophy. Here, details, their organization and interactions will contribute to and exemplify an overall picture of how a stratified universe "operates." The study and application of business and mathematics would also be a good example of the domain that the *Third Ray* encompasses.

Although I've given some essentially tangible examples of the *Third Ray's* effect, it should be understood that the organization of the universe and the active intelligence that it operates by is well beyond our human comprehension. As our human life passes, first physically, then emotionally, then mentally and "ascends" up through the dimensions, each layer shed allows new light and awareness on how our responsibility and participation are involved in the universe. Our "need to know" is only acquired after each of our levels of awareness are transformed, mastered and then passed. The best *esoteric* example for the *Third Ray* is the concept of initiation.

The planets associated with the *Third Ray* are Saturn and the Earth. The triangle of signs are Cancer, Libra and Capricorn. Read back to my descriptions of the Saturnian and Earth energies and the three signs and you'll be able to see the connections and parallels with *Third Ray* energies. The aspect most closely related to the *Third Ray* is the *trine*. The chakra associated with the *Third Ray* is the throat center and the master representing its qualities is Paul the Venetian. Its human representatives would be the *business man* and the *philosopher.* The symbol is the *spider web.*

THE RAYS OF ATTRIBUTE

As you can see, the *Third Ray* encompasses many dimensions of universal life. The interaction of all these qualities is divided further into four "separate" rays each with their own contribution of a type of specialized energy and perspective used to organize and activate the universe. Don't be fooled. These rays are *not to be considered as subservient* to the *Third Ray.* They are complimentary to each other and interact on every level with equal intensity and function.

The *Fourth Ray* is an energy that embodies all aspects of *harmony through conflict*. The universe is composed of polarities which are perpetually moving toward rebalancing any inequities left over from the big bang. This action reaches all the way down to the tiny scale of humans throwing things off balance by attempting to assert themselves in accentuating personal differences in order to establish their dominance over each other through creating what they see as preservation and a secure identity. This constant repositioning for dominance creates a struggle between humans acting and over-reacting respectively to the karma they've set in motion through their egotistical pursuits. The resulting pendulum effect (Gemini) is the universe's response toward recreating *harmony through conflict* in a world where humans constantly reset it off balance. Remembering that Mercury defines the world by separating what is in it (Virgo) only serving to validate his representation of the *Fourth Ray*.

Although I've given a very mundane explanation of how the *Fourth Ray* operates, we need to understand that its dynamics go much deeper than just our human frailties and struggles. Every dimension of polarization in this world and the more subtle levels above it operate in a similar fashion. Polarities like light and dark, movement and stasis, distant and close, feeling and apathy, sound and silence, thought and detachment, spirit and matter, just to name a few, are part of our polarized universe.

Any kind of conflict or power struggle comes under the heading of the *Fourth Ray*. Our ability to look past personal gain and focus on a balancing of seemingly conflicting energies is being challenged. Can we contribute to the smooth operation of the world without overcompensating and recreating an imbalance in the other direction? Can we adjust the pendulum of physical, emotional and mental life's contesting energies so there is more of an ease and simplicity in its performance? Can we resist our libidinous urge toward orienting natural adjustment into personal favor? Can we resist our animalistic urges to control and dominate? Can we go with the flow? Although *natural selection* and *survival of the fittest* are natural characteristics of our animal side, are we able work with the more subtle energies and lessen the pendulistic swing life's rawest energies? This is what the *Fourth Ray* asks of us.

The planets associated with the *Fourth Ray* are Mercury and the Moon. The triangle of signs are Taurus, Scorpio and Sagittarius. The aspect most closely related to the *Fourth Ray* is the *square*. Read back to my descriptions of the Mercurial and Lunar energies and the three signs and you'll be able to see the connections and parallels with *Fourth Ray* energies. The chakra associated with the *Fourth Ray* is the root center or base of the spine and the master representing its qualities is Serapis. Its human representatives would be the *mediators, sociologists,* and *artists.* The symbol is the *balance* and *the scales.*

RAY FIVE

The *Fifth Ray* is an energy that embodies all aspects of *concrete science.* This *concrete science* relates to universal law. This must *not* be confused with present day human science and the well-known *scientific method* of which it is a part but which works specifically with the tangible effects that are observable by humans. *Concrete science* or universal law regulates the universe and is inclusive from the most physical to the most subtle of energy changes. This includes etheric energies all the way to pure energy without any known attributes. It regulates the spirit and the many dimensions and permutations of our growing consciousness and that of any other entity in the universe. It stretches all the way to the unknowable.

The best reflection of this type of concept can be understood through knowing that *as above, so below* is the basic tenet permeating the universe showing whatever happens on any level or plane exhibits or exemplifies laws that uniformly affect every facet of the entire universe and its "operation." Even here, our comprehension of *cause and effect* has no bearing even though our human understanding expects its function to be present on every level of existence. The fact that existence and non-existence are part of the whole scheme of things makes human understanding of natural law unknowable.

The *Fifth Ray* encompasses any social organization, movement, culture or race from a scale past any personal egotistical influences. It has domain over its movements, growth, energy, values or any other quality that will in any way affect its action or inaction. This includes any influence of humanitarianism, genocide, extinction, species or race domination and effect, and in what way any living creature may interact with it and to what extent. Please recognize that the *Fifth Ray* concerns life's "direction" of *movement* within these dimensions, however, the *Third Ray* will maintain its dominion over its *structure* and the *Seventh Ray* with have dominion over the *order* that is present or created.

The planet associated with the *Fifth Ray* is solitary Venus. The triangle of signs are Leo, Sagittarius and Aquarius. The aspect most closely related to the *Fifth Ray* is the *quintile*. Read back to my descriptions of Venus energy and the three signs and you'll be able to see the connections and parallels with *Fifth Ray* energies. The chakra associated with the *Fifth Ray* is the third eye and the master representing its qualities is Hilarion. Its human life representatives would be the *medicine, behavioristic psychology* and our *human capacity to think* and construct our world. The symbol is the *crucible*.

RAY SIX

The *Sixth Ray* is an energy that embodies all aspects of *idealism* and *devotion*. It represents our dedication to someone or something and our reasons for doing so. This may happen on many levels. It may relate to our love and felt responsibility toward our pet all the way to our undying commitment and allegiance to a principle or cause.

Here again, on a lower human level, our dedication or commitment to a person or cause may come from a purely selfish motivation. We may love or pledge ourselves to someone because they have the ability or are likely to provide the security that our ego requires to feel in control of the person and/or our situation. Our motivation is the strongest factor in any commitment we may choose to apply ourselves to or profess to others. It is the most human side of *cause and effect*. On a political level we might call this *quid pro quo*. Personally, or politically, this motivate may be conscious for us, and therefore strategized and planned, or may be unconscious so our personal ego may not want to face the fact that it's not "altruistic." Mind you, many forms of altruism may be personally motivated but removed from the consciousness of its perpetrator for fear of their recognizing them and having to accept the acknowledgement of direct personal benefit.

The *Sixth Ray* is the primary ray that our civilization is working to evolve past. Its chakra center is the solar plexus; the human center of possessiveness. Its love and dedication is fraught with conditions and expectations related to our emotional security. It's lowest form of love is regulated by a personal *quid pro quo* whether consciously acknowledged or not. Our higher *ideal* is the unconditional love that everyone demands of others but are unable to offer themselves, or others, as a result of our own self-doubts and insecurity. The solar plexus and the *Sixth Ray* symbolize the primary originations of our need and wish to control our universe.

The planets associated with the *Sixth Ray* are Neptune and Mars. The triangle of signs are Gemini, Virgo and Pisces. The aspect most closely related to the *Sixth Ray* is the *sextile*. Read back to my descriptions of Neptunian and Mars energy and the three signs and you'll be able to see the connections and parallels with *Sixth Ray* energies. The chakra associated with the *Sixth Ray* is the solar plexus and the master representing its qualities is Jesus the Christ. Its human life representatives would be the *religion, ideology* and all *aspirations* toward the "good" and true. The symbol is the *chalice*.

RAY SEVEN

The *Seventh Ray* is an energy that embodies all aspects of *ceremonial order*. In the tangible arena this extends from human magical practices to the natural order and structure of nature and the universe. We might also say that *Ray Seven* is exhibited through the protocols for the "blueprint" of the universe. It is what to be expected in terms of the process of the working universe, its appearance and our awe and reverence of the magnificence in how it manifests. Our best tangible example is the way nature follows a self-sustaining and predictable pattern of life and maintains its renewal. *All That Is* builds on what is present and has come before and after.

Nothing is wasted. Everything has a "purpose." Everything fits into and through the matrix. To emulate the pattern is to preserve the *protocols for creation* and the perpetuity of its structure.

In this we can understand procreation and the patterns of creation that are manifested throughout the flow of life. Its smallest examples are the "birds and the bees" and its largest creation is the "big bang." All the natural laws are the components involved in the creation of life. The *Seventh Ray* represents and exemplifies the interwoven matrix of *protocols for creation*.

In human terms we can see this in the chain of command, the protocols for family, tradition, belonging and working with select and private groups, eccentricity, human mating rituals, magical groups, military organizations, government pomp and circumstance, etiquette, and our veneration of our most highly respected people and their positions. Reverence, respect and recognition are hall mark behaviors required of people of "lower" or non-inclusive stature. Its opposite perspective might include human diversity, inclusivity, commonness or any position or status devoid of specialness, effectiveness or reverence. In this listing of qualities and perspectives we can easily see that any involvement of human egotistical attitudes and perspectives can severely twist the meanings and expectations associated with positive manifestations of the *Seventh Ray*.

The planet associated with the *Seventh Ray* is Uranus. The triangle of signs are Aries, Cancer and Capricorn. The aspect most closely related to the *Seventh Ray* is the *septile*. Read back to my descriptions of Uranian energy and the three signs and you'll be able to see the connections and parallels with *Seventh Ray* energies. The chakra associated with the *Seventh Ray* is the sacral center and the master representing its qualities is Saint Germain. Its human life representatives would be *institutions, ceremonies, protocols* and *rituals*. The symbol for the *Seventh Ray* is the *torch*.

SACRED & NON-SACRED RULERSHIPS

In terms of our evolution as a species, not all of the planets can be considered of equal "stature." Like humans, some planets are known to have evolved much further in growth, awareness and effect than others. This is evident in the "rulership" of each of the *Seven Rays*. As per the domain of the *Seventh Ray*, planets can be considered *sacred* or *non-sacred*. Each ray has a sacred "ruler" associated with the it. Those with a second "ruler" may, in understandably human terms, be mentoring a non-sacred planet. Those that are sacred "rulers" are Vulcan, Mercury, Venus, Jupiter, Saturn, Neptune and Uranus. Those of a non-sacred status are Sun, Moon, Earth, Mars, and Pluto. Those of Sun and Moon are said to "veil" the influence of one of the sacred planets Vulcan, Uranus and Neptune. Which sacred planets are "veiled" will remain a mystery involved in the mundane rulerships, the point of *our* evolution and their configuration and positioning with the other planets and signs. The aspirant who is advanced and savvy enough to understand what issues they are working on will likely be able to discern which planets are "veiled" and why.

FINDING THE SEVEN RAYS IN THE CHART

There are primarily three ways to find Ray representation in a chart. The first is having planets in the three component signs. The second is having the ascendant being a member of one of the triads. And the third is having a Ray planetary "ruler" in a specific sign or house.

COMPONENT SIGNS

When planets are in the three signs that compose a Ray, they will be the primary energies that activate the Ray and the signs composing it. They will also activate a specific chakra center. With planets in all three signs, it's considered a full Ray influence. The native can respond to and carry out the influence independently of others. When there are two of the three, it's considered a partial influence.

For example, if there are planets in Cancer, Libra and Capricorn the native has a full *Third Ray* influence. This means that the Ray influence can be experienced solely by the native and without any input of another person or situation. If Saturn or Earth are in any of the three, the intensity and concentration of the Ray and the houses and signs they are found in are increased. If Saturn and/or Earth are in other signs, it brings the influence of the other signs and houses into the delineation of how the Ray might operate in the native's life.

Relative to this influence, if another person connects with this person with a planet of theirs landing in a third unoccupied or even occupied sign, not only will that person be integral to the native's expression and manifestation of the Ray but their combined efforts may either activate or obscure the effects of the Ray. This is the most common execution of the Ray's activity since more people than not are only sensitive to the tangible manifestations of the Ray. They are essentially, mentally and emotionally, unable to process its activation with only their own experience. They must have a tangible input from the physical world to even get their intention. It must also be understood that either one or both must be aware and evolved enough to be constructive with the Ray. Remember, to consciously evolve with the Ray, the native must be *inclusive* of its physical manifestations but also be willing to work with and contribute to what is operating at levels well beyond those tangible inclusions.

ASCENDANT SIGN COMPONENT

One of the more obvious manifestations of a Ray can be seen through the expression of the ascendant. Since the ascendant is how the native perceives the world and how the world perceives the native, this will be a primary venue for exchanging energies that activate a Ray and bring an awareness of it.

There are two planetary representatives that this can be accomplished through. The first is the *esoteric* rulership of the sign on the ascendant. The sign and house placement of this planet will show the area of life the native will first become aware of the effects of the Ray. For example, if the sign on the ascendant is Pisces, the *esoteric* ruler will be Pluto. The sign and house placement of Pluto would indicate where the native would feel the effects of the Ray and where they could begin an awareness of its operation. However, because the ascendant sign is a member of two Rays, the Second Ray and the sixth Ray, the ascendant will be involved in the evolution and expression of both.

The second planetary representative will be the planet(s) that are most closely representative of the Rays themselves. Since the ascendant is a member of two Rays, there will be *four* planets delivering the effects of the two Rays. These would be Jupiter and the Sun for the Second Ray and Neptune and Mars for the Sixth Ray. Needless to say, the signs and house placements of these four planets, plus Pluto, would permeate an effect virtually over half the chart. On top of this, remember that each other planet, in addition to these five, would integrate the effects of *their* Ray representations to the remainder of the chart. The effects would be subtle and pervasive to the entire chart and only awaken in the native as they began to mature beyond physical tunnel vision. Remembering that the Rays themselves operate much like the prism dispersing the colors from white light, the discrimination of their individual effects would be challenging at best, especially, since the white light that the Rays emanate from, "go through" the prism of the universe, and are perceivable individually but still blend into each other with no definitive borders.

When delineating the houses and the planets that land within them, please be cognizant of the Ray energies that each house harbors by virtue of the planets that fall within them. In this light planetary pictures will make a lot more sense in terms of the recognition and balancing of these energies from a conscious perspective. Remember, the unevolving native will be totally *reactive* and the evolving native, as he slowly gains awareness and begins to achieve consciousness, will then consequently and intentionally become proactive relative to the influence of the Rays.

SACRED & NON-SACRED POSITIONING

Relative to understanding sacred and non-sacred rulership, perhaps the best way to present an analogy would be to say that the sacred planets would be more "directive" in terms of the energy awakened in us as opposed to the non-sacred planets being more "applicative" and "supportive" in their effect since their "directiveness" has not fully become universally "matured." Much like we have avatars and aspirants, the same hierarchical structure may be thought to be applied on a more universal scale. Make no mistake that even the non-sacred planets are eons ahead of any human consciousness and are not to be thought of in any fashion as being diminished in terms of their importance and effectiveness relative to the "purpose" of the Ray that they sponsor.

PART II
RAY APPLICATIONS BY HOUSE & SIGN

Each planet in a sign or house brings the influence and effects of at the least one of the Seven Rays. If the native is an *aspirant* and working diligently on incorporating the *esoteric* energy of the Ray, its influence will slowly begin to come to light in their consciousness. The following delineations will give us an idea of what influences to look for and the attitudes that must be induced in order to consciously work with the Ray and manifest its effects in the *aspirant's* life. It should also be understood that the Ray awareness may be easily lost if the *aspirant* slips in his or her diligence, efforts and application. We can go through lifetime after lifetime drifting in and out of awareness over and over again depending on how often our personal ego takes charge of our focus.

ARIES & THE ASCENDANT/SEVENTH HOUSE AXIS

MERCURY – brings a Fourth Ray influence of *harmony through conflict* to Aries and the first-seventh house axis. *Exoterically*, Mercury brings a tangible, separating discrimination between conflicting options. One of the major expressions of this perspective is confrontational, especially, when posited in the first house and in Aries. The *esoteric* influence requires the application of intuition which allows us to step back from Mercury's viewing the conflicting options in a contentious manner so we may no longer be tempted to align with one side or the other. This changes *how* we perceive the world around us and *how* others see our part in it. The challenge for *esoteric* growth is in detaching ourselves from being a combative force. The Fourth Ray influence encourages us to use our intuition in seeing the physical, emotional and mental worlds as a whole and *inter*dependent picture. This gives the aspirant enough detachment to see *what* is needed for balance and *how* to proceed. The Moon as co-ruler will also show us *where* we will draw the circumstances to process the wisdom inherent in Fourth Ray energy. Please note that Mar's sign and house position will also bring issues and areas of life that influence the first-seventh house axis.

VENUS – brings a Fifth Ray influence of *concrete science* to Aries and the first-seventh house axis. *Exoterically*, Venus brings us choice and preference as a standard toward our understanding how the world works. We look for evidence that supports those choices and preferences. This brings us the scientific method. But that method aligns us only with the senses. In Aries and the first house, our choices polarize us with the world. How they see us and how we see them is a product of our choices. Hence, we make comrades and enemies through our choices and commitments. When we broad cast our choices and commitments, this tells the world who we want to be seen as. And as a consequence, they decide whom *they* want to see us as. Our commitments, how we project ourselves and our chosen actions may also create competition and envy. It becomes a separative influence. Please note that Mar's sign and house position will also bring issues and areas of life that influence the first-seventh house axis.

In contrast, the third eye sees a much larger and more inclusive picture of the world rather than mono-focusing through their choices and preferences. The challenge for the aspirant is to make life's required choices quietly and inwardly while allowing others to think of us as they prefer. Where *exoteric* Venus needs to choose and broadcast their choices to the world and promote their desired social status, *esoteric* Venus prefers to go quietly about their lives without creating competition or drawing attention to themselves. They pioneer through the world creating accountable examples of maturity and confidence for others to observe, assess and then, perhaps, emulate. *Choiceless awareness* permits the *aspirant* to detach from the need to assert themselves based on their values and choices.

MARS – brings a Sixth Ray influence of *idealism and devotion* to Aries and the first-seventh house axis. In Aries or the first house *exoteric* Mars is primarily an outward or externally directed movement. This will be applied to any cause or commitment that appears to demand an outward show of energy. The motivation behind it is the external alignment of the native's actions with a cause or ideal that can be seen, felt and applauded by others. That is, an externally motivated commitment where the native is perceived as being a warrior or savior by their observers. This action may also just be a play to control the environment of others through not letting them perform needed functions themselves or without the input of the native. In this light the native may then be perceived as being pushy, aggressive, a bully or takeover artist.

Esoteric Mars is not obsessed with appearances. Although personal recognition might be appreciated by the *aspirant*, its acknowledgement will be nowhere near the egotistical degree of the *exoterically* oriented native. *Esoteric* Mars possesses a humility unknown to the *exoteric* native. If there is need for dedication or tangible action toward the needs of a truly idealistic cause, the aspirant will humbly apply the energy regardless of its outward appearance or responses obtained from observers. Since the *aspirant* knows that the outer world is simply a reflection of his or her inner world, they will be content to take action with only the motivation toward making all energies run more smoothly for everyone, including themselves, while remaining in alignment with universal principles. The *aspirant* has become evolved and confident enough in their ideals and commitments that there is no need or desire for outer recognition.

JUPITER brings a Second Ray influence of *love and wisdom* to Aries and the first-seventh house axis and to people in the surrounding environment. Jupiter's expansive influence is *exoterically* directed toward tangible increases in our earthly endeavors. When we push beyond normally expected limits, we very often become aware of the effects of our actions when they exceed our expectations. It may be only then that we begin to listen to the responses that we receive from the universe. For some, only subtlety is required. For others, a two-by-four upside their head is required to get their attention. Please note that Mar's sign and house position will also bring issues and areas of life that influence the first-seventh house axis.

Jupiter's main influence is to push us past our limits so we may recognize something beyond our own motivations and goals. Jupiter broadens our perception of the world and our part in it. *Esoterically*, it pushes us well past our intended egotism. In doing so, it helps us to let go of our protective and personal small world mentality. In Aries and in the first house it also concentrates the *effects* of empathy. That is, it doesn't create empathy itself but expands how the world influences us to a point that it's impossible for us *not* to listen. In partnership with the Sun, it also brings us awareness through the excessive light that he emanates.

Jupiter's *exoteric* energy pushes everything past its limits often creating chaos in over-inflating the importance and effectiveness of the tangible world. When it reaches a point of critical mass, the *aspirant* is able to see the futility of "more is better" at which time *esoteric* Jupiter "takes over" and we begin to see the transiency of the ephemeral security our ego attempts to protect. It reminds us that nothing is finite. "The only security there is is knowing that there is none" (from *The Wisdom of Insecurity* by Alan Watts).

The human love we consciously seek is almost always conditional. We may say or think that it is unconditional but our motives are often unconscious. The *esoteric* influence of Jupiter is unconditional in the respect that it does not filter the love exchanged through any limitations or prerequisites. Its function encourages us to allow and accept the universe's reaction to us as is needed to break down our security-oriented restrictions and inhibitions toward the free and natural movement of universal energy. That is, it allows others to reject us if they feel that it fits *their* current preferences and needs. Unconditionality is only created when and where Jupiter pushes us past our limits. The wisdom comes in our learning when to let go and recognizing it again when it repeats itself.

SATURN brings a Third Ray energy of *active understanding* to Aries and the first-seventh house axis. It emanates this through the throat center. The throat center is the center of personal will. It is also the engine behind activating intention. *Exoterically*, the Third Ray boils down to personal control. That is not only control of the world but control of ourselves. In this way, control of the world is the main focus of an *exoterically* oriented native. Control of ourselves is more part of an *esoteric* arsenal. Both of these exhibit different forms of discipline. Discipline, structure, and control are very similar in nature. The *exoteric* is externally oriented and the *esoteric* is internally oriented. But these are qualities of a universe organized and patterned in very specific ways. This organization is much like the formation of a spider web where every action or inaction has a broadcasting and receptive effect across the spider web due to the intricate interconnection of its points of anchor. The cyclic structure of how nature perpetuates itself on its many levels and dimensions is the factor that is recognized by the *aspirant* who is *not distracted* by the external prospects of protecting personal security. In recognizing these cycles, the *aspirant* is internally cognizant of the cycles and stage of action current in each. With this knowledge he knows when to act and when to refrain from acting. In the case of refraining from acting, we can equate this energy to the sacrificing described in the previous description of how *esoteric* Saturn recognizes the need for refraining from action. Please note that Mar's sign and house position will also bring issues and areas of life that influence the first-seventh house axis.

Active understanding paves the way for recognizing the way the world is intertwined and the perpetual cycles that it follows. *Exoterically*, Saturn rules tangible structure, organization and the patterns that they follow. This tangible vibration of Saturn utilizes boundaries, limits and restrictions; all the things that the human ego uses to immobilize external control of themselves by others while eliciting the illusory feeling of personal security. *Esoterically*, Saturn rules the concept of the *aspirant's internal* and *intangible* structure and organization with and through his recognition of the fact that his internal structure is simply reflective of how he *perceives* the external world.

Relative to Earth, there, may be voluntary participation in getting involved in worldly affairs but without the awareness of the connectedness to the web and only from the perspective of not wanting to be left out. Remembering the placement of the Earth in opposition to the Sun reminds us that the native's Earth positioning is actually the perspective that they use to understand the Sun's influence. In this the *exoteric* native usually only recognizes the Sun in front of them. The *esoteric aspirant* is much more aware of his surroundings and the part they play in the overall scheme of his or her dawning awareness. Please note that Mar's sign and house position will also bring issues and areas of life that influence the first-seventh house axis.

In spite of our intentional interference, the external world is organized and works according to the structure of natural law. It's dynamic is just beyond most of our perceptions because we are so hyper-self-focused on our personal concerns that we don't recognize the larger picture beyond what we're immediately doing. Those of us who are adept enough at seeing past the personal are more able to recognize these patterns and choose when to act and when to refrain from acting in order to insure our alignment with and smooth transition of natural energies. The more we can see past the personal, the more far reaching will be the effects that we can generate karmically through aligning with the energies of the natural universe.

Since the co-ruler of the Third Ray is the Earth, her manifestation is the exemplification of the diversity and multi-leveled effects that Saturn produces in the many worlds of awareness that the *aspirant* is moving toward understanding and then willfully contributing to.

URANUS brings Seventh Ray energy of *ceremonial order* to Aries and the first-seventh house axis. This focuses on sacral center energy and brings us into alignment with seasonal nature and the inevitable cycle of birth and death. *Exoteric* Seventh Ray energies also encompass ritual man-made orders such as the Masons, government congressional rules and protocols, magical ceremonies and rituals, military chain of command procedures and other traditionalized patterns tied into repeated conduct and the practices of mental and physical disciplines.

One of the qualities that Uranus is often paired with is eccentricity. That is, odd behavior that seems to come out of nowhere. Remembering back to the functioning of Uranus as a returning of the energy to the natural forces as opposed to human design, we can see how Uranus can be operating in an *esoteric* fashion putting us back on track with the universal energy flow and our spiritual life path.

This quality is the most visible in Aries and the first house, especially, if he's on the ascendant. There are many behaviors that humans hold on to in order to maintain their perceived control of the environment and each other. During this attempt Uranus is constantly building energy and stress *against* the way *we* believe things should be and toward the way the *universe actually works*. In our projection toward the world through our ascendant, our human objectives predominate within most of us. But every once in a while, one of these energies cascaded by Uranus moves past our limits to keep our assumptions about the universe from staying within our desired perceptual boundaries. Then with explosive force our egotistical attempts at preventing their loss are overcome and the energies are snapped back into a normal universal flow. When people who have Uranus in Aries, the first house or on the ascendant are observed as this occurs, the onlookers perceive them as eccentric, erratic or "innovative." When the *esoteric aspirant* has Uranus in one of these positions, they have gained somewhat of an understanding as to how Uranus and the universe actually work and, consequently and hopefully, actively assists toward the Uranian goal of realigning with the natural universal energies. *These* are the true innovators. These are the spiritual warriors.

Please note that Mar's sign and house position will also bring issues and areas of life that influence the first-seventh house axis.

NEPTUNE brings a Sixth Ray energy of *idealism and devotion* to Aries and the first-seventh house axis. The center he works mostly through is the solar plexus. *Exoterically*, this is our possessive or lower mind. This is where our feelings and emotions are connected to the personal image we hold about ourselves. Neptune's tangible effect on this is a constant *dissolving* and draining away of the logic and reasoning that we use to defend against any worldly contradictions of ourselves as solid and unchanging. Through Aries, the first house and ascendant we employ a constant push to be seen by the world in a way that justifies our beliefs about ourselves and our solidity. Here, Neptune disagrees with that perception. He constantly shows us how we deceive ourselves through our beliefs. Yet, we continue to work feverishly at maintaining what we wish to believe about ourselves. *Exoterically*, Neptune is the master of self-delusion, especially in the first, fourth, seventh and tenth houses. The cardinal houses are where we interact the most with the world. Please note that Mar's sign and house position will also bring issues and areas of life that influence the first-seventh house axis.

Since the first house is our window on the world, it is also how the world sees us. Neptune on the first brings that home through the reactions of the world to our beliefs about ourselves and others. Here he serves as an emotional mirror. The question becomes will that be a one way or two-way mirror? Will we listen and hear what the world tells us? Do we put people on a pedestal? Do we see them as irrelevant? Do we pledge ourselves to someone based on who they actually are or what we choose to believe about them?

In possessive, *exoteric* love we devote ourselves to someone based on what we believe that they can do for us, aka, maintain our self-image of ourselves as a good, proper, loving and honest person. But what happens when the returns prove us wrong? What happens when the pedestal under what we expect to confirm that turns to clay? Neptune has done his job. He has given us a reality check. He has brought us back to seeing the world as it truly is. The same will be true for when we dedicate ourselves to causes, religious or otherwise, that we believe reflect the illusory beliefs we hold about ourselves and the security we believe that will be provided to us for doing so. Neptune is the arch enemy of our delusional human security. Hence, its *esoteric* rulership of Cancer.

Esoteric Neptune appears to show us to ourselves much kindlier when we become an *aspirant*. As an *aspirant* we're much more open to how we might be deceiving ourselves or others. We have a much clearer picture of where our ideals should be placed and what we should devote ourselves to. Humility and compassion, not conditional sacrifice, become factors in how we perceive the world. Kindness becomes a tool for reducing the pressure most insecure humans feel when their idealistic and illusory beliefs begin to crumble.

PLUTO brings a First Ray energy to Aries and the first-seventh house axis which is not fully manifested yet as our species has not evolved far enough into emotional maturity. Its focus is on *will and power*. However, this is neither the personal will nor the personal power represented by the Ray. *Exoterically* and in Aries, the first house or on the ascendant Plutonian energy can be overbearing to and for those who are not aware enough or strong enough to handle it. With an inflated ego or a diminished ego Pluto and the First Ray energy is a severe problem. Those who are over-inflated become bullies and megalomaniacs and those who are diminished become suckers and pushovers and allow themselves to be used whether through ineptness or strategy. For them, this energy usually works from unconscious origins. They are most often not even aware of what they are doing or how they are acting. They work subconsciously at maintaining their preferred personal image and security. Please note that Mar's sign and house position will also bring issues and areas of life that influence the first-seventh house axis.

Esoteric Pluto is a completely different energy and focus. It's much like handling a bucking bronco by hand. It takes skill and knowledge in understanding and anticipating how the horse will react. The understanding and anticipation are needed as the overall energy to be harnessed is well beyond the resistive power of a single human's effort. In this it takes guidance and skill in directing. It works very much like using Tai Chi Ch'uan where no resistance is used but strategic placement and small adjusted forces in directing the application of force. *Exoterically*, the native is unaware and unable to apply these forces and as a result create tremendous opposing resistance to and from whatever is contested. *Esoterically*, the *aspirant* knows the pitfall of using head on resistive force and learns to skillfully use strategy in the application of energy and force.

First Ray Plutonian energy in Aries, the first house and, especially, on the ascendant, is both consciously and unconsciously recognized by the public and often serves as a magnet to bring the native into public notice. Here emotional maturity is necessary so as not to become intoxicated by the power that the attracted public offers behind the native and his focused endeavors. Magnetic people like Hitler and Charles Manson are failed examples of properly used First Ray energy. Mahatma Gandhi and Franklin Delano Roosevelt are positive examples.

VULCAN brings First Ray energy of *will and power* to Aries and the first-seventh house axis. But since his tangible existence has yet to be acknowledged, his energies are only perceived by those with an *esoteric* awareness. For the *exoteric* native there may be no awareness available but, on the positive side, there yet remains a forging ability in gathering surrounding supplies and elements and forming tools for the self-awareness and functioning of others toward becoming an *aspirant*. On the downside, the native may be perceived by others as always "changing things" and producing impediments preventing their acquisition and the accomplishing of their preferences and earthly security.

On the positive side, Nicolai Tesla would serve as a positive and progressive representative of First Ray energy who has matured enough to wield and use the energy in alignment with universal law and the *Plan* behind it. Negative examples would be the will and power behind government agencies that create restrictions and impediments to individual freedoms.

Remembering that Vulcan is never more than eight degrees away from the Sun, we can generally assume that the influence supplied by the Sun, usually in or close to the house and sign Vulcan is found in, will work in tandem with whatever tools that Vulcan is moving toward forging. Please note that Mar's sign and house position will also bring issues and areas of life that influence the first-seventh house axis.

MOON again brings Fourth Ray energy of *harmony through conflict* to Aries and the first-seventh house axis. *Esoterically*, the Moon is again only a veil for one of the other sacred planets and operates as an unaware partner to Mercury and the activity of the Fourth Ray. The sign and house that the Moon rules will show what area of life the most obvious conflict will be found in. Mercury's house and position will show where intuition for easing or solving the conflict may be found. Please note that Mar's sign and house position will also bring issues and areas of life that influence the first-seventh house axis.

TAURUS & THE SECOND-EIGHTH HOUSE AXIS

MERCURY brings Fourth Ray energy and *harmony through conflict*. In the sphere of the second-eighth house axis resources and self-identification through values, assets and abilities are the issues brought to consciousness. For the *exoteric* native, what I and you have or don't have becomes painfully apparent. The differences and their polarizing effects create *conflict*, especially, if we assess ourselves according to what's external. This exacerbates the power struggle inherent in the tangible part of what's normally the Taurus-Scorpio axis. Since the *exoterically* minded native believes that their worth is determined by external and tangible sources, their assessment of themselves and their resources may bring either a sense of superiority or inferiority. Self-worth is intrinsic in feeling composed and confident. Too much or too little throws us off balance and makes us seek external confirmation of our worth. Since the Forth Ray is connected to the root center, its positioning in the second-eighth house axis brings the issue of survival to our consciousness and the resources we have or not to accomplish that. This intensifies our struggle involving our possessions and self-concept. Please note that Venus' sign and house position will also bring issues and areas of life that influence the second-eighth house axis.

The *esoteric* emphasis of the Forth Ray in Taurus and the second-eighth house axis brings the *aspirant* the opportunity to balance their sense of self and the use of their resources and abilities into alignment with the universe's use of them. Since the upper vibration of Mercury leans into our intuitive receptivity, the job for the *aspirant* is to begin moving from an intellectual "doping it out" tendency toward intuiting the small changes needed to reduce the tension produced by the Ray's *exoteric* functions. In doing so the *aspirant's* overall skill in mediating earthly matters will develop much more along intuitive lines thereby making them much more receptive to the more subtle vibrations of the Forth Ray. This will give them greater access to the universal energy available to them.

VENUS brings Fifth Ray and *concrete science* energy to Taurus and the second-eighth house axis. Here Venus feels right at home. Here *exoteric* Venus has us deciding what is beautiful, proper and valuable. The primary influence is one of choice and priorities. Here also the scientific method functions tangibly well in terms of the statistics, analyzing the native's assets, proficiencies and potential. These are all applied toward being used to compare with or gain advantage over the physical world.

Rather than looking for more efficient survival, the *aspirant* assesses how their abilities and assets may contribute better toward how universal law manifests itself. The native's self-assessment is viewed more in terms of a humble and universal tool for the White Brotherhood. The concern is not about the individual self and how well we'll fare in the tangible world but how the larger picture operates and what is needed to make it run more smoothly for the larger *Plan*. Venus here also brings emphasis to the third eye center. What's seen *exoterically* as a sacrifice is viewed *esoterically* as a contribution. Also understand that their well-being is not sacrificed in the process. The *aspirant* also decides and pursues what is necessary to keep their minds and bodies healthy and functioning efficiently in the world but only as necessary to maintain the wider manifestation.

MARS brings a Sixth Ray *idealism and devotion* energy to Taurus and the second-eighth house axis. Generally, in this house Mars *exoterically* pursues resources and qualities that will heighten their public and self-image. This will come as a compensation from a feeling of an exaggerated or diminished importance. The native will likely be more physically driven than their counterparts. Their physical possessions will hold a dominant place in their perceived self-assessment and how they believe the world will "grade" them. Please note that Venus' sign and house position will also bring issues and areas of life that influence the second-eighth house axis.

Esoterically, the focus is more on what issues the *aspirant* is dedicated to. Mobilizing energies and resources toward a cause or spiritual effort is foremost in the *aspirant's* mind. In recognizing the world and its imbalances, their attention is then drawn toward examining their own internal motivations and how they are reflected in the worldly circumstances they observe. This has a powerful effect on reducing the possessiveness centered in the solar plexus. This also becomes a high priority "cause" to be worked on within themselves in order to produce a cleaner and more efficient vehicle for the White Brotherhood to move toward expressing a more perfect universal manifestation. The process of purifying their own motivations is one of the most fundamental actions to be taken before any *initiation* may be undertaken.

JUPITER brings a Second Ray energy of *love and wisdom* to Taurus and the second-eighth house axis. *Exoterically*, the native with Jupiter placed here will attempt to expand their resources, their skills and their reach for the most effectiveness in the physical world that they are able. Bottom line, they may believe that "more is better." Jupiter's placement here may have the effect of blowing their perceived self-importance and self-image way out of proportion. These are often the people who over-extend themselves while looking for the "big deal" that will solve all their fears and insecurities. Please note that Venus' sign and house position will also bring issues and areas of life that influence the second-eighth house axis.

Here *esoteric* Jupiter has a very different focus. The accumulation of experience contributes to the wisdom the *aspirant* has at their disposal. There is a strong potential for providing guidance and education for themselves and others. Based on their own abilities and understanding that the world they observe is a reflection of themselves, they are able to provide insight for, not only themselves but, for others to understand and apply their own abilities. Here Jupiter connects the *aspirant* to the heart center. Through a calm, expanded and centered perception of themselves, they have the ability reduce the stress of a person who has difficulty in "getting into gear" through showing them how to access their own potential and diminishing self-doubt. A placement here is also the opportunity for the *aspirant* to fully perceive the extent of the more subtle abilities that are in their spiritual "toolbox." The Sun's position will show the most powerful place to draw on for developing awareness of our resources and gaining self-realization.

SATURN in Taurus and the second-eighth house axis brings the Third Ray energy of *active intelligence. Exoterically*, this can operate in one of two ways. First, it can give the native a refined ability for strategy in using their resources and abilities in the tangible world, especially, in business. Second, it may work as a severe impediment on the native through encouraging them to see the world as a difficult place with insurmountable barriers resulting in their inability to access their own resources. *Exoterically*, Earth here may bring an obsessive quality to the native. Please note that Venus' sign and house position will also bring issues and areas of life that influence the second-eighth house axis.

With Saturn's *esoteric* representation there is an uncanny knowledge of how everything is put together. The aspirant knows what is needed for a strong sense of self, personal and otherwise, and is able to pinpoint the qualities needing to be tweaked or adjusted in order to keep the universal world running in a smooth and undistracted manner. Saturn here offers the *aspirant* a connection to their throat center through dealing with their resources and those of others. The *aspirant* also has a refined sense of timing in knowing when to use those resources and abilities and when to refrain. Earth here *esoterically* will bring the opposing part of the axis to complete the whole picture of resources available to the *aspirant.*

URANUS brings a Seventh Ray energy to Taurus and the second-eighth house axis. *ceremonial order* is the focus. *Exoterically*, the native may rely too much on patterns and protocols in order to access their resources and abilities. They may also behave erratically when attempting to apply their finances and talents. At times it may bring genius quality and at other times, those of someone who is handicapped. Their dominant tangible quality is unpredictability, especially, in how they view themselves and their values. Please note that Venus' sign and house position will also bring issues and areas of life that influence the second-eighth house axis.

Esoteric Uranus is a much more intuitively powered energy. It gives the *aspirant* an unparalleled understanding of how their resources and abilities are tied together in a timeless matrix of interrelations. The order reflected can be felt through the sacral center. This enables them to feel and "see" projects in their completion before the work on building them even begins. *Esoteric* Uranus is a visionary. In their visions they recognize how to manifest the energetic fabric of the universe through its tangible elements.

NEPTUNE brings the Sixth Ray energy of *ideals and devotions* to Taurus and the second-eighth house axis. *Exoterically*, this would bring secrets to this axis. The secrets here would be in the form of abilities and assets that we don't know or believe that we have. Often, when we don't believe that we have or are what we need, we attribute what we wish we had to someone else to whom we then we idolize, put on a pedestal and label as a hero. In this way the quality drawn to our attention is still acknowledged but attributed to someone else free of our being responsible for it. Hence, we can admire it and not have to risk failure in trying to actualize it in ourselves.

The other side of the *exoteric* picture makes the native with this placement fearful about and deceptive toward others about their resources, abilities and self-image. This occurs through the connection through their solar plexus. What is unfortunate is that this type of deception is one step deeper into the hole of compounding their self-denial. Now they then find themselves in the position of having cover for what they've told others that they can do or know. After that comes, their need of keeping track of the lies that they've told others increases on top of what they've already told themselves. After enough lies have been told, they lose track.

In another light, Neptune in this position can represent a refined but latent talent far beyond the average person's capabilities. Again, they might not realize what they are capable of. *Esoterically*, the *aspirant* has gained a desire to and an understanding of how to assist those with special talent to recognize their gift, move past their faulty self-denial, trust their spirit and to be able to access and develop their skill. Neptune here definitely indicates a placement that can yield a special calling for the native. Please note that Venus' sign and house position will also bring issues and areas of life that influence the second-eighth house issues.

PLUTO brings the First Ray of *will and power* to manifestation in Taurus and the second-eighth house axis through intensifying the psychological structures that support the egotistical side of their self-concept. In this, Pluto may also manifest in two ways. First, there may be a tremendous sense of power that the native senses is at their disposal. It may bring megalomaniacal tendencies based on the perceived assurance that nothing can stop them. Contrarily, they may be manipulated by everyone professing to provide them with an edge on "getting ahead." In this they can become locked in an unconscious obsession with their own lacking of resources. Please note that Venus' sign and house position will also bring issues and areas of life that influence the second-eighth house axis.

Esoterically, the regenerative abilities of their self-concept and resources on an energetic level are almost immeasurable. The *aspirant* can tap into the combined energy of the public for their own recharge while assisting others in refocusing their energy on a clearer path to their self-realization. This is one of the positions for a natural healer.

VULCAN's position here will be the most comfortable and bring the First Ray of *will and power* to Taurus and the second-eighth house axis. It will be intrinsically involved with the Sun (never more than eight degrees away) in exposing constructive materials for the native's forging of resources and self-perception. There will be a decided absence of compassion, feeling or mercy in the application of Vulcan's energy. It will create tremendous ability and talent but bring an attitude that will be sorely lacking in social connections, cordiality or consideration. Please note that Venus' sign and house position will also bring issues and areas of life that influence the second-eighth house axis.

Esoterically, Vulcan will bring a strength and power in the resources and abilities forged by the *aspirant* for the purpose of educating and assisting themselves and others in developing their talents, confidence and strong self-perception. The *aspirant* will have to work especially hard at including kindness in the brew as the tendency toward ruthlessness will be overwhelming.

MOON will bring a Fourth Ray energy involving *harmony through conflict* to Taurus and the second-eighth house axis. The native's emotional focus likely will be based almost entirely on what they have, who they are and what is important to *them* alone. *Exoterically*, the native's major lesson will be learning to detach themselves from comparing and judging themselves through comparison with others and what they possess or are able to do. Please note that Venus' sign and house position will also bring issues and areas of life that influence the second-eighth house axis.

Esoterically, the Moon's energy will be veiling either Vulcan, Uranus or Neptune. These planets will either purge (Vulcan), burst (Uranus) or dissolve (Neptune) any egotistical dynamics that attempt to preserve materialistic or emotional security used to compensate for perceived inadequacy or indoctrinated incompetence.

GEMINI & THE THIRD-NINTH HOUSE AXIS

MERCURY brings Fourth Ray energy and *harmony through conflict* to Gemini and the third-ninth house axis. The *exoteric* focus is communication and the exchange of energy. Generally, Mercury in Gemini or this axis brings a photographic memory. With a major focus on self, as in an having an *exoteric* mindset, the native will have a great deal of difficulty listening to others. Often, the only listening that will occur will be when they are waiting for what they need to hear in order to validate their pre-chosen response. When this occurs, they rarely hear what another has to say other than what they "selectively hear." In a worldly competition they will often switch sides if they find that they are losing an argument. Since the Fourth Ray is connected to the root center, projecting the self and saving face are of the utmost importance.

Esoteric Mercury finds this positioning a very challenging perspective to overcome especially since it is so strongly rooted in tangible validations. However, the facility to be aware of and to move between alternate foci is a tremendous tool for the *aspirant* to bring self-realization and mirroring to those who are stuck in a static viewpoint. Remember that Gemini is the pivotal sign in the Second Ray energy of *love and wisdom* which is connected to the heart center. Learning to "see the other viewpoint" is a tremendous tool for awakening a broader perspective in those who might be close to becoming an *aspirant*.

VENUS brings Fifth Ray energy and *concrete science* into the realm of communications. In Gemini and the third-ninth house axis Venus levitates the native, in spite of their tangibility, toward an *esoteric* understanding of diversity, especially, since she is connected to the third eye. To those observing, they may seem fickle and capricious. They may appear to have passionate choices and preferences but they will also switch them as often as they hear about alternative options. Venus in Gemini and the third-ninth house axis will also mimic the people they are found with; however, this will unsuspectingly acquaint them with alternate perspectives. Please note that Mercury's sign and house position will also bring issues and areas of life that influence the third-ninth house axis.

Esoteric Venus feels right at home in Gemini and the third-ninth house axis. Here the *aspirant* can recognize the polarizations in their choices and the choices of others. Through the mutability of Gemini, they have the talent to alternate apparent perspectives enough for those stuck in a specific viewpoint to see other available options without the loss of their identity in acknowledging alternate choices. To see diversity in the form of *choicelessness awareness* is a blessing and a perspective to be strived for by the *aspirant*.

MARS brings Sixth Ray energy and *idealism and devotion* to Gemini and the third-ninth house axis. *Exoterically,* this will provide a soap box for the cause fighter. True to form, listening will be difficult for the native as their need to project their beliefs and opinions far outweighs the two-way communication venue of the position. No doubt, they will be a very forceful speaker, and it will include a very forceful solar plexus energy, but the information projected may or may not necessarily have substantial validity for the recipients. Nevertheless, the native will push on. Writing and digital vehicles will have equal force and intensity. Please note that Mercury's sign and house position will also bring issues and areas of life that influence the third-ninth house axis.

Esoterically, this gives the *aspirant* a tremendous augmentation of energy toward the use and understanding of universal energies. This also give them the ability to clearly discriminate the diversity of values behind all types of ideals, dedications and devotional issues. This will assist the *aspirant* in revealing to others a clear perception of their motivations powering their *ideals and devotions*. It will also teach them when to restrain their enthusiasm in favor of reason.

JUPITER brings a Second Ray energy coupled with *love and wisdom* to Gemini and the third-ninth house axis. Although the *exoteric* native may be mono-focused on what they feel and know, the Second Ray component of Gemini will offer enough diversity of focus to at the least make the native project a broader perspective than what they individually feel and know. This will enable the Jupiter component to push them beyond their limits breaking their individual mental restrictions. His position here will also widen the avenues of expression through additional communication mediums. The native may appear to "never come up for air" when it comes to projecting themselves.

Since the *exoteric* world is so conditional, it follows to reason that Jupiter and the Second Ray must powerfully emphasize unconditional acceptance of others in order to simply compensate for the tremendous insecurity inherent in the average native's attempt to close themselves off from perceived threats of feeling diminished by the outside world.

Esoterically, the first step in countering this direction is one of *allowing*. That is, *allowing* others to have different opinions, *allowing* others to have different preferences, and *allowing* others to bumble through their attempts at secularizing and segregating themselves from anything that might diminish their personal egotistical identities. It's a tough task for the new *aspirant* to allow the world to behave as it does, even if it doesn't agree with their personal beliefs and preferences. *Esoterically*, one of Jupiter's primary foci in Gemini and the third-ninth house axis is to initially foment a sense of tolerance. Once this has been accomplished, the *aspirant* has a fledgling unconditionality to work from and can move on toward promoting the Second Ray characteristics of *love and* wisdom and its resulting expression of compassion. The Sun's sign and house position will also show the circumstances where energy may be drawn from to augment Second Ray manifestation. Please note that Mercury's sign and house position will also bring issues and areas of life that influence the axis.

SATURN brings Third Ray energies of *active intelligence* to Gemini and the third-ninth house axis. In spite of having an organizing effect, Saturn's influence here often takes the form of suppression by a family's dampening effect on a child's mobility and communication skills. *Exoterically*, this may also take the form of stuttering or some other communicative defects leading toward stunted emotional growth. A child's perception of authoritarianism will determine whether they become inhibited in expressing themselves or become an inhibitor themselves when they finally escape the family suppression. This is one of the harder positionings for a child to overcome. Please note that Mercury's sign and house position will also bring issues and areas of life that influence the third-ninth house axis.

Once the child is able to move past the ill effects of this positioning, the potential for leadership, organization and discipline is staggering. If they remain in a reactive frame, their efforts will stay focused only on gaining advantage in the material world. However, if there grows a leaning toward the *esoteric* side of things, the teaching ability will be well above par. In this position the *aspirant* can explain the framing of the world to others in a way that their understanding may encompass the multi-level perspectives comprising the structure of the universe. Here the *aspirant* also has the knowledge of how to organize and structure all forms of communication, business and movement in productive groups and agencies that actively and knowingly promote universal law as opposed to being limited only to the physical, emotional and mental planes.

URANUS brings the Seventh Ray energy of *ceremonial order* to Gemini and the third-ninth house axis. This position may bring eccentricity to the native's communication skills. *Exoterically*, it may be very disruptive and chaotic. However, there is a very thin line between genius and insanity. Thoughts and ideas may be very innovative and progress in way well beyond common thinking or may become bogged down in irrational protocols that cater to personal idiosyncrasies and interfere with a smooth exchange of energy. Either way, the native's input to the world around them may be intermittent at best further promoting a feeling of chaos. Mercury's sign and house position will also bring issues and areas of life that influence the third-ninth house axis.

For the *aspirant*, Uranus *esoterically* adds a modicum of intuition to mobility and communications. There will also be a subtle and consistent quiet input that the *aspirant* will feel and *know* beyond the usual communications coming from the people that he interacts and converses with. This will let him know where the conversant's motivation is coming from and allow them to encourage them into conversations broadening their universal perspectives. If writing is a dominant force, the verbiage will be such that an underlying thread leading to detachment from relying on the tangible world for validation will be felt by the native. Mental exchange will become the vehicle for awakening intuitive faculties. Fodder for communications will come from Mercury's positioning.

NEPTUNE brings a Sixth Ray energy promoting proper *ideals and devotions* to Gemini and the third-ninth house axis. For the *exoterically* oriented native, their concern and expression will always seem to involve what is important to *them* from a worldly perspective or whatever group they've dedicated themselves to. This may be a function of being largely connected to the solar plexus. They may also get lost in romanticizing things or promoting unrealistic utopian concepts and hopes. They may severely deceive themselves into believing an illusionary reality of what they're espousing. In the same vein, Neptune here also aids the deceiver of others with smooth salesmanship and the promotion of action toward unrealistic goals to the disadvantage of the listener. Please note that Mercury's sign and house position will also bring materials from areas of life that influence the third-ninth house axis.

Esoterically, Neptune increases empathy with and sensitivity to others. Although the *exoteric* native might find this distressing, the *aspirant* welcomes the feeling as they have become emotionally mature enough to be able to discriminate what is pertinent for them to pay attention to and what is not. The *aspirant* has learned what to detach from and what to listen to as a way of guiding the *exoteric* native and what they feel toward establishing universal mindedness. This helps the *exoteric* native in first, developing accountability, and then only addressing what might influence the larger whole but not to the exclusion of themselves (they are also part of the larger whole). The largest task for both, but at different levels, is developing a balance and refinement in knowing and choosing what to act on and what to allow.

PLUTO brings a First Ray energy of *will and power* to Gemini and the third-ninth house axis. In an *exoteric* perspective, Pluto's presence here poses a danger to others. The power implicit in the conversational and persuasive skills of the native can be overbearing if not dangerous. They can be seen as a forceful and convincing orator. In its worst expression, this person can convince another to doubt even their own experience. It its best expression, this is someone who can gather a following and totally and emotionally empower them to follow whatever cause or project that they deem necessary. Here, Pluto's regenerative qualities are well above par and should be used to redeem energy that is used for action that is non-egotistical. Unfortunately, for the *exoteric* native, this is usually not the case. This is one of the reasons that First Ray energies are only minimally manifested on our plane of action. Mercury's sign and house position will also bring materials from areas of life that will influence the third-ninth house axis.

Esoterically, Pluto's energy is devoid of any subtlety. In this light it must be carefully manipulated to produce effects that are in line with what our consciousness is able to handle. The *aspirant* knows that our reservoir of personal power goes far beyond what most of us realize that we are capable of. Too much runs the risk of us becoming megalomaniacal with power. Too little runs the risk of never getting past our own perceived limitations. The evolving *aspirant* often knows at what limit to assist others in regenerating their personal power and moves with this very slowly.

VULCAN brings First Ray energy of *will and power* to Gemini and the third-ninth house axis. Remembering also that Vulcan is never more than eight degrees away from the Sun, we know that the Sun's position here or in adjacent houses will bring additional light to all the issues of communication more than any other position. Here, and in spite of their own egotistical focus, the *exoteric* native will unknowingly bring an understanding of how to build and forge productive exchanges between people, organizations and businesses to others. This native may become a "get things done" individual. Their level of emotional maturity and recognition of the same will tell to what extent and at what level the world around them will benefit from their ability to create as a forge. Please note that Mercury's sign and house position will also bring issues and areas of life that influence the third-ninth house axis.

Other than minimally operating as a physical forge, *Vulcan* only operates mostly on an *esoteric* level. However, the *aspirant* knows that full manifestation on the physical plane would produce complete chaos. Knowing this the *aspirant* works at only assisting others in acquiring minimal materials and minimal Plutonian energy for their personal goals until they see that the native is not going to go overboard attempting to control and dominate others. They will monitor their skills and attitude while directing them toward a goal that will not only benefit themselves but others on a wider scale and in line with universal guidelines.

MOON brings a Fourth Ray energy facilitating *harmony through conflict* to Gemini and the third-ninth house axis. Since the Moon is probably the planet most involved in self-absorption for humans, her position here will be mostly concerned with communication to others about themselves. Since they may be self-absorbed, the native may be unable to hear or understand what others are communicating. Here and according to the dynamics of the house, recognizing both sides of every story is available and necessary. Stepping outside of self is very difficult for the *exoteric* native. They may also see everyone else by virtue of reflection as not listening to or understanding them or being in opposition to their needs and wants. Please note that Mercury's sign and house position will also bring issues and areas of life that will be used for communication in the third-ninth house axis.

Esoterically, the Moon's energy will be veiling either Vulcan, Uranus or Neptune. This positioning will tie in heavily to the dynamics occurring in Cancer and the fourth-tenth house axis.

CANCER & THE FOURTH-TENTH HOUSE AXIS

As with the ascendant or the first house, this house is an angle or cardinal house contributing greatly to the physical manifestations we create in the physical world. Its circumstances almost inevitably become much more visible than the succedent or mutable houses. Hence, the *exoteric* results will be much more tangible and observable. Knowing this must make us much more prudent and observant in examining angular houses over the succedent and mutable ones. With this in mind, let's continue.

MERCURY brings Fourth Ray energy and *harmony through conflict* to Cancer and the angular fourth-tenth house axis. *Exoterically*, the prominent energies are foundations, traditions and security. These are energies that are based on consistent patterns of behavior that create a stability of protocols geared toward producing generational continuity and the illusion of "guaranteed" family security. However, not everyone recognizes or abides by each other's family traditions. This perspective exemplifies the action of the Fourth Ray. Even family members frequently don't recognize or abide by the rules carried by their elders. Through preserved traditions, emotional family patterns are perpetuated whether they function harmoniously or not. Strategic dynamics, whether conscious or not, form the basics of many family difficulties resulting in members either avidly staying within traditions because they give them an edge on life or intentionally and energetically escaping them because they produce impediments to their life and desires. Mercury's ability to produce perspective differences contributes tremendously to an individual's desire to stay with or abandon the security and traditions established by their family's prior generations. Their desire to stay with or abandon ends up being deeply embedded in their psyches. These desires resonated strongly with the *exoteric* side of the Fourth Ray. Please also note that the Moon and her south nodal sign and house positions will bring issues and areas of life that strongly influence the fourth-tenth house axis.

They say that the closer we get to the family circle, the more difficult it is to be able to change our behaviors and motivations and have them acknowledged and accepted by the people we surround ourselves with. Strangers will accept our personal changes much more easily than family members. *Esoterically*, thinking through the needs for these changes only scratches the surface of dealing with the emotional components that establish our perceived security. These personal security protocols, conscious or not, are the basis for the *harmony or conflict* we feel within our family, let alone with the non-family members we gravitate toward after leaving the nest and then unconsciously replacing them. We instinctively, and usually unconsciously, seek to connect with friends, associates and other non-family members who reflect the struggles and patterns we grow up with. These are comfortable to us and recreate or perceived securities…we hope. These circumstances and causes are the root issues that the *aspirant* must recognize and work through before an *esoteric* mind set is able to take hold.

VENUS brings the Fifth Ray energy of *concrete science* to Cancer and the angular fourth-tenth house axis. *Exoterically*, Venus brings choice and prioritizing to the traditions we grow up with. These often polarize us within the family structure. What we find pleasurable and valuable may endear us to and please some of our family members but may not align with what other family members like or approve of. Cancer and the fourth-tenth house axis are karmic positions and set the stage for the paths we are to tread. The traditions and the securities we grow up with comprise the perspectives that we begin life with. This then leads us through a sequential set of circumstances and reactions from other people which solidifies and stratifies our thinking and then the preferences decided as a result of those encounters. This sets up the polarities that we hold and live through. The native has now chosen traditional or anti-traditional values or a mix of them to live by. Remember, the *exoteric* side of Venus is a process of deciding and incorporating beliefs about what is to be cherished and what is to be avoided. Tradition and security are major components contributing to those decisions, pro and con. Please also note that the Moon and her south nodal sign and house positions will bring issues and areas of life that influence the fourth-tenth house axis.

For the *aspirant* and this axis, we are brought back to the *choiceless awareness* expressed in our prior description of *esoteric* Venus. She is also strongly connected to the perception of third eye. The *aspirant* knows not to struggle with others if the beliefs of others conflict with their own unless physical and emotional harm may occur through their inaction. When honor or public image are involved for someone who is *exoterically* bound, we know that resistance to them only creates a more intense conflict. The Chinese say that "to acknowledge your enemy gives them power." The *aspirant* knows this and knows when it is necessary to contend and when the best course of action would be to let it go. Egotism is one of the major factors in accelerating resistance. The *aspirant* also knows this and has worked hard to move past his reacting to an insulted or contentious ego. Harmony often comes through a sacrifice of personal choice leading to *choiceless awareness*. The *aspirant* also knows "what hill they're willing to die on."

MARS brings Sixth Ray energy of *ideals and devotion* to Cancer and the fourth-tenth angular house axis. If not anything else, Mars will bring tremendous energy and action to this position. *Exoterically*, it usually brings turmoil and conflict to the issues of this position but will also bring a vehement dedication to whatever action is chosen. Mars' placement here will bring fierce defense of family traditions or strong resistance and rebellion against them. The actions taken here can be anything from simple verbal squabbles to physical abuse or altercations. Remembering that Mars is connected to the solar plexus, we know that any interaction, good or bad, will be an intense one. We also know that rational thinking is not usually a component of a struggle when emotions are in play. The feeling can run anywhere from intense passion to ruthless aggression. "True believers" are probably the most difficult to dissuade from their quest. Reason does not usually produce the best results. Once Mars has been engaged, the resultant force usually must follow through to conclusion before cooler heads can prevail. Please note that the Moon and her south nodal sign and house positions will bring issues and areas of life that influence the fourth-tenth house axis.

Esoterically, when the *aspirant* takes action, the focus must be clear and concise to avoid any misconceptions on the part of the *exoteric* person being dealt with. There must be no doubt in the *aspirant's* mind about what they are doing. However, they must also be sensitive to recognizing changes in the energy that may defuse a situation before full force is needed to be applied. "True believers" need to be dealt with a little differently from the average native. They are single minded an often need to be left to run their course before they will listen to reason.

Overcoming the influence of the solar plexus is one of the most difficult tasks for the *aspirant*. In human evolution, the major focus for the average evolving human is to move the center of consciousness from the solar plexus to the heart center. This requires a diminishing of the possessive quality we all are trained into through the implantation of family traditions, doctrines and protocols. Since we are essentially still part animal, this "territorial" component of ourselves is more difficult to overcome than most any other of our *involutionary* qualities.

JUPITER brings a Second Ray energy of *love and wisdom* to Cancer and the fourth-tenth house angular axis. Whatever issues or traditions are found here, you can bet that Jupiter will exaggerate them and then the family will claim that *they* are the essence of wisdom. *Exoterically*, Jupiter essentially just expands the importance of the Cancer and fourth-tenth house issues. It will make the family larger and/or the issues larger. Jupiter will accelerate them so much that you can't help but notice them. It's then that they will become noticeable issues for everyone concerned. Please note that the Moon and her south nodal sign and house positions will bring issues and areas of life that influence the fourth-tenth house axis.

Esoterically, Jupiter in this position makes openness and awareness the priorities. The more we can see of the world and the fullness behind it, the more we can accept things *as they are* because we begin to see all the connections. This brings less of a need to cloister us in family protocols as a protection against being absorbed by the world and losing our egotistical identity. Our traditions can best be used as a vehicle for bringing everyone to a common understanding of who we are and what part we play in dealing with in the world. The *aspirant* instinctively knows this and diligently works at helping us unfold our traditional "onion layers" of defense that have been historically constructed against losing ourselves in our perceived unpredictability and openness of the world's unconditionality. The *wisdom and love* of the Second Ray begins with the recognition of our being a smaller reflection of the world surrounding us and feeling okay with it.

SATURN brings the Third Ray energy of *active intelligence* to Cancer and the fourth-tenth house angular axis. *Exoterically*, his position here only serves to strengthen the solidity of our traditional barriers held against the world protecting or debilitating our individualized identities. This effectively results in producing a very strong ego and protective shell for the native against the world, or perhaps the family, while reducing any outside interference with the family's historical continuity and preferences. Although this may also yield a very powerfully structured family organization, it may also produce a highly restrictive one. The results may run from being mildly suppressive to feeling trapped in emotional or physical abuse. Please note that the Moon and her south nodal sign and house positions will bring issues and areas of life that influence the fourth-tenth house axis.

Esoterically, the need for tradition serves as a template for recognizing the patterns and cyclic nature of our life on earth. For some who may be ungrounded, it brings the recognition of the need for order. For others who are too traditionally entrenched, it brings the recognition that we are stuck in something that prohibits the free and proper manifestation of the *Plan*. To whatever degree the dysfunction may be, there needs to be an understanding of how the universe is balanced and connected so we may consciously add to its proper manifestation. Saturn's position here affords us that opportunity if only we're able to move past our pride and need to control our surroundings to our advantage.

URANUS brings the Seventh Ray energy of *ceremonial order* to Cancer and the fourth-tenth house axis. Here Uranian eccentricity will make itself known within the family structure. *Exoterically*, the native will appear to be a rebel or an oddball to the rest of the family. If their eccentricity expresses itself in a way that threatens the continuity of the traditions held, fireworks usually ensue. The native will likely become a scapegoat or the "black sheep" of the family. Uranus' nature is to return earthly dealings back into the channels of universal fluidity. The native may be aware of this and work with it but odds are, they will be totally unconscious of what they are doing in helping the universe realign the family back within natural law parameters. Please note that the Moon and her south nodal sign and house positions will bring issues and areas of life that influence the fourth-tenth house axis.

The aspirant knows that working with Uranian energy in an *esoteric* frame will put them in situations that demand one of two foci. First, the need to redirect the energy in a way that is harmless to the people concerned while returning them to a balanced state with the universe. Second, and this is a bit more difficult, makes the *aspirant* appear as if *they* are the problem. How? Sometimes the natural energies are so off track that back peddling is impossible due to the fact that too much ego has been invested by the contestants for anyone to save face by backing off. This requires the *aspirant* to push the tension further to the breaking point beyond the limits of those who are contesting and perverting natural energies to the point where they are forced to let go. They then can blame the *aspirant,* thereby, saving face. But the *aspirant* must remain humble knowing that the release has occurred due to their efforts.

NEPTUNE brings a Sixth Ray energy promoting proper *ideals and devotions* to Cancer and the fourth-tenth house axis. *Exoterically*, this would bring secrets to this axis. Either there are things the family members hide from each other or that they hide from themselves. This would also indicate that there are many things that they simple do not understand about their expected traditions. It may also indicate that their basis for reason is based on fantasy or contrived beliefs about themselves and their interrelation with the world. Family members may also have dedicated themselves toward being overly religious as a tradition or escape. Additionally, sensitivity will be a problem. Either they might be hyper or hypo-sensitive to each other's actions and interchange. This may lead them to over-react or under-react to each other and family stimuli. In the extreme, this may bring the need for therapy. On the positive side, they may be warned by knowing at a distance what is happening to specific members of their family without any physical world indications. Please note that the Moon and her south nodal sign and house positions will bring issues and areas of life that influence the fourth-tenth house axis.

This positioning of Neptune is his *esoteric* rulership. *Esoterically*, part of the dynamic that Neptune's over-sensitivity brings is an augmented immersion into their fantasy perception bringing the need for detachment to the forefront. The delusional quality of total immersion into any situation or feeling may push the *exoteric* native well past their comfortability in controlling any fantasy that they may be hiding behind.

The hiding, conscious or not, is usually done to avoid some real-life situation that doesn't match their expected preferences about their position in the family or the outer world. Again, for those who are *exoterically* held by their delusional beliefs, therapy may be required.

On the positive front, this may bring someone forward with tremendous sensitivity and ability in the art field or any other venue that allows for the refinement of a skill or talent. Since the *aspirant* has a strong sense of how the universe is supposed to work, they have an understanding of how to assist talented others in re-channeling or diminishing their hyper or hypo-sensitivities that might obscure their sense of reality into the most creative venues.

PLUTO brings a First Ray energy of *will and power* to Cancer and the fourth-tenth house axis. Pluto's *exoteric* positioning here brings an intensity to home, tradition, family and heritage. This is especially noticeable in how the Pluto in Cancer generation depended on the family for support through World War II and the Great Depression. For this generation and for people with Pluto in this position, family closeness and connectedness are imperative and a fundamental prerequisite for their health and prosperity. This perspective also reflects through crime "families" like the Mafia, the Cosa Nostra and even gangs since Pluto is such a staunch exhibitor of the underworld. Whether the family experience is positive or negative, we know the experience will be an intense one and reach to the core of one's being. In this light this position may also be indicative of much larger family connections than just its immediate members. Others may be brought into or included in family identifications through race, ethnicity, profession, people who are simply in need and many other connecting factors. There is power and safety in numbers. Please also note that the Moon and her south nodal sign and house positions will bring issues and areas of life that influence the fourth-tenth house axis.

For the *aspirant,* the *esoteric* side of Pluto in this position brings almost unlimited power. He knows how to handle it without confrontation but with a gentle redirecting in conflicts answering the intensity of those "under the influence." The *aspirant* also knows of the tremendous regenerative and healing power that Pluto brings. His task is to assist "stuck" natives in removing their persistent and obsessive mindsets of being locked in limiting traditions and belief systems. Once free from restrictions, the energy becoming available far exceeds the energy wasted in holding the obsessions in place. This liberation is where the true regenerative energy of Pluto comes from.

VULCAN brings First Ray energy of *will and power* to Cancer and the fourth-tenth house axis. Remembering also that Vulcan is never more than eight degrees away from the Sun, we know that the Sun's position here or in adjacent houses will bring additional light to all the issues of family and tradition more than any other position. For families who have no connection to any tradition, Vulcan will likely help them to create one. But on a deeper note, Vulcan is not only the blacksmith of the universe but he brings the purging fire since he lives within the corona of the Sun. He works in tandem with Pluto by purging outlived structures and patterns and utilizing the materials and energy that remain to forge a stronger and more effective pattern in alignment with the universe. So, although *exoteric* natives may find the purging fires of Vulcan undesirable and antithetical to their idea of provisional security, in the long run a better structure will be provided in spite of their fears and trepidations. Please note that the Moon and her south nodal sign and house positions will bring issues and areas of life that influence the fourth-tenth house axis.

Esoterically, the *aspirant* understands how to work with Vulcanic energy. They are able to assist the native by pointing the purging force into areas of their life that will make room for the new and more efficient protocols for behavior. Although some of his actions may be agreed with by the native, other actions suggested by the *aspirant* may not endear the *aspirant* to them due to the fact that they may feel that they will lose too much security if followed. They also may simply be unable to envision the advantages of the newly intended protocols. The bottom line for Vulcan's power after purgation is the unification of the elements left behind into the most solid and efficient structure for manifesting the universal *Plan* despite what us humans may think or believe.

MOON brings a Fourth Ray energy facilitating *harmony through conflict* to Cancer and the fourth-tenth house axis. She feels quite at home in this position. Since the Moon is probably the planet most involved in self-absorption for humans, her position here will be mostly concerned with family, traditions, gaining personal and family security and maintaining it. Others in the family may feel differently about us and how this should be done. This in itself will create the struggle inherent in the Fourth Ray. Establishing our security is a wider expression of establishing an identity that gets us treated in ways we want. Once we have that rapport, we usually want to keep it.

Exoterically, the Moon is the densest part of our chart. It represents past life qualities that have yet to integrated into our burgeoning personality in this new incarnation. It is also the universe's way of giving us impetus in a direction that will rebalance those karmic issues. The desire that the Moon provides forms the essence of our conflicts. Herein lies the issue that *harmony through conflict* gives us the most understanding of. It polarizes us with the world through what we *believe* we lack. Hence, the conflict. The tradition we are born into gives us a not only backdrop that sets the stage for the proper placement of our Moon's karmic residue but gives us our beliefs about ourselves and what we think we have and lack as scripted by the tradition that we're born onto. Through Cancer and the fourth-tenth house axis, the Moon provides us a personality, and as such, a path for identity resolution. Please note that the Moon's south nodal sign and house position will also bring issues and areas of life that influence the fourth-tenth house axis.

Esoterically, the *aspirant* knows that our Moon is a powerful polarizer for how we perceive the world. The best route for him to assist us is to help us see that we already have what we need to live life according to the *Plan*. Remembering the *Wizard of Oz* and the three characters that traveled with Dorothy? They all believed that they lacked what they needed to live life "properly." In the end, they all came to understand that they already had what they needed to follow the path. They just had to trust their spirit. For each of them, the man behind the curtain in the *Wizard of Oz* was actually just the energy being veiled by the Moon.

LEO & THE FIFTH-ELEVENTH HOUSE AXIS

MERCURY brings Fourth Ray energy and *harmony through conflict* to Leo and the fifth-eleventh house axis. The *exoteric* focus is on our children, childhood, creativity and recreation. It brings playfulness, vacations, recreation and any form of tangible creativity as a result of this placement but it may also bring laziness and sloth.

Our childhood experience has a tremendous effect on how we approach the world. If our discipline and communication lines with our parents are strained, overbearing or even absent, our attitude toward doing pleasurable things for ourselves may be affected. Mercury's position here leads us to assess our childhood and how we believe we have been treated. This may be done consciously or not. This affects whether we see creativity, pleasure, recreation and leisure as something that is either enjoyable, necessary and allowed or whether it should be perceived as wasting time and producing a characterization of us in the eyes of others as lazy, careless or avoidant of our responsibilities. Our attitudes toward creativity, pleasure and enjoying ourselves are very much dependent on our perception of our childhood experience and how much our rapport with our parents was either permissive, demanding or balanced. The Sun's sign and house placement will show where influence might be drawn from other areas of life. All the qualities and circumstance applied here may also be reflected through the personalities of our children, especially, the first and third.

Exoterically, Leo, the fifth-eleventh house axis and our childhood determine how we believe we *should* behave in the world. Mercury's *harmony through conflict* influence will determine whether we follow the rules of the world or rebel against them. If our childhood has produced too much restriction or too much freedom, our perception of our place in the world will be out of balance one way or the other. In these cases, we may even become belligerent or submissive.

Esoterically, the *aspirant* knows that there must be a balance between manmade rules and universal rules for the world to run and manifest smoothly. They also know that for most natives these rules must start off out of balance for the native to gain the correct direction and impetus to fulfill the manifestation of their chosen path. The native knows this because their own path has led them through an imbalance ultimately leading them to the realization that if they hadn't had the struggle that they did, they would never have arrived at the understanding that they have now.

VENUS brings the Fifth Ray energy of *concrete science* to Leo and the fifth-eleventh house axis. *Exoterically*, Venus brings choice and prioritizing to the rules we grow up with. How we see ourselves will have a tremendous effect on what we choose to do with our time. Will we allow leisure? Will we burn the candle at both ends? Will we be the responsible one? Will we play to the exclusion of all else? Here we choose between enjoyment and responsibility, work and play. Depending on what our childhood has told us about ourselves and our value, we will decide what is important and who we align with in the world. This choice defines our friends and enemies. Whose rules do we follow? The more tangibly oriented we are, the more we will lean to either acquiescence or rebellion. The less materialistic we are, the more we will trust our inner guidance. Our parenting and the indoctrination we received will determine which one we feel that we are allowed to choose. The Sun's sign and house placement will show where influence might be drawn from other areas of life. All the qualities and circumstance applied here may also be reflected through the personalities of our children, especially, the first and third.

Esoterically, the *aspirant* knows full well the consequences of the choices he's had to make. He has examined his childhood very carefully and has recognized which experiences he's had to detach from and not "take personally." The *aspirant* also realizes that choice polarizes him, so he "chooses" *choiceless awareness* on his path. This allows the karmic residue he incarnated with to flow naturally toward its own resolution without interference from his urge to control the outcome or the image it creates as the world perceives him. He knows when to act and when to abstain. His third eye helps him to see the "Razor's Path."

MARS brings Sixth Ray energy of *ideals and devotion* to Leo and the fifth-eleventh house axis. *Exoterically*, Mars will bring tremendous energy and action to this position. It will also bring a strong dedication to whatever action is chosen. Depending on the native's values and what they *feel* is important to them, their approach to their recreation, creativity and enjoyment will range from mild application to full vigor. Remembering that this axis is about rules and how things "should" be relative to how our childhood has trained us, there may be an intensity that feeds a lacking self-image and goes far beyond just simple enjoyment or creativity. This is the axis that the "true believer" draws their energy and intensity from. Sixth Ray energy can apply simple *ideals and devotion* or may have the intensity and drive associated with a fanatic or cause fighter. Depending on how far the native's identification and alignment with the rules takes him will determine the strength of his commitment and intensity. The Sun's sign and house placement will show where influence might be drawn from other areas of life. All the qualities and circumstance applied here may also be reflected through the personalities of our children, especially, the first and third.

Esoterically, the *aspirant* has weened himself off the need to fight causes in order to justify his self-perceived value and identity. He knows that there are many people in the world who need to validate themselves through victory in causes connected to the rules of their childhood indoctrination. These natives see a competitive loss as reflection of their diminished personal value and social stature. This dynamic is seen not only relative to personal causes but in sports and the business world as well. Rather than rationalizing the reasoning behind the native's cause and adding intensity to the imbalance as would therapy, the *aspirant's* job here is to use their third eye in finding an avenue for the encouragement of the native's self-esteem in *other* areas of life that are not connected to their indoctrinated childhood phobias and insecurities.

JUPITER brings a Second Ray energy of *love and wisdom* to Leo and the fifth-eleventh house axis. *Exoterically*, Jupiter will exaggerate any influence dealt with in this position. If the native is concerned about their rules to live by, they will be augmented to an extreme. If they are dealing with creativity and recreation, it will be done beyond reasonable limits. If they have directed strong energy toward a cause or calling, they will become fanatic or go overboard with it. Jupiter here will push things past the limits expected by the native in order to make it obvious enough to them that the issue(s) needs some attention or adjustment. His function is to either loosen or tighten restrictions or permissions to an extreme so they are noticed by the native. Their recognition will then, hopefully, allow a deeper and more extensive understanding of the issues and boundaries they're dealing with. The Sun's sign and house placement may show where a supporting influence might be drawn from other areas of life. All the qualities and circumstance applied here may also be reflected through the personalities of our children, especially, the first and third.

Esoterically, Jupiter broadens our horizons bringing *love and wisdom* and understanding to our otherwise tangibly bound world. He also brings compassion *for ourselves* relative to our difficult childhood experiences and indoctrinations. The *aspirant* knows the power of breaking locked beliefs about ourselves and others, good or bad, by pushing them past our expected limits. He also knows *when* to do this and that there are times where this will only exacerbate a problem. This comes through having lived through similar experiences and having come through cleaner and clearer in spirit on the other side. The energy Jupiter brings is not always pain free. But the energy that is released when this does occur is tremendously free flowing. Freedom from the boundaries of personally imposed limits, whether induced by childhood or traumatic experience is the key to the free flow of our *love and wisdom.*

SATURN brings the Third Ray energy of *active intelligence* to Leo and the fifth-eleventh house axis. *Exoterically,* his position here only serves to consolidate the issues he touches. Childhood of the native is apt to be overly restrictive. Saturn's position here often creates barrenness or impotence and the native's attitude toward children and creativity is also apt to be very restrictive if not prohibitive. Whatever the circumstances here, seriousness will be the dominating force. Learning will be an austere experience whether through enforced parameters, which is most likely, or dedication of some sort. The occurrence of a "normal" childhood will often be absent and leave the native overly structured or even abused. The Sun's sign and house placement may show where contributing influences might be drawn from other areas of life. All the qualities and circumstance applied here may also be reflected through the personalities of our children, especially, the first and third.

Esoterically, the *aspirant's* knowledge of how the universe is organized and constructed may be very helpful for the *aspirant* and the *exoteric* native. Understanding how everything is tied together often eases the stress in feeling the restrictive quality of what is learned. In light of the possibility that in past lives the native may have ignored accountability and responsibility in favor of "fun" or personal creativity, Saturn's placement here is a reminder that "fun" and responsibility are *both* necessary for the proper expression of universal energy. Whether "fun" or responsibility were overemphasized, a new look at their balance is necessary. Also, Saturn's placement here may also be the potential for organizing the *aspirant's* and the native's creativity in a much larger venue providing benefit for a much larger populace. This may also provide the indication of a "calling" needing to be actualized.

URANUS brings the Seventh Ray energy of *ceremonial order* to Leo and the fifth-Eleventh house axis. Here Uranian eccentricity will make itself known within the framework of children, childhood, rules, creativity and recreation. *Exoterically*, the native will appear to be a rebel or an oddball when it comes to these areas of life. They may do things that are unexpected or even unwanted. The *exoteric* native of this tendency may have been driven to employ this positioning, mostly unconsciously but possibly consciously, as a tool so they will be perceived as someone who is "different" and to be taken notice of. This perspective is often a consequence of someone whose childhood and creative ability have been shamed, diminished or in some way deflative of their self-image and self-respect in their upbringing. They may also have become the "clown of the class" or an entertainer looking for constant validation or applause. Their children may also inherit the same disposition from the same repeated child rearing practices whether done consciously or not. The Sun's sign and house placement may show where contributing influences might be drawn from other areas of life to add to Uranus' effects. All the qualities and circumstance applied here may also be reflected through the personalities of our children, especially, the first and third.

Esoterically and on the positive side, this positioning is extremely creative since it looks for options for applications and behavior that reach beyond the current scientifically or socially structure protocols. The *aspirant* recognizes this quality in those who have been able to move past or diminish the perceived shaming or devaluation that happens to some children through their childhood. The creative power inherent in Uranus' proclivity to direct them past *exoteric* "stuckness" may not necessarily be conscious or make the native aware of what they are actually doing but gives them an impetus toward making things "better" for all concerned.

The *aspirant* recognizes this in their hearts and takes steps to make those affected, including themselves, to feel better about feeling "different" while understanding and dropping the need to impress others.

NEPTUNE brings a Sixth Ray energy promoting proper *ideals and devotions* to Leo and the fifth-eleventh house axis. *Exoterically*, this would bring secrets to this axis. Since Neptune clouds or fogs the perception of the *exoteric* native, a child may not have a memory of their own childhood. It might have been a total blur. They may even be self-deceptive about the experience that they've had. They may tell "fish stories" or have an imaginary friend to solidify their recognition of who they are. Since this axis is childhood, recreation and pleasure, there may have developed a strong preponderance toward experiences or substances that would allow them to "forget" their discomfort. There may also be a strong tendency to daydream and get lost in a fantasy world. Sensuality may be a quality used to distract from discouraging feelings or missing self-definition. However, if this is not an issue involving self-identification, this is an extremely effective agent for creativity. This may include artists, musicians and writers who may not be grounded in the "real" world but produce works of art with sensitivities that go far beyond ordinary perception. The Sun's sign and house placement may show where contributing influences might be drawn from other areas of life to fulfill Neptune's effects. All the qualities and circumstance applied here may also be reflected through the personalities of our children, especially, the first and third.

Esoterically, Neptune brings sensitivity, perception and their refinement to this axis. Here *ideals* are refined and our *devotion* to compassionate venues are refined as to their influence and effect on others as well as on ourselves. The *aspirant* understands the dynamics of empathy which Neptune brings to this axis. He understands how easy it is to get lost in our feelings, especially, when we don't realize that we are picking up on those arounds like radar and assuming that what we pick up are our own feelings. This is where the refinement ability within Neptune's arsenal comes into play. Neptune brings the potential for the refinement of our sensitivity to the point where we know in an instant what we are picking up and from whom. Many of the spiritual disciplines that align our *ideals and devotions* with the universal *Plan* utilize the qualities of Neptune to improve the quality and clarity of our *ideals* and the disciplines and causes we choose to *devote* ourselves to.

PLUTO brings a First Ray energy of *will and power* to Leo and the fifth-eleventh house axis. Pluto's *exoteric* positioning here brings an intensity to the creativity and recreation we choose to participate in. Whether we're playing, painting, designing or making love, Pluto adds an intensity and strength unparalleled by other agents. Pluto may also bring an obsessiveness to this axis. In this there may be strong feelings about mingling with the others in terms of wanting to participate with many people at once in recreational activities or the feeling may be in the opposite extreme of wanting to avoid them as a result of an unconscious fear or repulsion.

Pluto's connection to the underground and fascination with people of an unsavory character may draw the *exoteric* native to people and activities that involve danger or even the thrill of getting away with something unlawful. The extreme may even present as a daring attitude risking the native's body and health. They may even indulge in substance abuse to the extent of potentially harming themselves or others. All these qualities and issues may also be applied to the native's children, specifically, the first or third child. The Sun's sign and house placement may show where contributing influences might be drawn from other areas of life to augment Pluto's effects.

In a positive vein, there may be a tenaciousness available to the *exoteric* native, or their children, in overcoming obstacles and roadblocks to the activities or projects they are involved in. The difficulty arises in knowing when to stop. Sometimes the native will push well past the law of diminishing returns creating frustration and wasting time and energy for all concerned.

Esoterically, the *aspirant* has most likely been through many of these scenarios and come out on the other side physically and emotionally rebalanced and giving them personal control over the *will and power* available to them. In balance the *aspirant* can use this power to assist and direct others in bridling their own intensity with consciousness and common sense. With Pluto in this position the *aspirant* may also be able to influence large groups of people in terms of their creativity, rules, children and childrearing.

VULCAN brings the First Ray energy of *will and power* to Leo and the fifth-eleventh house axis. Remembering also that Vulcan is never more than eight degrees away from the Sun, we know that the Sun's position here or in adjacent houses will bring additional light to all the issues of creativity, recreation, children and childrearing more than any other position. Since Vulcan is technically non-existent and unmanifest at this time, his action will silently and from behind the scenes forge many situations that will streamline and clarify the Leo and fifth-eleventh house axis tools that we have at our disposal. *Exoterically*, Vulcan's position here may bring an unconscious ruthlessness and selfishness to the activities of the position or may even manifest these qualities in the all the children or just the first and/or third child of the native. The lessons of this lifetime, usually indicated by the Sun's sign and house, will have a focus and intensity, applied impartially, as forged and intensified by Vulcan. He will also provide the function of purgation in removing all outworn or useless patterns that the native may have developed through his childhood or past life concerns. Here, even pleasurable things may be burned away in spite of every effort put forward by the native to maintain the security provided by their presence and affect.

Esoterically, Vulcan brings a unity and single-minded focus to any activity undertaken through Leo or the fifth-eleventh house axis. This in itself brings *will and power* through the *unification* of focus much like a blacksmith might integrate the components of a tool to be forged. The Sun's position will additionally, and more than likely, contribute to the unity and intensity but also provide the potential for the native to actually see and recognize who and what he's working with and why.

MOON brings a Fourth Ray energy facilitating *harmony through conflict* to Leo and the fifth-eleventh house axis. *Exoterically*, she brings tradition to bear on our childhood. Her presence may also indicate a happy childhood while providing a comfort, familiarity and even a sense of security with any creative and pleasurable activities associated with this position. The Moon's position here may also produce a very strong connection between a mother and her children or even a grandmother, especially, since the Moon represents a family's traditions. If to an extreme, this may even result in overprotection and consequently undermining a child's ability to detach enough from the mother to be self-sufficient. This may lead to many issue invoking *harmony through conflict* contributing to the comfort or discomfort throughout the native's childhood.

Exoterically, one of the more important outcomes of the Moon in Leo or the fifth-eleventh axis activities may become a preoccupation with the native's personal feelings to the exclusion of the recognition of the outside world and what other people might be feeling or doing. The native may also in turn overprotect their own children to the point of incapacitating their self-sustenance.

Esoterically, the Moon will bring emotions to the surface based on our childhood. Remembering that emotions are feelings experienced, attached to a thought through *exoteric* Mercury and committed to memory, we can understand why this process may be a reflection of the Fourth Ray, *harmony through conflict*. We can also remember that the goal of Mercury is to transform thinking into using intuition as a directive tool rather than relying on thought for direction. The *aspirant* knows this and remembers that the Moon veils one of three other planets, Vulcan, Uranus and Neptune. They also knows that Vulcan purges, Uranus redirects and Neptune detaches. The challenge for the native and the *aspirant* is to figure out whether the Moon's placement in this position is there to purge, redirect or detach from the childhood experiences that inhibit the native's responses to their "outside" world. The potential for the native to do this themselves is strong and they may do it through added focus, innovativeness or release. However, the *aspirant* recognizes the factors playing in the native's responses and knows which of the three planets are veiled and which quality to assist in: purging, redirecting or detaching.

VIRGO & THE SIXTH-TWELFTH HOUSE AXIS

MERCURY brings Fourth Ray energy and *harmony through conflict* to Virgo and the sixth-twelfth house axis. The *exoteric* focus is on our service, health, work and discrimination. Mercury's position here is very comfortable. However, it does bring conflicting energies through the polarizations of the Fourth Ray. Physical maladies and imbalances in health are a direct result of malfunctioning processes in the body thrown out of balance by the combined effect of our hereditary predispositions and personal habits. Whether we're looking at auto-immune issues or simple obesity due to poor diet, we are always the cause of our diseases whether the causes are self-inflicted or because of the stressful situations we put ourselves in. It is our responsibility to discriminate what habits and patterns are good for the maintenance of our physical body, not to mention our emotional, mental and spiritual selves. However, as humans, unaware ones at best, we usually let our body and emotions direct the foods we supply it with, our degree of movement and exercise or the lack of same.

The extent of the *harmony through conflict* extends to our daily habits and work environment. On the physical and emotional planes, we are constantly adjusting how we relate to the physical environment. Any resistance to the natural movement of energy, usually directed toward our comfort and preference, produces polarized situations. The resistance we pose causes friction with others and can produce a contentious attitude toward our environmental circumstances if or comfort level is not attained. This would seem normal to most of us since our western way of dealing with our universe is based on the assumption that we should be controlling it. Our beliefs about service can easily fall into an *exoteric* perspective under the expectation that we must change things for others believing that it is our obligation to do so. Even there, service, consciously or unconsciously is polarized and as such can be perceived as a series of favors resulting in obligations; ours to others and others back to us as "payment." The Moon, the other polarizing agent, will also provide influence from the sign and house that she is found in.

Esoterically, the *aspirant* knows that almost any straight on resistance to any situation usually causes extra stress on the part of both individuals. He or she also knows that sometimes extra energy must be applied simply to push *through* the resistance far enough so at least one of the parties are willing and able let go. Discriminating which to do when takes experience and skill but, most importantly, an understanding that any egotistical tendencies, such as needing to be "right," *must* be abandoned. Resistance creates friction which is a hallmark energy characteristic of Fourth Ray energy. Naturally, there will always exist a polarizing effect on the physical plane, simply because human physical, emotional and mental capacities are based on polar opposites if only to enable the ability to establish the identification of our options to choose. Mercury and the fourth Ray are the primary facilitators for showing our worldly options by virtue of their polarizations through opposition. Mercury and the Fourth Ray bring conflicts of energy to our attention. All health difficulties are a result of unresolved polarizations. To diminish or cure an illness we must discriminate which conflicting elements oppose each other and then determine what we must do to ease or abate the tension.

VENUS brings the Fifth Ray energy of *concrete science* to Virgo and the sixth-twelfth house axis. *Exoterically*, Venus brings choice and prioritizing to our health and our environment. How we see ourselves, which is the bailiwick of Venus, will have a tremendous effect on how we choose what to do with our health and our time. If we see ourselves as healthy, then no matter what the physical signs are, we are likely to ignore signals and/or simply take medication to diminish any symptoms. If we believe that we are "supposed" to serve others, then we will do that regardless of what the lessons or actual needs of others might be. Our decisions about who and what we value are the dominant authorities in how we approach our health and our service, not only to others but also, to ourselves.

Our daily and work environment will also be good measures for assessing our health, mentally, emotionally and physically. If our environment is in disarray, so will our mental state, our feelings and/or our physical conditions. What we *do* need to realize, above all else, is that ill health progresses from the subtle to the gross. So, problems will first start in our mental condition. If we don't pay attention to that, it will "thicken" into an emotional effect. If we *still* don't pay attention, it will manifest physically. At each stage we have the opportunity to recognize issues affecting our health and set them right *before* they manifest on a more tangible level. Even here the scientific method may prove useful. Mercury's sign and house position will contribute influences that will affect Virgo and the sixth-twelfth house axis.

Esoterically, the *aspirant* recognizes the obvious signs of deteriorating health. His efforts will be made at directing the native toward recognizing how their choices and behavior are affecting their health. The skill comes in encouraging the native see the signs themselves, recognize the implications and then make a decision putting a plan into action that will mitigate any harmful influences. The action *must be taken by the native* in order to gain the understanding of the long-term effects so their harmful actions won't be repeated. *No one can heal another person unless the person allows and/or participates in the healing.* The decision for health *must*, essentially, come from the native. The *aspirant* knows this and sometimes must, reluctantly, let people make their own decisions and take actions that are harmful to themselves and, perhaps, to others.

MARS brings Sixth Ray energy of *ideals and devotion* to Virgo and the sixth-twelfth house axis. *Exoterically*, Mars will bring tremendous energy and action to this position. It will also bring a strong dedication to whatever action is chosen or ignored. The native's ideals will be observed through the daily routines that they set themselves to. The solar plexus will be a prevalent player in what the native decides to do, or not. Feeling will also be a strong component while instinct and intuition will play a dominant roll.

Action is the imperative and will not necessarily be performed through the result of thinking. Remember, Mars is simply action. Whether the motivation comes from instinct or intention is immaterial. The imperative for Mars is to act, not think. This can lead to difficulties in identifying what action may be taken in lieu of an unconscious application or an idealistic cause. The result will always be action. So, when it comes to health, diet and other issues pertinent to Virgo and the sixth-twelfth house axis, that action taken will be impulsive, feeling motivated and automatic. Binge eating may occur. Body building and health-oriented action may be taken to an extreme or become totally negligent as the native's impulse and desire motivates him or her past reasonable limits. Blind devotion or obsession may become a problem.

Thought is ruled by Mercury. Mercury only connects to Mars through Aries *esoterically* and Scorpio *hierarchically*. Where Mars is concerned, thinking is an afterthought. Once the intuitive aspect of Mercury is developed, it is only then that Mars will partake of action that is considered *esoterically* sound and reasonable. This limits the action of Mars to *exoteric* parameters unless that development has taken place. In this light there is a danger that fanatic or obsessive action can be taken by the native only to be seen by others as irrational. Remember, the Sixth Ray is also ruled by Neptune who may totally obstruct the native's perception of the proper values and reasoning behind the actions that they might take. This may apply to the cause fighter, the obsessive healthcare worker, the ambitious gymnast, the binge dieter or any other native in the "helping" fields.

Esoterically, action must be taken as a result of our heart's perception. In Virgo and the sixth-twelfth house axis, this action must not be taken indiscriminately where the *aspirant's* own health and service are threatened or that his action deprives those whom he or she assists in being self-accountable and autonomous in *their* action. *Ideals and devotion* must not be taken lightly. Relative to service, tremendous discrimination must go into the choices that the *aspirant* makes as to who is to be assisted and how. Instinct and intuition tell the *aspirant* where to apply this energy but their acquired wisdom and growth must tell them at what point their application of energy is sufficient to where those he or she assists become self-sustaining. Those self-sustaining efforts also might not carry on and the *aspirant* must let them go.

JUPITER brings a Second Ray energy of *love and wisdom* to Virgo and the sixth-twelfth house axis. *Exoterically*, Jupiter will exaggerate any influence dealt with in this position. When we deal with Virgo and the sixth-twelfth house axis we primarily think of health and service on both sides. That is, our health and the health of others and service to others and ourselves. Both sides need to remain in balance in order for it to work both ways. Working for ourselves to the exclusion of others and working for others to the exclusion of ourselves runs contrary to the balance inherent in *love and wisdom*. Whichever perspective is dominant, Jupiter and the Second Ray will produce circumstances that will exacerbate the conditions farther out of balance so the attention of the native will be acquired. If these two perspectives are in balance within the native, the work that they will do will benefit all concerned. No "correction" will be needed. If not, they will need a "push" from Jupiter toward the same dominance of the imbalance to push their awareness past their current belief system so they will realize that they have gone too far. Once they realize this, they can take action to restore a harmonious energy flow.

There are many natives who are *exoteric* in their focus attempting to overwhelm the circumstances that seem to oppose their current belief system. Remember, Jupiter has a strong connection to Sagittarius, the ninth house and the beliefs we hold in our highest estimation of perfection. In this we are often blind to the veracity of conflicting factors. Jupiter is needed to overemphasize what we need to pay attention to. When he does, we often feel like we've been shot out of a cannon.

Esoterically, the *aspirant* knows how to use the Second Ray and Jupiter energy. He knows that a Jupiter influence will create a runaway train if created without proper direction and limits. In Virgo and the sixth-twelfth house axis a balance of health, service and our daily and work environment are of paramount importance if we are to energize the Second Ray energy. Jupiter here will assist us in using compassion and mercy for the benefit of those who are less aware, are in overwhelmingly challenging situations and will provide the *aspirant* with enough energy to administer to others with enough left over to support their own health and well-being. Additional resources and support can be found in the sign and house that the Sun and Mercury are in.

SATURN brings the Third Ray energy of *active intelligence* to Virgo and the sixth-twelfth house axis. *Exoterically*, his position here serves to organize, consolidate or restrict the native's health, service and daily routines. Saturn's influence here may be resisted and, therefore, no discipline or organization may take place. Or, the native may become obsessive compulsive about organizing, structuring and disciplining. Remember, the Third Ray has a close relationship with the throat center. The key to using Saturn and the Third Ray properly depends on the native referencing their life and patterns against how the world moves around them. If they can integrate their action and discipline in alignment with the flow of the world around them, Saturn will contribute a constructive influence. But generally, Saturn's natal position here usually begins with a resistance to whom they see as an authority.

In a constructive sense but still *exoterically*, Saturn here contributes toward building the body, the work environment or even a structure of people and materials for administering service to self and others. This may take the form of a network like UNICEF or the tentacled internet. The success depends on the tenacity and ingenuity of the native and how well he or she is able to put his or her will (throat center) into action. There, caution is needed for the native to become balanced in their sense of authority. If the structure becomes an outward expression of the native's ego, there will be severe restrictions and the reach of what they are doing will only reach a small percentage of their target "audience." Even with honorable intentions, the organization itself can become progressively subverted to an individual's need for dominance and control at a later date.

Esoterically, the effectiveness of what the native does will depend on how oriented they are toward being an *aspirant*. If they have matured past the need to use their service as a badge for establishing an egotistical identity and have truly become an *aspirant*, the organization can reach an effectiveness far beyond the small group of people with whom the group was begun. Remember also that a co-ruler of the Third Ray is the Earth who represents the ultimate in diversity and group unification beyond the borders that Saturn would *exoterically* gain dominion over.

URANUS brings the Seventh Ray energy of *ceremonial order* to Virgo and the sixth-twelfth house axis. Here Uranian eccentricity will make itself known within the framework of health, service and working environment. The native will likely take an approach toward these issues if not in an eccentric way, in a more innovative way. *Exoterically*, this innovation may not be geared toward the needs or desires of those whom he or she might be serving. Nevertheless, there will be some effectiveness in spite of any extensive "personalization" of the services provided.

The native's diet and attitude toward their health is likely to be very unique. This may extend from doing things very differently and in a quiet way to producing a lot of flair and bravado in the production or administration of what their service is providing whether only to themselves or open to others' participation.

Early on in their upbringing the native may be observed as behaving a little oddly or quirky in the way that they handle their daily activities and how and whether or not they might assist others. Depending on how much encouragement or autonomy the native has been allowed in their childhood will determine to what degree their egocentricity will be developed. The more they might have been pressured or diminished, the more bravado and "specialness" will have been necessary for them to compensate.

Esoterically, the *aspirant* with Uranus in this position will be able to find ways of being of service that bypass the normal channels which might ordinarily provide restrictions and obstacles. Their own habits may be just as different relative to the rest of the population but be in line with what the universal energy might work best through. Many people are not in "sync" with the natural energies and to the *exoteric* native the *aspirant* may seem to be excessively odd. However, as the Seventh Ray is best represented through the sacral center and the natural order of things in nature, the *aspirant* may seem to be quite odd and eccentric to some but conversely, a miracle worker to others.

NEPTUNE brings a Sixth Ray energy promoting proper *ideals and devotions* to Virgo and the sixth-twelfth house axis. *Exoterically*, this would bring secrets to this axis. Since Neptune clouds or fogs the perception of the *exoteric* native, health issues, service issues and the awareness of the environment the native lives in will be scattered at best. They may be absent minded or at the least, unclear about what should or could be done concerning the issues of the axis. Their personal hygiene may be lacking or they may be fanatic about it. They may be extremely picky about their diet, their surroundings and the people the allow themselves to be surrounded by or totally slovenly and uninterested. Neptune in this position may bring hyper-sensitivity and/or hypochondria. Mars' sign and position will tell what any likely hypochondriacal or hyper-sensitivity issues might concern. Neptune's positioning here may make illnesses very difficult if not impossible to diagnose.

Anyone who works in the health or service field may be over-dedicated to the point of damaging their own health or have no compassion at all. Any illness contracted may be a result of surrounding people or the environment presenting harmful circumstances or energies to them, however, the native may be totally oblivious to them.

Esoterically, and in contrast to the above circumstances, the *aspirant* with Neptune in this position may be unusually aware and sensitive to the energy flow and patterns of the people around them. Neptune bears a strong connection to the solar plexus and the Sixth Ray energy directed by *ideals and devotion*. They may also be tremendously empathetic and know and feel what everyone around them is feeling, aware of or oblivious to. Once they have mastered recognizing and controlling the empathic aspect of their own persona, they may become an outstanding healer or advisor. Neptune's position here will bring a high-level devotion to the universal *Plan*. Mars' sign and position will also show where influences can be drawn from and where Sixth Ray action may take place.

PLUTO brings a First Ray energy of *will and power* to Virgo and the sixth-twelfth house axis. Pluto's *exoteric* positioning here brings an intensity to the health, service and/or daily routines we choose to participate in. The native with Pluto in this position has an outstanding ability to heal and regenerate, however, this may manifest as an obsession over the issues that the sign and axis presents.

Depending on whether the native has experienced depreciation or confidence building in their childhood, they may either have an intense fear of working with the public or an immense joy. Any lacking or spoiling in the native's childhood experience may also manifest as a need to establish dominance over others or allow themselves to be dominated. Either way, their worldly experience will contain a strong exposure to the public and all the attending physical, emotional and mental interactions. *Exoterically*, the intensity felt will almost be palatable.

Exoterically and *esoterically*, the *aspirant* has an atomic stockpile at their disposal. They know this and know how careful they must be in applying energy indiscriminately. They know that whatever changes they effect will have a profound effect on themselves and any native that they assist. The *aspirant* is also aware that Pluto's placement here will give them expanded exposure to the public and their energy level. He or she also knows how quickly other natives will gravitate toward them for a "feeding" and is prepared to maintain his or her own levels to the benefit of themselves and others. The *aspirant* also knows how to use their tremendous healing ability. This position of Pluto often makes for an effective therapist provided the therapist's values are on a par with universal energy patterns.

VULCAN brings the First Ray energy of *will and power* to Virgo and the sixth-twelfth house axis. Remembering also that Vulcan is never more than eight degrees away from the Sun, we know that the Sun's position here or in adjacent houses will bring additional light to all the issues of health, service, daily routines and work environment. Here Vulcan's effect will enable the purging of any patterns or obstacles to the *esoteric* use of his and the Sun's energies. This may not be to the liking of many *exoteric* natives, especially, if those patterns and obstacles are the things that they use to assure the maintenance of an egotistically based life view. Since Vulcan has been viewed statistically as non-existent in the conventional astrology world, he generally will be perceived as working on an unconscious level by those who are *esoterically* aware. He removes anything that will stand in the way of realizing the Sun's *esoteric* goal. This will cause the *exoteric* native to "come clean" in spite of themselves or any attempt to maintain a preferably tangibly secure existence. Professions associated with this placement might be dentist, demolition, restoration, therapy or any capacity that strips away materials that are useless, outdated or worn if they will create an impediment to the Sun's function or service. This includes removing people, groups or counterproductive habits. Since Pluto is a co-ruler of the First Ray, his sign and axis will show where any restorative or regenerative energies might be drawn from.

Esoterically, gaining a full handle on Vulcan's purgative energy is virtually impossible for the *aspirant* to acquire. However, he does know enough and has had enough of his own purgative experience to guide others in the process of streamlining their spiritual lives and perspectives. The most common and most effective purging will be that of a native's personal and tangible securities in favor of a wider perspective and a deeper understanding their place in the universe. This may not always be obvious to the native at first and may often cause some consternation about why they should be concerned about others when their own feeling of security is to be abandoned. This remains true until they feel the freedom of their ability to act more broadly in the scope of their possibilities. The *aspirant* is also constantly streamlining their maintenance and adding to their concentration of their *will and power* toward becoming one with the universal flow of energy and feeling the joy of being part of perfecting the creation of the world.

MOON brings a Fourth Ray energy facilitating *harmony through conflict* to Virgo and the sixth-twelfth house axis. *Exoterically*, the Moon's position here is similar to Mercury's with the exception that the Moon makes the connection much more personal and emotional. One of the more important outcomes may become a preoccupation with the native's health and personal feelings to the exclusion of any awareness of the outside world's perspective of them or what other people might be feeling or doing themselves. They will likely be more concerned with themselves and how *they* are treated by others in terms of their health, their service and how others contribute to or interfere with their daily routines and environment. These concerns will usually resonate with the native's feeling of security and the familiarity produced by the traditional rules and patterns that they've grown up with.

The Moon's position here may also bring a predisposition toward being a hypochondriac with real and/or imaginary illnesses. Additionally, the native's daily routine would be of utmost importance toward maintaining their emotional balance. In an extreme case, obsessive compulsive disorder (OCD) might become an issue.

Because of the personal nature involving the Moon, the Fourth Ray of *harmony through conflict* will be a dominating factor, especially in light of the fact that the axis is mutable. The native will instinctively take sides in any dispute or contention. This will tend to intensify the polarization characteristics of the Fourth Ray.

Esoterically, it is likely that the *aspirant* will know which planet, Vulcan, Uranus or Neptune, is veiled by the Moon. He will likely use reverse psychology to edge the native into a more neutral viewpoint, then question what the native is feeling when they are in a less volatile position in order to allow them to get used to operating from a more neutral perspective. This will, hopefully, also partially free the native from clinging to any polarized perspective that they've used to make themselves feel secure in childhood. For the *esoterically* minded native with this positioning, they will have a facility for marshalling others toward a less egotistical path while preparing a way to become *aspirants* themselves.

LIBRA & THE SEVENTH-FIRST HOUSE AXIS

As with the ascendant or the first house, this house is an angle or cardinal house contributing greatly to the physical manifestations we create in the physical world. Its circumstances almost inevitably become much more visible than the succedent or mutable houses. Hence, the *exoteric* results will be much more tangible and observable than the other houses. Knowing this must make us much more prudent and observant in examining angular houses over the succedent and mutable ones. With this in mind, let's continue.

MERCURY brings Fourth Ray energy and *harmony through conflict* to Libra and the seventh-first house axis. The *exoteric* focus is on the "other," relationships, long term partners and "open" enemies. Contrary to the emphasis on independence in first house, the emphasis in the seventh house will be on sharing, balancing needs and wants with the other and whether the native will be able to do so in important relationships. Sharing doesn't come innately unless the native has had a significant issue with this axis in past lifetimes. Ordinarily, sharing must be taught. Mercury's Fourth Ray energy will resist this inclination. It may be viewed as a loss by the native. There may be squabbles about who comes first or last and who deserves more or less. We can also see how "open enemies" exemplifies the Fourth Ray energy.

Remembering that opposites attract, repel and mirror each other, we can see how a Fourth Ray energy might over-emphasize polarities and discourage any balance between all three relationship perspectives. However, it will be the mirroring that will eventually produce the longer range of possibilities for growth. When we are made to see ourselves, it is then that the wheels start turning and we come to the recognition that some of our beliefs about ourselves and others might just be off a bit. This begins the painfully slow process of maturing into sharing at a balance.

Esoterically, the *aspirant* recognizes the need of the native to establish their identity through comparison and opposition. He knows that the lower the self-image and confidence of the native, the harder the change will be and the longer it will take them to arrive at manifesting balance. This positioning produces patience and penchant for listening in the *aspirant*. It also allows for a deeper understanding of how relationships operate ranging from being childish to emotionally mature. The *aspirant* knows when to interject advice and when to hold back. This quality allows for the finest development of mediators and arbitrators.

VENUS brings the Fifth Ray energy of *concrete science* to Libra and the seventh-first house axis. *Exoterically*, Venus brings choice and prioritizing to dealing with the "other," relationships, long term partners and "open" enemies. Here we determine who and what premise we will use to either include or exclude others from our worldly rapport. Will someone be a close friend? An enemy? An intimate partner? This positioning will also fuel in an ongoing process constantly re-evaluating who deserves to remain within our circle of association. These conclusions may not always be within the parameters of common sense, compassion or reason but they will always be based on our experience with them or based on the opinions of people we trust aligning with *their* experience and preferences instead of our own.

Based on our prior definitions of Venus and its rulership of how we see ourselves we can see how this positioning may have a tremendous influence on whom we decide to trust or align with and why. Have we learned to trust ourselves and our own judgment or have we been taught that others know better who and what are best for us? Our self-image is a major factor in our choices concerning others.

So, Venus' positioning here will give us clues as to whom the native may include in their circle of relationships and what values are used to make those decisions. This can be done based on feeling and personal experience (internal) or it can be done based on the rules of the family and culture the native sees themselves part of (external). To understand which rules the native will follow, we must first know whether in the native's childhood they have been encouraged toward autonomy and personal accountability or to follow the rules of their perceived superiors along with the assignment of blame.

Esoterically, the *aspirant* has arrived at a place of balance between his own needs and desires and the needs and desires of the circle of people he has chosen to put himself in. He has moved well past the effects of how others may perceive him to what his presence in a relationship or group will have on the overall effect on the surrounding world of natural law. The *aspirant* has taught themselves to see whether the native trusts themselves and their experience or have they given away their personal power to those whom they seek approval of and whom they see as being more important than themselves.

The *aspirant* has trained themselves to operate in alignment with the Fifth Ray and the *concrete science* in the universe. He or she has learned to see things as they are in the larger scheme of things and is able to guide others in their choices. First, they teach them to trust their own inner judgment, and then to have the courage in making choices in lieu of not receiving the approval of or advantage over individuals or groups seeking personal security in *their* choices based on *his* approval and alignment with them. The *aspirant* recognizes this dynamic as "the blind leading the blind."

MARS brings Sixth Ray energy of *ideals and devotion* to Libra and the seventh-first house axis. *Exoterically*, Mars will bring tremendous energy and action to this position. Either the native will be very active, or even contentious, in and toward relationships or they will attract relationships that do the same. They will be very strong in their drive and devotion to their partners, enemies and close associations. Their action will come from a place of impulse rather than pre-thinking their actions. Because Neptune is also connected to the Sixth Ray and is centered in the solar plexus, they may not be aware or conscious of what they are doing, let alone, the effects they may have on their relationships. This may make for some contentious discussions or arguments speaking about the effect each person will have on each other.

The dedication to whatever action is chosen might be mindless, especially, since thinking is not a prerequisite for Mars' action. For the native with Mars in this position, the ideals behind the action are likely not assessed, only blindly followed. This will also be one of the positions of Mars for the "true believer."

Esoterically, the *aspirant* knows that it is likely that the native they're assisting may not rationally assess their actions before taking them. They know that their first priority is to assess the native's awareness levels. Once determined and then established, the *aspirant* can ask questions about the motivation and values behind their actions to draw them toward being more in touch with the energy behind their actions. This will tend to make the native more conscious about his or her worldly participation.

This Mars position will keep the *aspirant* moving toward others regardless of any privacy or solitude he may attempt to seek. This universal drive is an impetus and invitation to re-integrate with the tangible world in order to ferret out resistive qualities that might prevent a deeper understanding of the *aspirant's* own conscious motives and re-balance their participation.

JUPITER brings a Second Ray energy of *love and wisdom* to Libra and the seventh-first house axis. *Exoterically*, Jupiter will exaggerate any influence dealt with in this position. In this light the native will have a large repertoire of people connected through various types of relationships. There may be wide cultural difference. Their relationships may seem to be the most important thing in their lives. Every issue with others will be a "Godsend," a "catastrophe," a "life changing experience" or any other over-emphasized experience. From the perspective of the native, this will also inflate their own importance or the importance of the person focused on through the experience. Which is usually dominant will depend on whether the native has been diminished or over indulged in their childhood.

Jupiter's positioning here is to draw attention to the area of relationships through over-emphasis. Karmically, the native may have ignored relationships in past lives or based all they are and do on their rapport with others. Jupiter here simply blows imbalanced relationship issues out of proportion so they can be recognized and dealt with. The Second Ray deal with the heart center. Its activation attempts to nudge the native into opening their heart enough to allow the consciousness behind *love and wisdom* to come to light when dealing with their interpersonal relationships. This will lead the way toward bringing balanced humility, empathy and compassion into awareness. The Sun's sign and house position will show other areas of life that will bring relationships in the native's life to the forefront. Venus' position will bring the values used for assessment.

Esoterically, the *aspirant* has likely already passed through a crisis in dealing with their own ego and has come to recognize their own strength in using empathy, humility and compassion as a tool in dealing with others. The *aspirant* has learned to assist the native in either backing down from their self-generated intensity or increase their intensity and stress to the point where they will finally let go enough to be able to listen to their own heart.

SATURN brings the Third Ray energy of *active intelligence* to Libra and the seventh-first house axis. *Exoterically*, his position here serves to organize, consolidate or restrict the native's relationships. The native may see the "other" as the authority in relationships. They may also perceive *themselves* as the authority within their relationships. Which perception is felt will be determined by how they were programmed to see themselves and others in their childhood. Precociousness may also be present.

Saturn brings a seriousness to their relationships. Laughter and joyousness will be severely reserved. Rules for behavior in relationships will be extremely strict. Discipline may be a focus or an issue. Partners solicited may also be significantly older or younger depending on which way authority is assigned. Remembering that the Third Ray is connected to the throat center, thyroid imbalance may also be an issue. This position may also reflect a quality of narcissism. The sign and house position of the Earth and Venus will also give insight as to what issues will be brought into questioning who is in authority.

Saturn's position here shows the connections between all the people in the native's life. What the native says or does with one person will eventually get back to or have an effect on themselves as well as others. Transactional analysis in *Games People Play* by Eric Berne will offer many clues as to the native's self-image within a relationship.

Esoterically, the *aspirant* knows the seriousness that the native assumes in their relationships and uses their discipline and forbearance as a tool for understanding their motivations and to stimulate their *active intelligence*. The *aspirant* knows how powerful the structuring side of discipline can be in bringing an awareness as to where authority should emanate from. The *aspirant* will attempt to show the native how the worldly tangible web (not to be confused with the internet) is interlaced and that no one person or component is any more or less powerful than any other and that it is universal law that determines the ultimate authority. Hopefully, this will encourage the native to let this "higher authority" direct their worldly actions and disciplines and release themselves from "earthly" domination.

URANUS brings the Seventh Ray energy of *ceremonial order* to Libra and the seventh-first house axis. Here Uranian eccentricity will make itself known within the framework of relationships. The people that the native is attracted to will *not* reflect their traditional upbringing. This may happen through choice or unconsciously depending on the native's level of interpersonal awareness. Uranus in Libra and the seventh-first house axis are geared toward reorienting the native's perspective and attitude toward relationships. Whether being consciously or unconsciously directed, being "different" will enable them to detach from how they were traditionally trained to perceive and respond in relationships differently. In keeping with Uranus' connection to the sacral center, their "differentness" will be used as their point of balance in facilitating their detachment. In an extreme, this may even be manifested through a rebelliousness.

When depth is eventually established in the native's relationships, they may ultimately revert to their culturally traditional upbringings encouraging them to break the relationship because its quality comes to close to the childhood training that they are trying to disconnect from. Hence, Uranus in this position often results in relationships that are only temporary in nature. At departure the native may quote them as becoming boring, stagnant and limiting.

Esoterically, the *aspirant* has become aware that all relationships are only temporary. They are usually aware that those whom they attract and who appear to be different are merely the universe's way of drawing their attention to their own characteristic behavior in relationships that might need to be reassessed and perhaps broadened.

The *aspirant* also recognizes that this qualitative occurrence changes the lives of natives who find it difficult to develop depth and consistency in their relationships. The *aspirant* can assist the native in releasing themselves from feeling trapped by their traditional upbringing and to see it as only a reference point for understanding themselves in relationships and not as a prerequisite for their future emotional behavior.

NEPTUNE brings a Sixth Ray energy promoting proper *ideals and devotions* to Libra and the seventh-first house axis. *Exoterically*, this would bring secrets to this axis. Since Neptune clouds or fogs the perception of the *exoteric* native, relationships issues may confuse their awareness or understanding. They may likely have unrealistic ideas about how their relationships are proceeding and the logic and values behind them. They may also have the tendency to deceive themselves by putting their partners on a pedestal by assuming things about them that are not real. *Ideals and devotion* may be an honorary concept for the native to dedicate themselves to but for the *exoteric* native they may be based on erroneous assumptions or missed information about who or what they have pledged themselves to. Neptune can produce circumstances that are deceptive or lead the native to deceive themselves. Venus' sign and axis position will provide the values used to assess.

The Sixth Ray is centered in the solar plexus so anything felt by the native will likely have intensity. Neptune's influence here may bring a hypersensitivity to the things that others may do and/or say. Whatever they believe will be strong and somewhat unshakable, even if it's delusional. Neptune is a contributing factor toward behaving as a "true believer." Neptune in Libra or the seventh-first house axis also makes the native susceptible to being easily deceived by others. The sign and axis position of Mars will give added energy and influence to the workings of Neptune, especially, since he acts generally on impulse.

Esoterically, Neptune can produce a refinement in understanding the nuances in relationships. The more grounded the native is in universal law and reality, the clearer they can become with handling life in between the tangible and intangible. The more refined the balance between the two, the clearer will be their perception. The *aspirant* has had enough experience to move past most of the potential for self-deception, but will still be improving on their refinement in their understanding of how the universe functions. Please note that the *aspirant must* remain on their guard as it is quite easy to slip back into confusion and self-deception if their egotistical side regains a foothold. The recognition and refinement of reality is and will always be an ongoing process.

PLUTO brings a First Ray energy of *will and power* to Libra and the seventh-first house axis. Pluto's *exoteric* positioning here brings an intensity to relationships. Whatever or whomever the native's relationship is with, you can bet that it will be at an intensity most people are not comfortable with. In an extreme, it can seem obsessive.

Pluto brings the public to whatever sign and axis he falls in. The native will have extra-ordinary experiences with more than just his circle of acquaintances. The exchange of energy will usually occur below the threshold of awareness and may produce undercurrents that shape the relationship in ways that neither the native nor the "other" may be aware of. It may bring an uneasy feeling on both their parts if they are not astute enough to recognize their motives for investing in the relationship. Those who are the least aware are likely to be the most easily manipulated. Pluto in this position often results in power plays whether conscious or not. His positioning brings a *will and power* that will either be under the native's direction or under the direction of the person he or she has a relationship with. This energy can often become consciously contentious or at the least, subliminally coercive. Whatever the type of energy, you can bet that it will have a regenerative quality allowing for a tenacious push of *will and power* by either the native or the receiver. Venus' sign and axis position will determine the values being contended.

The *aspirant* deals with Pluto from an *esoteric* perspective. He knows the potential for intensity and is careful to direct this energy in a constructive way rather than letting it settle into the unconscious of the native to produce undercurrents that escape their understanding and control. The goal of using this energy must be conscious, in alignment with the universal forces and have the potential to activate the compassion and humility that connect *esoteric* Pluto to Pisces. The *will* must be coupled with these qualities before the *power* should be used. The main reason that the first Ray is not yet manifest is that our civilization has neither gotten a handle on our egotism nor perfected our use and recognition of universal empathy, compassion and humility.

VULCAN brings the First Ray energy of *will and power* to Libra and the seventh-first house axis. Remembering also that Vulcan is never more than eight degrees away from the Sun, we know that the Sun's position here or in adjacent houses will bring additional light to all the issues concerning relationships. Pluto's sign and axis position will provide the regeneration for all the issues that Vulcan's position brings to the forefront.

Vulcan's position here will allow us to purge relationships that inhibit our ability to connect with people who will benefit our emotional maturity. The *exoteric* native is not usually aware of who those people might be and often resist letting go of people who provide their security or who verify the narrative that they have chosen to believe about themselves. *Power* comes from aligning with an energy that is directed by the mind and the heart. When directed by the mind, usually lower, the native ends up in places that need to be purged. When directed by the heart, they usually align with the universal force but it is often not recognized by the native who has a narrative that is egotistically oriented. Having a strong ego is necessary as it provides fuel for the *will*. Being egotistical is being invested in the security provided by our narrative. Vulcan's purging ability is antithetical to security. He is ruthless and has no considerations for our feelings or beliefs. His *only* objective is to free the light of the Sun so awareness may prevail and a solid base for universal *will and power* may be forged. This is terrifying for the *exoteric* native.

Vulcan operates *esoterically* and works antithetically to the understanding of the native. He usually produces results that are threatening to their security. When Vulcan is in Libra and/or the seventh-first house axis, the Sun is usually with him. This positioning of both tends to put the major attention on relationships but may purge the ones that the native *believes* are good for them. In essence, the ones purged would only perpetuate their dependency and emotional stunting. This is very confusing for the *exoteric* native. It makes them feel that the universe keeps short-circuiting their preferred and expected happiness in relationships.

Esoterically, the *aspirant* uses Vulcan's purging ability to clear the way for evolution and the implementation of the universal *Plan*. He or she understands and accepts that this will bypass any personal preferences they may have in favor of the larger picture. His or her emotional maturity enables him to accept this and assist others in moving past their insecurities in close relationships. Pluto's sign and axis position will also indicate where regenerative forces may be available from, both for holding on and for purging.

MOON brings a Fourth Ray energy facilitating *harmony through conflict* to Libra and the seventh-first house axis. *Exoterically*, the Moon's position here is similar to Mercury's with the exception that the Moon makes the connection much more personal and emotional. One of the more important outcomes may become a preoccupation with relationships of all kinds – romantic, platonic and inimical.

The native's experience in learning about relationship in their early upbringing will be paramount in how they handle any subsequent relationships. They will handle them the same way they handled their family and assume the same rules and circumstances apply in the new relationships. In this way their security will depend on how the partners act and what they do. This puts tremendous pressure and responsibility on the partners for the emotional welfare of the native. This may create an unconscious resentment for both parties. If the native had a difficult upbringing, the partner will feel either suffocated or abandoned. If the native had a free and happy childhood, the partner may feel ease in the relationship but perhaps no grounding or responsibility on the part of the native. The key here is that the native will determine the basis for the relationship through the identity that they are projecting on their partner. This struggle aligns with the polarizing energies that the Fourth Ray of *harmony through conflict* operates under. This positioning of the Moon polarizes the relationship until the native is able to mature into autonomy.

Esoterically, the Moon veils either Vulcan, Uranus or Neptune. These bring the prevailing qualities of purgation, reorientation and detachment respectively. The *aspirant* knows this and has also gone through a major part of their own purging, reorienting and detaching bringing them to a point of relative emotional maturity. This enables them to "see" what the *exoteric* native needs and which of the veiled planets and their position will be of major involvement in the maturing of the native in relationships.

SCORPIO & THE EIGHTH-SECOND HOUSE AXIS

MERCURY brings Fourth Ray energy and *harmony through conflict* to Scorpio and the eighth-second house axis. The *exoteric* focus is on "other people's resources" which includes finances, assets, support, banks, loans and a whole host of people and organizations that provide physical, emotional and mental support to the native. The axis itself includes two of the three signs that comprise the Fourth Ray of *harmony though conflict*. In its grossest connection to ego, it represents the power struggle between individuals and organizations where assets, tangible or not, are the medium of debate. Mercury's position here can often represent consideration of strategies which assess and plot for advantage over each other's resources. This could represent a subtle dominance in a relationship all the way to the hostile takeover of a corporation. This strategy can be business oriented or even sexual.

Exoterically, Mercury here is involved in the assessment of the assets of others, the self-image of others, what or whom they use to value themselves and what they perceive of importance in their lives and the lives of others through comparison. This represents the height of human polarization – conscious and unconscious. Since we are speaking of the Fourth Ray, we know the energy is connected to the root or base of the spine center and the native's perceived survival. Their perception of survival can range from simply belonging or not to an elite social group all the way to duels and physical combat. The Moon's sign and axis position will tell where more fodder for the process will emanate from.

How a child is taught to value what he or she is or what he or she has or not has a profound effect on how involved this power struggle may become. The more the native has been trained into being balanced, the less important what someone else has or is capable of except for those individuals for whom assisting others is a joy to perform. The more the native has been trained into a mindset of lack or being inadequate, the more what someone else is or has will be of importance. The Moon's sign and axis position will add personal emphasis and emotional content.

Esoterically, the *aspirant* knows that the *exoterically* oriented native will exist in a mindset of comparison. The only way the *aspirant* can show the native that the power struggle can be abandoned is to assist them in accomplishing what they believe they lack with only the resources that they already have. This was clearly shown in the end for the lion, the tin man and the scarecrow in *The Wizard of Oz*. Otherwise, envy and obsession with one's perceived lack or another's possessions is virtually impossible to disarm except through "winning" a competitive struggle.

VENUS brings the Fifth Ray energy of *concrete science* to Scorpio and the eighth-second house axis. *Exoterically*, Venus brings to consciousness choice and prioritizing in dealing with the assets and abilities of the "other." What does the native feel is important? What does the other value? What has the comparison shown? Most of this occurs within the tangible world. This includes the emotional and mental planes. However, the Fifth Ray works through the third eye center. This mostly deals with things that are intuitive and unseen to the native. Some natives intuitively know what others are capable of without any physically confirming evidence. Inversely, they may also be afraid of what others know about them.

This axis is where the native decides how much and what support they will give their partner, their enemies and the world. It is also the place where they will judge what it is they want from others and what they believe that they can expect from others in the way of support. The more tangibly oriented the native is, the more this will be of importance to them. Venus' position here will often lead them to decide on a strategy for the control of the assets and abilities of others in relation to their own. The native will attempt to rebalance them to favor their own feelings of security.

This sign and axis are where the native will determine what he or she values and finds desirable or not in other people. Here will be specific likes and dislikes about what other people are capable of and what they could provide to the native. At its deepest level this will also be the sexual encounter and how the native participates in physical intimacy. This is the place where the native will decide how much and how close they will allow another person to be with them. This can range from a mere indulging in a minor pleasurable sensation all the way toward allowing and feeling total nirvanic abandon.

Esoterically, the native's self-perception of value and self-image are the primary basis for determination on how they will assess their own values and those of others. The *aspirant* knows this and will direct the native toward becoming more aware of the value and assets that they already have. The *aspirant* will also show the native that value must come from their own perception of themselves devoid of outside influences and opinion. They themselves have already passed through and eliminated the illusory perspective of comparing and judging their own value by virtue of what the outside world has stipulated is appropriate. This will tend toward a lessening of the envy or jealousy that the native may feel which always occurs as a consequence of feeling a perceived lack or inadequacy stemming from their childhood indoctrination by their caretakers. In this light the *aspirant* with this positioning may also be involved in professions that enlighten to and encourage natives toward realizing their hidden talents and potential and assist them in choices that activate them in a heart centered way.

MARS brings Sixth Ray energy of *ideals and devotion* to Scorpio and the eighth-second house axis. *Exoterically*, Mars is very comfortable in this position and will bring tremendous energy and action to the axis. Either the native will be very active, or even aggressive toward dealing with the self-image and resources of others. They will be active in either soliciting or applying support from or to the people near and close to them. All the qualities and issues ruled by this axis will be heightened in terms of energy. As this is the ray of *idealism and devotion*, the native must examine their motivations in taking or receiving action through this axis. The native's actions here will always bring them into contact with the self-image and resources of others. They, in turn, will be very much drawn to and affected by how others use *their* resources and assets. In this way our self-image is connected very strongly to the solar plexus and the seat of our tangible identity.

The draw to intimacy will be very powerful for the native. They will constantly be drawn into everyone else's business. They may even be seen as being intrusive. They may feel simply unable to help keeping themselves from doing so. This will also show up as a need to investigate secrets whether sanctioned by others or not. Anything that is hidden will be fair game for the native, even if it invades the privacy of others. The inclusion of Neptune as the ruler of the Sixth Ray may also bring deceptiveness into the things that are hidden from the native or from the other. This may be intentional or not. The native must uncover their motives behind their actions in this axis. The *ideals and devotion* that are motivated in this axis may be self-deceptive for or simply elusive to the understanding of the native. Any of the native's tendency toward blind devotion facilitated by the Sixth Ray may contribute to the native's further lack of understanding but add to the momentum of their experience.

Esoterically, the *aspirant* knows the deceptiveness that can occur through the Sixth Ray's *ideals and devotion*. He or she has done enough inner work to understand their own motivations for action and has aligned them with the universal law in spite of any of their own earthly desires or advantage. The *aspirant* knows that this is an ongoing battle and that they could easily slip back into impulsive action motivated by their ego. They also know that the native's action is often taken impulsively and without forethought. The *aspirant's* primary focus will be to lead the native toward an awareness of what is motivating them to act and to also keep a tab on their own motivations so that they remain clearly aligned with the universal *Plan*.

JUPITER brings a Second Ray energy of *love and wisdom* to Scorpio and the eighth-second house axis. *Exoterically*, Jupiter will exaggerate any assets or resources dealt with in this position. In this light the native will have a large reservoir in which to observe what people have and are capable of. If there is a power struggle in the eight-second house axis, of which there often is, Jupiter and the Second Ray will push it out of proportion. The native may give or gain a lot from this axis but will also become a lot more attentive to it due to its exaggeration. This positioning is also a point of potentially broadened awareness, however, the native's focus, *exoteric* or *esoteric*, will determine the type and level of influence that will be perceived, understood and then used.

Jupiter's position in this axis will augment the attention and concern of the native for issues concerning intimacy and its potential. It will also bring empathy and an intuitive knowing of how other people feel about themselves and what they feel their capabilities and inadequacies are. The native will either receive tremendous support from others or the well will totally dry up. There will be no middle ground. In this light there will also be an expanded contact and participation with people and organizations that provide or receive support from others. This will include banks, finance institutions and many other organizations who deal with the resources and capabilities of others and their groups. The Sun's sign and axis position will give more insight as to where more connections may come from.

Esoterically, there is a lot of *wisdom* that can be learned by observing what others have, are capable of or how they use it. The *aspirant* with this positioning has patiently come to an observance of many of the interactions that *exoteric* natives have by allowing their own reactions to what others say or do to fall by the wayside. *Wisdom and love* are fostered by patience, compassion and humility. In using these qualities and forgoing any egotistical reactions intended on preserving their own preference and security, the *aspirant* gains *wisdom* in leaps and bounds simply through their observation and non-action. There is *wisdom* that can be expanded by Jupiter through allowing others to act and react unhampered. It is then that the *aspirant* can assist the native in applying their resources and abilities without prejudice or motivated by personal advantage.

SATURN brings the Third Ray energy of *active intelligence* to Scorpio and the eighth-second house axis. *Exoterically*, his position here serves to organize, consolidate or restrict the native's assessment and use of other people's resources and abilities. Support from others for the native may be sparse at best. Saturn's position here will certainly make sure that support is organized and structured but in its harshest scenario, there may still be slim pickings. Access or use of others' resources and capabilities will have its requirements and restrictions. There may be protocols that must be adhered to. There may be conditions that others have imposed before the native can have access to or partake in the use of others' resources. These conditions may be part of the larger web that the Third Ray is distributed through. Whatever happens on one side of the web is felt and often recognized on distant web "fibers." The interconnectedness of all things broadcasts throughout the structured world. Since the Third Ray deals with *active intelligence,* what the native may know about another's resources gives them clues as to their larger picture and its organization through the process of deduction. The Earth's sign and axis position will give more validation.

On a personal level, Saturn in this position is often felt by the native as they're being deserted or ignored when it comes to feeling supported by others. This may also manifest as a responsibility for them to provide support to others in the form of time, energy and resources at their own expense. The native may also find that others may appear to be in an authoritative position by virtue of their control and ownership of the resources that the native wants or needs to function. This could result in a mild form of extortion or emotional blackmail on the part of the native or others coercing the individuals into performing in ways preferred by the resource keeper. This may manifest as being responsible for things such as paying a mortgage or, in the extreme, being subject to loansharking.

Exoterically, Saturn in this position brings heavy lessons involving responsibility and accountability. This positioning teaches the native that paying dues is a necessary activity if they are to receive the benefit that the eighth-second house axis has to offer. However, the polarized world works according to cause and effect. If the *aspirant* can assist the native in easing the pressure from their *exoteric* push toward worldly security by showing them how their actions *create* the polarity creating their perccived lack, the native may be able to consciously reduce the push and the frustration.

Esoterically, if the *aspirant* can show the native how to see the larger web (not to be confused with internet) expressed by the Third Ray of *active intelligence* rather than simply staying within their own small personalized perception of needs and lacks, they would be able to recognize the energetic benefit of going with the flow of a universal acceptance and awareness beyond the purview of simple cause and effect. Unfortunately, Saturn's involvement in karma and the structuring of the *exoteric* native's belief system is extremely powerful and rarely does the native move past the perception of his personal polarization. The throat center is an extremely powerful tool that must be ultimately used to align the native with universal energy rather than attempting to mold the physical world into the native's security-oriented preference by simple persistence through force. The *aspirant* has made tremendous progress in being more universally inclusive, but as with every structured plane, his slow growth of perception, awareness and ascension must still follow a similar cycle of "life and death" that is prevalent to every plane.

URANUS brings the Seventh Ray energy of *ceremonial order* to Scorpio and the eighth-second house axis. Here Uranian eccentricity will make itself known within the framework of other people's resources and the native's intuitive assessments of them. The native's objective and thrust using Uranus will be to separate others from what it is that limits *their* accessibility to those same resources. Whether it benefits the native or others, the resulting objective will be the same. The Uranian "pattern" of action is usually one of sudden release or change. This is characteristic of what some people would label "excitement" and others would label "insecurity." This dynamic brings the increase of pressure to an eventual release or explosion of restrictions toward the natural flow of energy. Anticipation, or fear, is an energizing force. The native with this positioning will encounter sudden changeability in the availability of support from and to others. Suddenly the flood gates are open and the next minute there is nothing and often with no apparent cause.

In Scorpio and the eighth-second house axis Uranus' unpredictability of support is an applied dynamic for making people depend on themselves for what they need or want to live. This forces the native to organize themselves in ways that align with the natural flow of energy rather than any contrived means for coercing others to provide for them. For the native who is insecure with his or her own abilities and resources, the availability of another's is very important as an emotional crutch providing the illusion that they will be taken care of. Their sudden evaporation or appearance can be unnerving.

In a similar light, the sudden disconnect characteristic of Uranus might be an OBE or an out of body experience. Remember, this is the axis of secrets and the unseen. What better example could there be for a sudden exposure or disconnect from the tangible world?

Esoterically, we know that the Uranian dynamic is a sudden disconnect from worldly security. And as a trans-Saturnian planet, he is a vehicle for our realignment with the immutable universal laws of the universe. His effect or "job" is to remove us from the need for personal control over our universe. Accepting this can be terrifying to the *exoteric* native. However, there is comfort in learning that our care and well-being exist in a much larger framework than our human consciousness. If the *aspirant* can bring the *exoteric* native to the awareness of the freedom and power that is available in this mindset, the native's personal pain and need for control will be lessened and his or her journey back to the creator will be a smoother and less contentious one. However, the acquisition of this freedom will not preclude the karmic "lessons" that still remain to be experienced in the native's akashic records.

NEPTUNE brings a Sixth Ray energy promoting proper *ideals and devotions* to Scorpio and the eighth-second house axis. *Exoterically*, Neptune would bring secrets to this axis. Since he clouds or fogs the perception of the *exoteric* native, assets here may seem hidden. They could be hidden intentionally by others like attempting to avoid taxes on investments. They may simply not be seen because they are in a place not accessible to the native or others. Or the native and others may be self-deceptive in their beliefs to a point that makes them unable to perceive their own resources or those of others. In light of the fact that they are hidden from view, Neptune may even allow them to fantasize that there is something much more idealistic and available to them beyond their common sense.

With Neptune in this position *exoterically*, what we believe we see as assets or debits will most likely be deceptive, either intentionally or by faulty perception. In this light, both emotional and business dealings may be at risk of not being seen as they truly are. Neptune can easily deceive our senses. Our dependency on our senses must be reduced to a minimum if we are to evolve spiritually. Additionally, our solar plexus will have a much more dominant part to play with Neptune in Scorpio and this axis. Mars' sign and axis position will tell where much of the utilized energy will come from.

Our ego and how we identify ourselves as compared to others and their possessions must be reduced to a point where our own inner assessing can take place *based on our own experience* not what or who others appear to be in the external world. This is a call to listen to our heart not our insecurities. Any preconceptions about ourselves or others *must* be dissolved.

Esoterically, Neptune's position here is extremely tricky. Remember, Neptune is the *esoteric* ruler of Cancer, the home of *exoteric* security and tradition. Since the *exoteric* native's ego compares themselves to everyone else, Neptune's job, especially in Scorpio and the eighth-second house axis, is to dissolve any preconceptions about how they think other people and the world *should* be. Who or what they consider *ideal or devote* themselves to should be carefully discriminated. The *aspirant* has faced the Neptune experience of self-deception and has struggled and worked hard to move past deceptive worldly illusions as perceived about other people and to consciously align with universal protocols.

PLUTO brings a First Ray energy of *will and power* to Scorpio and the eighth-second house axis. Pluto's *exoteric* positioning here brings an intensity and depth to the issues of resources and capabilities. In some cases, the native may develop an obsession with them.

Exoterically, Pluto gives the quality of regeneration to the tangible world. The support that comes through this axis may be long lasting. It may indicate a trust or legacy left for or by the native. Conversely, it may also indicate an obligation or connection to the underworld. In any case, there will be a strong connection to the public and the resources available to the native through this axis or the native's involvement in providing the same to the public.

Having information about others gives the possessor power and influence over others. This positioning may indicate an ability for investigative work or to establish the hidden qualities of others. It may also become an obsessive quest for the native. There will be an urge or sense in the native that they must know everything about anyone they have a serious connection to. It may even lead to becoming an agent for an investigative agency as the *will and power* (tenacity and proficiency) necessary for this kind of work is well beyond the limits of the average person. The native may also become a valuable asset to any organization that values hidden information about others. Privacy may become a moot point for the native or the people he or she connects with.

Pluto's positioning as an outer planet contributes tremendously to his *esoteric* qualities. The *aspirant* knows that his or her regenerative ability will have a profound effect on those that they assist. But they also knows that his or her self-examination of their own motives is an important prerequisite for working efficiently and "cleanly" with the universal energies connected to others. Pluto's intensity makes this quality a valuable component in the healing field. The ability for the *aspirant* to assist others in rising like a Phoenix is staggering. In this capacity, the *aspirant must* be clear of any alternative or personally oriented agendas. The effective *aspirant* will have conducted an intense "soul searching" of his or her connection to the public and the advantages and resources that could be provided to them on a solely selfish level. This clearing will allow for a laser focus on the assistance for the rebuilding of the unrealized potential in the average person's ability for self-sustenance. The balance must also consist of enough of the *aspirant's* own self-sustenance to remain healthy and energized in their universal Plutonian objectives. Vulcan's sign and axis will tell where most of the rebuilding and forging will take place.

VULCAN brings the First Ray energy of *will and power* to Scorpio and the eighth-second house axis. Remembering also that Vulcan is never more than eight degrees away from the Sun, we know that the Sun's position here or in adjacent houses will bring additional light to all the issues concerning the resources and capabilities of others.

Vulcan's positioning here results in the forging of projects, abilities, patterns and protocols that utilize the abilities and resources of others. Although his action is primarily *esoteric* in nature, his energies are used to build the possessions, securities and futures of those who provide these resources whether by voluntary contribution, unsuspecting participation or being deceived and swindled by *exoteric* natives.

Before Vulcan forges, his pattern is to first purge. Supplies, possessions and even abilities and tendencies that might be outdated or inappropriate for what is to come must first be eliminated and burned away. For the *exoteric* native, this will often be an undesirable experience as most natives will prefer to retain the security of what they have until a better option presents itself. But nature doesn't work this way. As what is dead or useless falls away in nature it makes room for new growth. Nature abhors a vacuum. However, the human ego cannot easily handle the void produced by the birth/death cycle. Humans attempt to hold on to what is familiar; living or dead. The human ego requires security to feel "safe." *Esoteric* Vulcan strips away what is worn out or obsolete whether the human is holding on to it or not.

Esoterically, the *aspirant* knows that Vulcan primarily works in an *esoteric* fashion which always contradicts the holding on tendency of the *exoteric* native. He or she knows that the best option for assisting the native is to convince them of the potential that exists for growth using only what they are able to perceive as an asset or a resource. When a change of life circumstance presents itself, preferable or not, the native is usually unable to see past the loss of what they will have to give up in order to realize their new potential. Short of painting a vision for the native, the *aspirant's* only other option is to remind the native of the *will and power* that they might have exhibited in the past to get them to trust that the universe will bring a desirable replacement over their past security. Hand-holding and commiseration are *not* qualities in keeping with the patterns utilized by Vulcan. The ultimate choice for everyone is by virtue of their own *will and power* which is, essentially, allowing the universe to take its course.

MOON brings a Fourth Ray energy facilitating *harmony through conflict* to Scorpio and the eighth-second house axis. *Exoterically*, the Moon's position here is similar to Mercury's with the exception that the Moon makes the connection much more personal and emotional, especially, with the issues this axis deals with. One of the more important outcomes may become a preoccupation with what other people have or are capable of. If this becomes the basis for judgment of other people, this could become a huge problem for the *exoteric* native, especially, if this also becomes a reason for connecting or disconnecting from other people.

The polarization that the Moon brings to this axis is a major detractor for allowing personal growth. It intensifies the separation of the natives through their judgment of the quality or quantity of the assets and resources that others may possess or not. This keeps their perspective locked on their physical, emotional and mental planes. Remembering that the Moon is the densest point in our charts and that it veils either Vulcan, Uranus or Neptune, it makes sense that the native's childhood learned attitude toward the comparison of their abilities and assets with that of others would need to be either purged (Vulcan), separated (Uranus) or dissolved (Neptune).

Esoterically, the *aspirant* will likely know which of the three planets are veiled and what dynamic needs to be used to realign the native's physical, emotional or mental perspective on other people's resources. This, in essence, will enable the native to properly place the "left over" qualities of the Moon that have been brought into their life. As this occurs, the *aspirant* will also become sharper in aligning their own perspectives and gain deeper insight on how to assist others in doing so. Mercury's sign and axis will give additional insight as to where information can be had to work with the thinking behind the Moon's position.

SAGITTARIUS & THE NINTH-THIRD HOUSE AXIS

MERCURY brings Fourth Ray energy and *harmony through conflict* to Sagittarius and the ninth-third house axis. The *exoteric* focus is on "other people's" philosophy and view on life. In this position Mercury brings many opinions on how better to live one's life. There can be very strong debates and common-sensical opinions on life style, circumstances, values and the potential for end results. Polarization will be an influential factor and the Moon's sign and axis position will tell which areas of life will provide the most "evidence" with a potential plethora of "should's." The *exoteric* native may be very opinionated and offer unsolicited advice to others. Details and discrimination will comprise the major thrust of what is put forward, sometimes missing the "big picture."

Because of Sagittarius and the axis issues, Mercury's positioning here may also bring religious, cultural or racial issues to consciousness. There may be a lot of travel or talk of travel. The native may be a powerful advocator of a specific way of life. They might appear to be a zealot or fanatic. "Preaching" may become a problematic projection. There may be talk about the big deal, "fish stories," fantasy plans, "pie in the sky" or a daydreamer type of perspective put forward by the native. However, this type of thinking may also bring unique ideas and problem-solving perspectives that that broaden problem solving potential. Good or bad, this positioning may allow the native to "think out of the box."

Education or any form of "higher learning" may be of primary importance for the native, whether in support of it or in disdain of it. Regardless of the issue, this positioning is likely to create polarization in the way the *exoteric* native communicates with the world and what they may expect or hope for as a response in return. This may include selectively listening for grounds supporting their opinion or being unable or unwilling to listen to others to really understand what they might be attempting to convey about themselves.

Esoterically, Mercury needs to be utilized in an intuitive manner. Hearing what others need or want to convey doesn't always mean sorting through and discriminating the "facts" that Mercury is able to tangibly discern. It means listening and expressing ourselves from a wider intuitive base of expression and perception. The *aspirant* has trained themself to listen to more than just what is said. The *exoteric* possessiveness (the solar plexus) and the need for egotistical survival (root center) have been minimized in the *aspirant* enough so that they are actually able to sense the motivation behind a native's communication. In this way they can ease most of the tendency of the native to polarize and can lead them to actually hear what they need to hear in order to free their mind and intuition toward a broader and more universal potential.

VENUS brings the Fifth Ray energy of *concrete science* to Sagittarius and the ninth-third house axis. *Exoterically*, Venus brings to consciousness choice and prioritizing in dealing with other people's communication, higher education, culture, religion, philosophy and life values. Venus here encourages the native to consciously decide their life values and who and what they're going to believe. Other people's philosophies and life styles will be explored for the value they might have for the native in choosing how they wish to live their lives. Since the sign and axis are mutable, this may be subject to many changes. As new evidence comes in, paths may change just as quickly. They may even seem fickle and even unstable to the observer. However, the mostly unconscious inner goal is a lot more solid than what may be evidenced by others in the "practical" world. For the intuitive native, they may be searching, unconsciously at first but later consciously, for intangible evidence directing them toward a life path that feels right. Whether developed yet or not, the third eye is a powerful contributor to the native's quest. A "knowing" of universal law may be present but not as yet a conscious understanding to abide by. Observation may be a strong tool but emulating the path will produce a sense and feel if it is right for them. The unconscious goal will be the search for life's purpose and an ongoing search for their idea of perfection.

The native with this positioning often seems undisciplined, erratic and irresponsible. However, the unobserved inner directive to pursue perfection is unshakable. There often exists a lightness of spirit and a trust that things will always "work out." Many types of life path will be explored and a worldly understanding may be acquired but unrecognized by the native or his or her observers.

Esoterically, in both the aspirant and the *exoteric* native there is a sense, if not a knowing, in how the universe works and the natural laws it follows. Their lightness of spirit and trust in the world often inspires others to seek a similar perfection in their own lives. The biggest challenge facing the *exoteric* native is to know and understand that there are accountabilities and responsibilities that must be found and adhered to in the tangible world while pursuing their idea of perfection. Once this balance has been established, their own persona as an *aspirant* may be realized. Other *aspirants* immediately recognize the native's unconscious quest and can strive to assist them in making it conscious.

MARS brings Sixth Ray energy of *ideals and devotion* to Sagittarius and the ninth-third house axis. *Exoterically*, Mars will be an explorer. Impulse will be a primary driving factor in what the native does. They could leave on vacation at the drop of a hat. They could walk out on a job on the turn of a mood. They could activate their passion in following a cause simply by being inspired, true or not, that it is a viable one. The freedom that this positioning energizes is a strong one. Dedication could occur instantaneously, especially, if the encouragement is strong enough. Here, the *exoteric* native's *ideals and devotion* are driven by impulse. As Neptune is a powerful contributor to the Sixth Ray and the solar plexus, the native must take care and learn to examine the validity behind the causes he or she is inspired to fight for.

With Mars in Sagittarius or the ninth-third house axis, listening to others is a foreign experience. No pun intended. Getting their own message across is much more important than knowing what anyone else is saying. This is not to say the Mars here is rude, but simply oblivious (Neptune) to the fact that there may be another viewpoint. Remember, Mars does not think. *Exoterically*, he simply acts based on impulse.

Mars in this position may indicate that the native does a lot of traveling and/or may have resided in a distance away from his current locality. There will be experimentation if not conscious investigation into cuisines, cultures, religion, international travel, and experiences that may satisfy immediate urges. Participation and acceptance of all these experiences and much more are just a sliver of what makes up Mars' *hierarchical* rulership of Sagittarius.

Esoterically, Mars is simply an energy driver that responds to impulse and intuition. Although he brings passion and intensity, the task for the *aspirant* is to make sure that his or her navigator is responsive to universal flow of forces and rules not just personal urges that are responsive to their need for adventure or security. As long as there is conscious intention behind the action taken and it is in line with the universal energies, Mars will have served his purpose. Energy has no mind. Mars is a perfect example. The task for the *aspirant* is to encourage the *exoteric* native to listen and observe where his or her urges are coming from. Becoming conscious of the motivations behind our actions is imperative if we are to evolve and grow to become aware or ourselves, let alone the patterns of the universe.

JUPITER brings a Second Ray energy of *love and wisdom* to Sagittarius and the ninth-third house axis. Jupiter feels very comfortable in this position. His purpose is to expand our knowledge and wisdom in accepting all types of lifestyles, religions, and cultures *in others*. This acceptance must occur within a balance. That is, we must not adopt any life style or world view simply because it is presented to us. The *love and wisdom* part has to do with a "live and let live" philosophy and urges us to understand that in the empathy and compassion that he brings to us, we should not allow the paths of others to direct our lives indiscriminately simply because this is what we were shown. Jupiter is here to expand our education and awareness of the diversity in the world and to be accepting of it but to keep our own counsel and inner trajectory.

Exoterically, Jupiter will exaggerate any belief or belief system that the native chooses, falls into or is led to by others. By exaggerating the live styles and philosophies of others, he only brings to awareness the many choices we have at our disposal leading toward the broadening of our awareness. What we follow as a life style should be a conscious decision. Jupiter brings the diversity of the world to our door so we have a wide variety of options to choose from. We must still maintain a responsibility and accountability for our choices and for whom and what we involve ourselves with. A proper inner navigator must always remain present in keeping with the highest values we hold.

This exaggeration is necessary because so many of us become stuck in a particular life view or philosophy only because it serves to maintain the security that we believe we need to preserve what we have and know about ourselves. In brief, the ego wants to keep things static so it can maintain control and universal life wants to broaden the potential of who we are able to be and what we are able to do. Jupiter here forces a crossroads of sorts. That is, do we stay on the path as we believe it to be or do we allow more diversity in so as to expand our love and wisdom? Sometimes we're just being shown something different in order to allow us to confirm the path we've already chosen. Not all life events need to be "dealt" with. The Sun's sign and axis position will add to the qualities and areas of life that will broaden our perception.

Esoterically, the *aspirant* knows that life and its options can be overwhelming. But that feeling of overwhelming is to push us past our limits so we don't remain limited within a life view that prevents our growth due to our perceived security needs. Unless the new options are exciting and provide life advantage in the appearance of our first exposure to them, most *exoteric* natives will be resistive to any kind of growth. The *aspirant* knows that appearances may be illusory and transient and must find a way to assist the native in seeing the entire depth of what the Jupiter experience is providing to them. This can only be done through *love and wisdom,* compassion and patience in allowing the *exoteric* native to see the advantage in moving past their solely tangible life view. Jupiter and the Second Ray (heart center) are immeasurably involved in our first spiritual *initiation.*

SATURN brings the Third Ray energy of *active intelligence* to Sagittarius and the ninth-third house axis. *Exoterically,* his position here serves to organize, consolidate or restrict the native's assessment and use of life styles and philosophies for his or her spiritual growth. It must also be understood that spiritual growth here may start with limited and conventional religions and philosophies but must eventually be shed in order to actualize a wider potential for *active intelligence* requiring accountability and a universal definition of responsibility.

Generally, the *exoteric* native's view of responsibility is comprised of motivations leading to a perceived advantage of their worldly status and control. This is wholly tangible and serves the native's idea of security. The responsibility that is needed to become an *aspirant* is a larger and more diversified inclusion of the *energetic* well-being of themselves and others relative to their spiritual growth and acceptance of their inner life path. This well-being does *not* serve egotistical needs that are limited to the native's appearance, status or control over themselves and others in the tangible world.

Saturn's position here may indicate a learned and/or developed life status allowing the native to have control over the beliefs of others and the temptation to use that control for personal advantage. This temptation could come in the form of a corrupt religious leader, a tyrannical business mogul, an admired Hollywood personality or many other positions that mix status and control allowing for personal manipulation. The native's egotistical side must be tempered. The heart center must be opened. Saturn's positioning here is a serious process and must be met with the dedication connected to the Sixth Ray of *idealism and devotion.*

Esoterically, the *aspirant* has his or her work cut out for them. Generally, *exoteric* natives who have "ascended" into this type of control or position have no interest in humanitarian pursuits. Their emotional security requirements are usually so deeply buried that all they are able to perceive is personal gain or loss in the tangible world. There is a tremendous amount of backtracking and historical examination of their upbringing required to allow them to see how and why they arrived at this position. The more power and control they have, the less likely they will be to even look at their childhood deprivations. The *aspirant* must have exorbitant amounts of patience and fortitude to stick with finding soft spots in the *exoteric* native's emotional armor to energize the *love and wisdom* that everyone has at their core.

URANUS brings the Seventh Ray energy of *ceremonial order* to Sagittarius and the ninth-third house axis. Here Uranian eccentricity will make itself known within the framework of other people's beliefs, philosophies, religions and culture. His position here will express itself through two possible scenarios. The first scenario will be in keeping personal freedom. The more "different" a life style is, the more attractive it will seem to them. The life style will also change at the drop of a hat. Whatever creates the most "wow" will be a persona to be played to activate attraction and admiration. The *exoteric* native with this positioning needs to be, seem and feel different and free of any restriction.

Life views and perspectives will go through quick but short phases after the sparkle and fascination with them wears out. New and different experiences will be sought to the exclusion of all else. There may also be travel to distant places presenting different cultures, religions and cuisines. Freedom and exploration of the new and different will be the primary goal.

The second scenario will be for the preservation of emotional security. Often times, Uranus appears here to acquaint the *exoteric* native with alternate life views and philosophies to break old fixed or stuck patterns from previous lifetimes. In this case, change will be unwelcomed and staunch resistance to any life philosophy that conflicts with the currently held "differentness" or individuality will be fiercely maintained. Differentness then becomes a rock to be held on to in order to preserve the emotional security offered by the beliefs that the *exoteric* native might currently be holding.

Esoterically, Uranus' perspective is to simply "encourage" the *exoteric* native into moving back into a life view that is aligned with the sacral center and the universal principles directing the balance of nature. Since the native's rules and restrictions are manmade, this influence often meets considerable resistance. Although *ceremonial order* is the energy associated with natural law and the Seventh Ray, the "ceremonial" part extends well past the conventional or manmade limits of traditionally or tangibly oriented protocols. This can be extremely stressful for the *exoteric* native. The *aspirant* who is working with this energy can offer insight to the native that will show the disadvantage of operating too far outside or to closely within the emotional limits that they have framed for the maintenance of their security. This will provide the native with an unbiased observation of the unbalancing effect of employing either scenario that provides too much freedom or too much constriction. Remember, the keyword for Uranus is *reorientation*.

NEPTUNE brings a Sixth Ray energy promoting proper *ideals and devotions* to Sagittarius and the ninth-third house axis. *Exoterically*, Neptune would bring secrets or delusions, about ourselves or others, to this axis. Since he clouds or fogs the perception of the *exoteric* native, their life path may also seem hidden. There are many dependencies that may manifest as a result of these secrets and delusions.

For most people this position blurs the principles behind our choices that lead us to decide who or what we dedicate ourselves to. Neptune can bring crystal clarity or severe delusion. It all depends on our consciousness, awareness, upbringing and how well we acknowledge our life circumstances. If we are emotionally grounded and mature, our *ideals and devotions* will be clear and focused. If not, we may end up living in a fantasy world of dependencies and expectations. Most people primarily operate somewhat in the latter but containing a mix of both depending on the areas of life that we've been indoctrinated in or given a mature awareness of by our caretakers. Which occurs more also depends on the maturity level of our caretakers. Most people begin their lives stuck in patterns that began with indoctrination from birth.

Generally, those with Neptune in Sagittarius or the ninth-third house axis are susceptible to any life style that activates their imagination. They are easily led and easily taken advantage of. Since the solar plexus is the dominant center, they go almost strictly by what they feel and how it contributes or detracts from their self-image. If someone is adept and twisting the facts and presenting the fantasy that the *exoteric* native finds pleasing to and supportive of their sense of security, they can manipulate the native who will be none the wiser. Neptune's position here is not only to *dissolve* the native's naivete, but to *dissolve* their investment in believing who they have been told that they are and that they are more responsible to others than themselves. This makes them eminently more manipulatable by others with a personal agenda.

Whether the deception is self-generated or influenced by others capitalizing on our naivete, the bottom line of Neptune's positioning here is to make us all aware and self-accountable for our choices. This clears the way for our understanding and acceptance of the universal patterns of which we are only a part. There is nothing wrong with having a sense of personal security but it must lie in balance with our participation in the universe and not a fantasy-oriented view based on acquiring and maintaining personal control. Neptune teaches us that personal control is only viable when being used on ourselves.

Esoterically, the *aspirant* knows the hazards of believing that they can control anything but themselves. When our upbringing has taught us that we are more or less than others, it becomes very difficult to break the beliefs that we were indoctrinated with that hold that assertion over us. The *aspirant* knows this after extensive soul-searching and analyzing their motivations behind their dependencies. If they have freed themselves enough from the parental delusion that trained them in believing that they must control and influence the world, they can also become a solid example for the *exoteric* native's acquisition of emotional freedom from these types of dependencies. Then the native will be able to utilize the refinement qualities of Neptune to align themselves with *idealism and devotion* toward the universal plan.

PLUTO brings a First Ray energy of *will and power* to Sagittarius and the ninth-third house axis. Pluto's *exoteric* positioning here brings an intensity and depth to the issues of this axis. In some cases, the native may develop an obsession with them.

Exoterically, there will be a drive to foster one's life views on the world. Convincing the public may become a priority. The native's views are embedded deeply and thoroughly. They will believe that they are unshakable. Conversations about them with others may become contentious. The question becomes, will their *will and power* be used to impress others into following *their* way, thereby justifying the validation of their own beliefs, or will they allow and encourage others to follow *their own* star and calling while promoting their own spiritual growth? The regenerative quality of Pluto here can be a formidable force to harness, especially, if it is egotistically committed.

If the native is mature enough in their perspective, there is a strong resonance with the general public. The native may have an innate understanding of what the public consensus will be on any of their important value-oriented issues. They may also have an understanding of what creates fear for them and be able to tap into this part of the public's psyche in order to influence them. This may manifest as leadership or, if the native is weak in their own self-image, there may result a tendency to follow the crowd instead. Confidence and *Self-Trust* are the qualities that must be present if the native is to be able to follow their own path, let alone lead others, with the intensity that Pluto promises to provide.

Esoterically, the *aspirant* knows the depth from which the *exoteric* native's beliefs may emanate from. This may give an edge to the *aspirant* on how to proceed in showing what and how the native may be able to adjust in order to release the pressure created by a dysfunctional upbringing. Pressure to follow the crowd comes from prior conditioning. Faulty parental programming that operates against the *exoteric* native's *Self-Trust* and autonomy must first be overcome before they can release themselves of performing for others for approval. The *aspirant* knows this and finds and emphasizes the circumstances in the native's life where they can see and understand where and when they *did* have *will and power* and followed their own counsel. In knowing and recognizing this it becomes easier and easier to trust following their star and calling. Then, the "proper" energy and perspective will take hold of the native's heart and provide the courage they need in following the laws of the universe that move so faithfully within all our hearts.

VULCAN brings the First Ray energy of *will and power* to Sagittarius and the ninth-third house axis. Remembering also that Vulcan is never more than eight degrees away from the Sun, we know that the Sun's position here or in adjacent houses will bring additional light to all the issues concerning the *exoteric* native's beliefs, philosophies and perspectives about life.

Vulcan purges any personal beliefs that no longer serve the purpose behind the native soul's calling. This process will likely not always agree with their projected beliefs that support their immediately perceived security. Vulcan operates very much like the way a dentist treats a cavity. First, the dead, useless and decayed tissue must be carved and drilled away. Then when a solid foundation in line with the body's mandates for healthy tissue is all that remains, new materials may be forged and added to build a more fitting structure. This is what happens to the native's values and belief in the presence of Vulcan.

The unsuspecting *exoteric* native may create circumstances for others that are akin to the above example. This may not endear them to the others that they encounter or associate with. Others may sense this quality in the native and avoid them, not even realizing why. The native may also not understand why others might duck them. Remember, Vulcan is only manifest on the *esoteric* level and "above." He or she may do this unconsciously.

Vulcan is an agent for change. For him to operate, consciousness is not required. For many, his action in their lives may be a complete mystery. For others, they may realize *what* is happening but be unable to understand *why* or *how* they bring it on themselves or others. All they know is that they, somehow, manage to manifest contentious circumstances to their belief systems and to those of other people. This will especially unnerve people who are attempting to keep faulty belief systems supporting their emotional security in place.

Educating and growing awareness of ourselves, others and the things we hold on to for security is the primary response that is needed to understand the dynamics of Vulcanic action. Sagittarius and the ninth-third house axis provide a prime field for this type of growth to take place. Some learn about culture. Some go to school. Some travel to different countries. Some just become immersed in sorting out philosophy. The bottom line is that this axis provides the space and tools to develop broader perspectives to handle and expand the beliefs we have been indoctrinated with that hamper our growth and emotional maturity. Vulcan is an agent for change, albeit, an unconscious one for most people. His strong connection through the First Ray to the position of Pluto and the underworld will also have a tremendous effect on our ability to purge what is "not working." It's no surprise that the First Ray is connected to the crown center of which we as humans have virtually no comprehension of let alone how it "works."

Esoterically, the *aspirant* knows that Vulcan, in conjunction with Pluto, is an extremely powerful tool that must be used with care, skill and proper intention. The heart center and the upper three chakras must be used in conjunction in order to arrive at the appropriate place for each soul's recognition of their path toward universal consciousness. The *aspirant* can only do this through example and perhaps relaying personally analogous life circumstances where the native can see how and why change must occur in order to become conscious.

MOON brings a Fourth Ray energy facilitating *harmony through conflict* to Sagittarius and the ninth-third house axis. *Exoterically*, the Moon's position here is similar to Mercury's with the exception that the Moon makes the connection much more personal and emotional, especially, with the issues this axis deals with. Situations dealing with personal values and life philosophies may become intensely personal. Any disagreement may meet with either a strong response, which is usually not as likely, or a disassociation with others who might disagree which is more likely. The main motif for Moon in Sagittarius is that of freedom. This will tend to lighten its intensity in this position.

Remember that Sagittarius is a member of the Fourth Ray and that the Moon is a dominant representative in *harmony through conflict*. Although the Moon in this sign and axis may bring a lightness, we must remember that she also veils Vulcan, Uranus and Neptune. If any depth is pursued in this axis, it will certainly ramp up the intensity.

Fodder that contributes to life views and perspectives will be found where Mercury is deposited. It is through the house and axis issues that Mercury stimulates that will give the medium or life circumstances that philosophies and values will be shown through.

Esoterically, the *aspirant* may find the *exoteric* native evasive when bringing up life values and philosophies. Encouraging the native to get serious about their values may be a challenge at best. The sign the Moon is in will show the type of emotional content and security being brough to the axis for examination. The hardest belief systems that need to be "cracked" will be those attached to a religious group dogma. They usually provide the strongest support for maintaining emotional security contingent upon approval. Their allegiance to principles indoctrinated in childhood may be unbreakable since their emotional security may be coupled with embedded traditions established over centuries and those traditions may actually be the "lessons" through which their understanding of universal law must be learned.

CAPRICORN & THE TENTH-FOURTH HOUSE AXIS

As with the ascendant or the first house, this house is an angle or cardinal house contributing greatly to the physical manifestations we create in the physical world. Its circumstances almost inevitably become much more visible than the succedent or mutable houses. Hence, the *exoteric* results will be much more tangible and observable than the other houses. Knowing this must make us much more prudent and observant in examining angular houses over the succedent and mutable ones. With this in mind, let's continue.

MERCURY brings the Fourth Ray energy of *harmony through conflict* to Capricorn and the tenth-fourth house axis. Career, social status and how we relate to authority are issues that the Fourth Ray will "take issue" with. As the axis for authority, there are two ways that the *exoteric* native will perceive their position in the world. They will either see themselves *as* the authority or *submit* to others for permission to express themselves. Both of these positions are perspectives based on the tangible world and the native's prior polarizing experiences with it. This perspective then filters through to their career, social status and every other aspect of how the native relates to the world through the lens of *harmony through conflict*.

Relative to authority, communication will be based on either listening or telling for the native who has been indoctrinated too far in either direction. That is, they have been trained into believing that they either instruct others because they "know" more than or follow others who they have been told know better than they. In this light, professions that are based on aligning with requirements or the making of them will exist in a push-pull Fourth Ray rapport. As a result of childhood indoctrination, emotional survival will be at the root (center) of this perspective, especially, since the other half of this axis deals with traditions that demand to be followed. Most of us learn to either follow them or rebel or specify that others must follow.

Exoteric natives that are balanced in their approach to the world are inner directed, were raised to have confidence in themselves and their decisions and exhibit life participation with an autonomy that doesn't relate to the world through the lens of perceived external authority.

The *esoteric aspirant* has learned to neither direct nor follow but to offer examples and options for the *exoteric* native to see that don't get caught up in the push-pull forces that are so connected to their need for personal security and advantage. They have developed a sense of detachment that allows them to see the *harmony through conflict* scenarios as they are: a manifestation of the polarized world. He or she also knows that those who are the least secure within themselves need a stronger polarized view of themselves in order to "verify" their belief in their emotional survival. The *aspirant's* role as "spiritual" mediator requires skill, patience and foresight in assisting the *exoteric* native to arrive at an emotional place possessed of a finer balance, especially, since the Moon is the co-ruler of the Fourth Ray. Here the native may detach from their dependency for approval by the world to a more inner directed non-possessive autonomy.

VENUS brings the Fifth Ray energy of *concrete science* to Capricorn and the tenth-fourth house axis. *Exoterically*, Venus usually brings choice and prioritizing to consciousness in dealing with our career, social status and authority. Manmade law and authority are two of the most poignant categories managed under Capricorn and the tenth-fourth house axis. Our social status and career are direct consequences of those choices. Venus' position here usually makes us aware of how we must choose to align or not with social laws and requirements. How other people treat us and qualify our social position and its effect on the public plays into the tangible way we and others define ourselves. Whether that choice is made consciously or not has a profound effect on how we see ourselves in the world. Those of us who are aware enough are a bit further in assessing their position. Those who are not simply react. Those who are aware strategize the control of their worldly positions. Those who are not usually follow or rebel.

In all this choosing and prioritizing, what we must come to understand is that our man-made laws are often antithetical to the dynamic that universal law imposes on us through the Fifth Ray of *concrete science*. The premise behind the making of man-made laws are that they preserve our social structure and create an ease in the flow in how we deal with each other. The reality behind this motivation is that we attempt to create and preserve personal security and continuity in that we may produce an advantage and egotistical safety over others in what we feel in our interactions with them. The publicly projected ideal appears "out front" while our true intentions remain hidden, sometimes, even from ourselves.

The *exoterically* oriented native is concerned with creating and maintaining a social standing that supports their preferred projected image. If they have come from an upbringing that has indoctrinated them with a feeling of lack or inadequacy, their primary goal will be to hide that perception and produce a projected image of authority and superiority over others. Most of the time that perception of inadequacy remains unconscious but the need to defeat a sense of "lack" takes conscious precedence. They will then strategize to acquire what they feel they have been deprived of. The "inadequacy" part will remain hidden. If they have come from an upbringing of spoiling and privilege, their drive will be one of expectation and entitlement. In either scenario, their drive will create a strategy that they believe will lead them to public dominance and recognition.

Esoterically, Venus' position here represents the universe's "need" for us to come to understand our true identity. Our quest for an identity that hides the insecurities that we may have been indoctrinated with always meets its polar opposite. Choosing anything almost *always* produces opposition from what we have chosen to reject. This includes people who are attempting to "become" their chosen and preferred image. In Capricorn and the tenth-fourth house axis Venus and the Fifth Ray become the "Great Leveler." On her highest-level Venus shows us that we must sacrifice any imbalance, like a perceived superiority and inferiority, in order to become an aligned and productive part of the universe and *its* laws. That sacrifice is *always* of our egotistically constructed self-image of either entitlement or inadequacy that *always* contradicts our actual universal "persona."

MARS brings Sixth Ray energy of *ideals and devotion* to Capricorn and the tenth-fourth house axis. *Exoterically*, Mars here will be an atomic engine. Impulse will be the primary driving factor in what the native does. There is an innate assumption that we *have* the authority or that that we *are* the authority enough to do or accomplish whatever we have the inclination to do. Our belief, even if it is not conscious, is that all we have to do is just apply the energy and what is wanted or needed will simply manifest. Energy has no mind. We simply apply it and it acts whether we think about it or not. Whatever profession, social standing or career is indicated by Capricorn and the tenth-fourth house axis, Mars will simply energize the movement in that direction.

Courage, in many instances, is a positive quality. However, sometimes thought and patience are needed. This is not always apparent to the native with Mars in this position. Just because an impulse exists toward doing something does not mean it is wise to pursue. We pursue our *ideals and devotions* mostly with the assumption, or even expectation, that any energy applied in that direction will result in a positive effect. This is often due to the fact that we believe that what we *devote* ourselves to is always proper and aligned with what's "good" for everyone and, hopefully, ourselves. Unfortunately, the result is not always in our best interest, let alone, that of others.

Although we may assume that what we consider *idealistic* and worthy of our *devotion* is always good for all, the manifestation of those circumstances is not the primary lesson that Mars brings to us in this position. There are many times that the *exoteric* native considers what is right and proper but lacks the courage or drive to put his or her ideals into action. This may be due to our upbringing or even a past life residue. Mars' effect has the tendency to bypass this hesitancy. That is, Mars bypasses through the processes that produces fear or a perceived lack of adequacy and enables us to pursue the ideal anyway. This is like saying, "Damn the torpedoes Gridley, full speed ahead." We may even say that sometimes the urge passes caution and common sense. The worst example of Mars in the position is someone who is reckless in their application of action and energy even to the point of endangering others.

Esoterically, having Mars in this position can be considered an asset depending on the circumstances. He aligns with Neptune in activating the solar plexus enabling passion to fuel our actions. The positive side will be that of a fearless warrior relentlessly pursuing the noble cause of manifesting universal law. The worst scenario is a true believer energized with deluded principles that may result in damage to themselves as well as others. The *aspirant* recognizes which is which since he or she is aligned with *love, wisdom* and universal principles. Sometimes it's easy to redirect the zealot with just a minor adjustment in their focus. Sometimes it's not. For the *aspirant*, it is truly a challenge knowing when to assist on their behalf and when not to.

JUPITER brings a Second Ray energy of *love and wisdom* to Capricorn and the tenth-fourth house axis. *Exoterically*, this is a very uncomfortable position for Jupiter to work through. Since this position is ruled by Saturn on both the *exoteric* and *esoteric* levels, Jupiter's placement here seems to run contrary to what is normally needed for the axis. He is here to let us know when "too much" occurs and it is past "enough." Remember, Jupiter brings *love and wisdom*. The aspect to be most understood is the *wisdom* part.

Although Saturn and his rulership here are the primary dynamics that regulates and organize our career, social status and how we relate to authority, the structuring and restrictions that might have been applied or learned, in this life or prior ones, may have been too much so that those areas of life may now be stunted or overly restricted by Saturn's influence. Some relief or "breaking free" may be what is needed. For example, the *exoteric* native may have become too serious, stingy, too bogged down with perceived requirements or may have become overly susceptible to the authority of other individuals who have imposed their restrictions on them. Jupiter's tendency to expand all he touches creates enthusiasm and encourages the native to push past excessive restrictions and allows them to open their heart center and trust that the universe will help them achieve their objectives. However, if the restrictions present have been accepted as an immovable and dominating force, his influence may "backfire" and he may intensify the restrictions that the native already feels.

Esoterically, Jupiter is here to expand the qualities of the heart center, *love and wisdom*. He will attempt to do this no matter what sign or axis his placement is found in. However, since there are lessons and experiences contrary to the essences of Jupiter that must occur in this axis, his work may *seem* to begin at a disadvantage. Yet, the influence he may apply are those of acceleration on the usual domain of Saturn. But perhaps a much softer and finer balance must be established. The basis of *active intelligence* may be there but *love and wisdom* must be added to the mix in order to also "even out" the austerity and discipline with empathy and compassion. For the *aspirant* to assist he or she must bring gentleness with firmness, compassion with discipline and enthusiasm with temperance. Earth's sign and axis placement may show where other assists may be drawn from.

The balance that must be established here in the tenth-fourth house axis is crucial if the potential for growth is to be accessed by the *exoteric* native. The only other axis with as much importance is the first-seventh house. These two axes represent the balance between spirit and matter, the balance that must be accomplished between the tangible and intangible world if the native is to be able to walk the "Razor's Path."

SATURN brings the Third Ray energy of *active intelligence* to Capricorn and the tenth-fourth house axis. *Exoterically*, his position here serves to organize, consolidate and structure how the native *appears* to others in the tangible world, how he or she perceives their social status and what his or her projected path is here to manifest. That is, the lesson here is not what is accomplished but what is learned along the way.

The circumstances ordinarily outlined by conventional astrology books indicate careers involving a material accomplishment as our primary goal in life. Although worldly accomplishment is the main focus for *exoteric* natives, experiences of a much more subtle influence are integrated through our worldly endeavor in an effort to bring our awareness to a "higher" level (more subtly aware) enabling us to perceive the universe as being more inclusive of feeling and intuitive influences. This is emblematic of Saturn's *esoteric* rulership as allowing for the potential for the sacrifice that is so characteristic of the higher vibrations of Capricorn and the tenth-fourth house axis.

Generally, Saturn's positioning here most often results in a tendency for the *exoteric* native to over-control, tightly structure and personally limit the efforts and actions of others connected to his or her career and social status. Personal authority is often assumed and even the concept of sacrifice is all but forgotten. Sacrifice then, *exoterically*, only occurs when personal advantage can be gained over his or her professional enemies *and* comrades. The tendency to restrict and over-control others comes from a childhood authority who has inflicted this on their childhood. This authority could have been, or maybe still is, either a male or female. This often makes the child feel out of control and thereby tend to dedicate their entire life toward regaining what they believe that they have lost.

Esoterically, the *active intelligence* of the Third Ray enables the native to see the interdependency of the tangible and intangible energies that act in our multi-level universe. Once this is observed by the native, their will and intention, as activated by the throat center, will have a firm grounding based on the natural laws of the universe. Where sacrifice needs to be made and force needs to be applied will become abundantly clear.

URANUS brings the Seventh Ray energy of *ceremonial order* to Capricorn and the tenth-fourth house axis. Here Uranian eccentricity will make itself known within the framework of their career, social status and authority. His position here will express itself through two possible scenarios. The first scenario will be in keeping personal freedom. The more "different" a career is, the more attractive it will seem to them. Their career can change at the drop of a hat. Whatever creates the most "wow" will create a persona to be played to activate attraction and admiration. The *exoteric* native with this positioning needs to be, seem and feel different and free of any restriction. For the *exoteric* native who is in an authoritative position and with Uranus in this axis, their application of discipline and their expectation for the behavior of employees and subordinates may seem erratic at best to those observing. In more extreme cases, the application of discipline and the rules may be totally unpredictable, especially, in light of the preferred specialness that the employer "needs" to feel. In cases where this positioning is reflective of an employee or subordinate, their adherence to job or project requirements may be sporadic and lack dependability.

Careers and social positions may go through quick but short phases after the sparkle and fascination with them wears out. New and different ways of exposing one's specialness may be sought to the exclusion of all else. Freedom to try what will create the best reflection of their social position may become their primary goal.

The second scenario will be for the preservation of status and power. Change will be unwelcomed and staunch resistance to any life work or position that conflicts with the currently held projection of "differentness" or individuality will be fiercely maintained. Uranus' position here may ultimately tend toward shattering any security or consistency that is attempted by the *exoteric* native.

Esoterically, Uranus' perspective is to simply "encourage" the *exoteric* native into working on a career and social position that is aligned with the sacral center and the universal principles directing the balance of nature. Since the native's rules and restrictions are manmade, this influence often meets considerable resistance. Although *ceremonial order* is the energy associated with natural law and the Seventh Ray, the "ceremonial" part extends well past the conventional or manmade limits of traditionally or tangibly oriented protocols. Intuition will be a main vehicle to bring this awareness to the native. This can be extremely stressful for the *exoteric* native, especially, if they are not yet in touch with their intuition. The *aspirant* who is working with this energy can offer insight to the native that will show the disadvantage of operating too far outside or too closely within the socially expected limits that they have framed for the maintenance of their power and position. This will provide the native with an unbiased observation of the unbalancing effect of employing either scenario that provides the "differentness" of too much freedom or too much constriction. Remember, the keyword for Uranus is *reorientation*.

NEPTUNE brings a Sixth Ray energy promoting universal *ideals and devotions* to Capricorn and the tenth-fourth house axis. *Exoterically*, Neptune would bring secrets or delusions, about ourselves or others, to this axis. Since he clouds or fogs the perception of the *exoteric* native, their focus on tangible career accomplishments and social status may preclude any perception of what actually needs to be followed in order to spiritually evolve. Also, there may be many dependencies that manifest as a result of their falling under the auspices of illusory *ideals and devotions*.

Since Neptune brings the possibility of distorting reality, any *ideals and devotions* connected to career objectives may be part of a perspective based on a fantasy or unrealistic expectations of what their career will or must provide for them. Remember, this is Saturn's domain and Neptune is antithetical to him. Neptune's primary mechanism on the *exoteric* level is one of *dissolution* and detachment from any concept, perception or construct that distracts from being able to see and use the more subtle laws of the universe "properly." Unless our career is involved in some form of art, music or creative endeavor that utilizes how our perceptions might be represented or fooled on a tangible level, Neptune is likely to create havoc in the practicality and responsibility driven world under the rulership of Saturn. On an emotional level (Neptune *esoterically* rules Cancer) this may include all the family patterns and tangible mechanisms that we put into place in order to assure ourselves that we exist and work in a world where we *believe* that we can control external circumstances leading toward our preferred illusion of security and permanency.

Except for the artistic fields and careers that depend on sensitivities for their proficiency, Neptune will likely create extensive difficulty for the *exoteric* native desiring any semblance security and permanence in their career. Additionally, their sense of authority, applying it or responding to it, will also likely be faulty when viewed from an *exoteric* perspective. The sign and axis position of Mars may tell much more about where worldly influences might come from, be focused and be energized from.

Esoterically, the *aspirant* recognizes the confusion that an *exoteric* native may experience in dealing with Neptune in this position. The best he or she can do is assist them in heightening their sensitivities to a point where they are able to see the universal laws in operation above and beyond their tangible world expectations. Ultimately, this may raise their perception of the world as a much more inclusive place than simply a reflection of their own personal lacks and preferred emotional securities.

PLUTO brings a First Ray energy of *will and power* to Capricorn and the tenth-fourth house axis. Pluto's *exoteric* positioning here brings an intensity and depth to the issues of this axis. In some cases, the native may develop an obsession about their career, social status or how they relate to authority. One of the most important aspects of Pluto's position here is that he influences the career through creating direct contact with the public either physically, through media or any other tangible connection.

There is power in numbers. Will the *exoteric* native follow the mob or lead them? Those who follow the mob usually do it for safety and to disappear from direct attention. Their perspective is that there is "safety in numbers." Those who wish to lead, and are able to, see the mob as an opportunity to facilitate their preferences through using others in addition to gaining recognition. Their perspective is that "it's better to lead the pack than be subject to it."

Both of these aforementioned tendencies emanate from our upbringing. Here is where our social experience and its public status are formed. It mirrors how we have related to our own family and how our family has related to the public. It is the place where our traditions are tested for social viability. Was our family fearful of others who weren't of their own clan and tradition or were they welcoming with no cautions, limits or restrictions? The habits, fears and confidence developed here are carried to the world. Pluto's presence in Capricorn and the tenth-fourth hose axis brings to the surface the deepest parts of our psyches as trained by our family. Until we have other than family experiences that are intense enough to pierce the emotional barriers we've had set in place in our childhood, nothing will change. When Pluto creates the opportunity to have life changing experiences that are intense enough to overwhelm our "security protocols" previously established at the root of our childhood psyches, it is then that we may act and become transformed by Pluto.

Pluto's position here gives a resiliency and an astounding ability to recharge whatever the native's career, social objectives and emotional patterns are at the time. *Exoterically* and as adults, their dysfunctional childhood behaviors may develop into patterns that are better hidden but prevail in public just the same. Please understand that these patterns will prevail until Pluto intensifies another experience enough to replace them. If nothing replaces them, wrong or harmful goals themselves will be recharged just as potently.

Pluto's primary rulership is *esoteric* but conventional astrologers have assigned his *exoteric* rulership to Scorpio as it meets the concepts of regeneration, the hidden and what is occult (unseen). His rulership of Pisces *esoterically* meets those qualifications but also adds an unconscious and more personally oriented perspective. The *aspirant* knows that whatever is touched by Pluto will be intensified and regenerated. In this light he or she is very careful in his or her assistance to the *exoteric* native to emphasize characteristics and traits that will advance the native toward a much less egotistical venue. Hence, any Plutonian intensity will create much less resistance in how the native is responded to by the actions of the universe.

VULCAN brings the First Ray energy of *will and power* to Capricorn and the tenth-fourth house axis. Remembering also that Vulcan is never more than eight degrees away from the Sun, we know that the Sun's position here or in adjacent houses will bring additional light to all the issues concerning the *exoteric* native's career, social standing and authoritative concerns.

Vulcan's presence in this axis is very simple. Whatever career, social status or authoritative goals we have, if they are not aligned with universal law, they will first be purged of counterproductive influences and then forged into potent tools for the universe's manifestation which will likely not be in line with what the *exoteric* native prefers. This will occur whether we agree or not. If we are not able to let go of egotistically oriented objectives, we will ultimately end up shooting ourselves in the foot every time we attempt to maintain them and never understand why. Remember, Vulcan's domains are only on the *esoteric* and *hierarchical* levels. Personal preferences are immaterial.

For the *esoterically* oriented *aspirant*, Vulcan is a tremendous tool for simplifying our evolving existence and our perception of how to sustain it. It resonates from the crown center. In this light we, as an *aspirant,* must consent to being led by our heart, our intuition and something much larger than all of us. Our personal will is immaterial. Whether we appear to others as a proper vehicle for "good" or not is immaterial. There is no guarantee that we will be "saved," favored, acknowledged or protected in any way from potentially undesirable circumstances that the universe might beset us with if we align with universal principles. Our total consent and dedication must be total. When we identify with the whole, we then become a productive part of the process.

MOON brings a Fourth Ray energy facilitating *harmony through conflict* to Capricorn and the tenth-fourth house axis. *Exoterically*, the Moon's position here is similar to Mercury's with the exception that the Moon makes the connection much more personal and emotional, especially, with the issues that this axis deals with.

The *exoteric* native's emotional patterning and traditions will be brought to this axis as either their attempt to publicly relate to the world that way or affirm their rejection of them. Whatever emotional patterning we were trained to fulfill in our childhood will play out through the Moon in whatever sign and axis she falls in. In this case, we will bring those patterns to our career, social status and attitude toward authority. As an example, we will relate to our boss the same way we related to the authority in our family. The expression may be a bit more refined so as not to look like the responses of a child but the rapport will, nevertheless, be a reflection of what we grew up with. If we rebelled against the authority in our childhood, there will be characteristics of rebellion toward those in charge in our career. If the authority was our confidant or friend in our childhood, our boss will be related to the same way we related to the authority in our childhood but likely with just with some adjustments to accommodate for manners and professional protocols.

Whatever the roles were that we played with our family in our childhood, they will be extended to the rest of the world and operate through the *harmony through conflict* of the Fourth Ray. It follows to reason here that any professions that are in sync with the Moon's patterns and traditions, such as cooking, homecare, real estate, childcare, foster homes, small business and more will either be benefitted or hampered by this positioning. However, unless we've matured enough into self-sufficiency and autonomy after our childhood, or actually were trained into being so, we will carry over any dysfunctional patterns that marked our childhood. Remember too that the Moon veils Vulcan, Uranus and Neptune who are antithetical to any childish or egotistical behaviors that contradict the smooth running of universal law. These childhood patterns, if dysfunctional, will be either purged, exploded or dissolved within the parameters of the professional sphere. Mercury's sign and axis will give further understanding as to how these patterns may operate and where.

Esoterically, the *exoteric* native as well as any assisting *aspirant* have their work cut out for them. To recognize dysfunctional childhood patterns is the first hurdle. Making an effort to replace them with mature and balanced responses to the world is an altogether different issue and likely will not align with patterns that preserve the emotional security of the native. Here, the Moon implores us to "put away childish things." In an *esoteric* perspective, this is the diminishing and eventual elimination of any egotistical behaviors that attempt to maintain the protection of our hidden perceived inadequacies, deprivations and insecurities. If we don't do this in a family setting, the public forum will surely become the next arena.

MERCURY brings the Fourth Ray energy of *harmony through conflict* to Aquarius and the eleventh-fifth house axis of group consciousness and identity, aspirations, love received and career resources and objectives.

What we aspire toward usually has a direct correlation to what we have been taught to believe about ourselves since childhood. If we've been brought up to believe that we are capable and autonomous, we will strive for goals that emphasize that. If we've been brought up in poverty or to be inadequate, the *exoteric* native will strive to become rich and fiercely defend their possessions or become an over- or under-achiever. Mercury is connected to the root center and the Fourth Ray and will tell us *how* to accomplish these goals as a function of ego survival. The sign and axis that the Moon is in, the co-ruler of the Fourth Ray, will bring added personalization and security seeking.

Aquarius and the eleventh-fifth house axis bring our attention to group consciousness and identification. For the *exoteric* native group consciousness is simply a wider view of their own self-identification from a worldly point of view. From childhood and on we grow in our identity with the world. Our personal ego expands past our internal identification (second house) then to our family identification (fifth house), then to our one-to-one relationship identification (eighth house) and lastly to express our group identification (eleventh house). Each level becomes wider and wider as we sacrifice a little more of our personal preferences in each step outward in order to broaden our scope of interaction. However, Mercury's Fourth Ray influence may bring some struggles and confrontations based on personal vs. group values, especially, since it might *feel* like a survival issue due to being concentrated in the root center. Remember, the *exoteric* native sees and feels things in terms of polarity or in a me vs. you mindset.

Since Mercury brings a polarized view perspective to the axis, love received becomes love *from* you or what you *give* to me. Sharing is essentially beyond the Fourth Ray dynamics. There is an innate separateness underlying all personal and group interactions. In the same light, this axis represents the assets and friends that are gained or lost from social status and career participation.

Esoterically, it would seem that the *aspirant*, from the *exoteric* native's perspective, should assist the native in strategizing gains and losses relative to their group consciousness and identity, aspirations, love received and career rewards and resources. But in reality, the *aspirant's* job is to assist the native in disconnecting from the "checks and balances" perspective and to enable them to diminish their materialistic approach to life where their aspirations are involved and bring a more balanced approach to life that is not so tangibly bound.

VENUS brings the Fifth Ray energy of *concrete science* to Aquarius and the eleventh-fifth house axis. *Exoterically*, Venus usually brings choice and prioritizing to the forefront in dealing with group consciousness and identity, aspirations, love received and career rewards and resources. This positioning is more of an assessing and planning aspect in relation to how the native sees their effect on others and how they would like to integrate with the world.

As the fifth house side of the fifth-eleventh house axis shows our childhood and what we believe might have benefited or hurt us, the eleventh house side weighs in on planning and setting our sites on how we are either going to capitalize on what we did benefit by or our plans and intentions outlining how we will regain what it is that we feel we might have lost or been deprived of in our childhood. Here, Venus first assesses, then chooses and then commits to what or who it is that we intend to add, remove or integrate into our world.

As we progress or fail in our intentions, we then, *exoterically*, use Venus to judge ourselves in light of the world and what it expects of us and we of it. If we have fundamentally learned to trust ourselves, our intuition will play a small part in where and to whom we are directed. This will activate rudimentary beginnings for using our third eye and the *concrete science* that it brings to us. On an *exoteric* level, this essentially allows the native to use the *tangible* science of using a modified scientific method, through planning, logic and practical discrimination. This perspective still comes under the Venutian umbrella of universal science. However, it will still only involve the tangible world addressing the native's egotistical needs. On the rawest level, this still only represents the *exoteric* native's planning and efforts to *acquire* what they want or feel that they lack. Egotistical aspirations here are still only a polarized objective. For the *exoteric* native, the whole idea of ascribing this positioning as being representative of "love received" might simply be an egotistical view of looking for what the world can "give" to us.

Esoterically, Venus' positioning here represents a much wider view of what our aspirations can contain. Remembering that the eleventh-fifth house axis represents group consciousness, we can understand that a group's values and goals aim toward a sharing and humanitarianism, even if only to a small group itself, is a larger objective than the possessive needs and wants of simply one person. Each group, small or large, is a microcosm of a much larger goal perspective for humanitarian aspirations. The *aspirant* knows this and attempts to open an awareness in the *exoteric* native of a much wider view for *their* goals and desires that include more than just their personal needs and wants. If or as the native begins to do so, the inclusiveness of the larger whole they feel, or the love received, begins to replace their smaller, more personally oriented objectives.

MARS brings Sixth Ray energy of *ideals and devotion* to Aquarius and the eleventh-fifth house axis. *Exoterically,* Mars here will be an atomic engine. Impulse will be the primary driving factor in what the native does. Here there may be an innate assumption that we have goals or aspirations that others are aligned with. This is a placement of *activism.*

For the *exoteric* native, group identity, personal aspirations, love received and career rewards are very important on a tangible level. They are tied into the native's worldly and polarized view of themselves. However, having consciousness about them is not always evident. With Mars in this position, their impulse and action toward these things is much more important than their knowledge about them. For them, action speaks louder than words. Thinking is not always present. Impulse always is, whether it's recognized or not.

The Sixth Ray brings *idealism and devotion*. This will bring a dedication to a cause, person or project that is inspired and triggered by impulse and feeling and is energized by the solar plexus center injecting passion and intensity into the action. The fact that Neptune is a major catalyst in the activation of the Sixth Ray also allows for the possibility that the narrative in pursuing the impulse may be deluded or deceived in the values presented behind the action or by people promoting it.

The usual objective of this positioning is to allow the *exoteric* native to move past their hesitation and mental restriction generated by the potential fear of failure or catastrophe that may ordinarily stop them from following their impulses. Often, there is so much mental interference that the native has been unable to move past their own mental chatter and inhibitions. Generally, this emanates from their being raised to doubt their own adequacy and capacity to make "correct" decisions that might be viewed as making a "mistake" by those to whom they have been trained to abandon their authority to. Mars often adds the impetus necessary for moving past any mental stalemates that might be created through intensifying the effects of the solar plexus.

Esoterically, the *aspirant* may assist the *exoteric* native in creating a balance between the self-limiting and inhibiting characteristics behind their indoctrinated insecurities and the impulse they might feel in doing things that their trained mental chatter tells them is reckless. It is likely that past life limitations may have brought in a "mental barricade" against allowing them to do what their impulses ask. Mars' positioning here may be simply a universal correction to move them past the self-limitation learned in past lives. Their present lifetime family training would likely be repeated in their current life in order to recreate the conditions that need to be overcome.

JUPITER brings a Second Ray energy of *love and wisdom* to Aquarius and the eleventh-fifth house axis. This is a contentious position for Jupiter to work. This position is Jupiter's *esoteric* rulership. Since this position is normally ruled by Saturn on the *exoteric* level, Jupiter's placement here *seems* to run contrary to what is normally needed for the *exoteric* axis. Jupiter's position here is to let us know when "too much" organization and discipline has occurred and it is past "enough."

Saturn's position here has been to form a healthy ego relative to the native's values and their objectives in the tangible world. However, once that occurs, what often happens is that sense of ego and the restrictions that keep it organized and structured get in the way of what is directed by the heart. Remember, Jupiter here brings *love and wisdom*. The heart center is the dominant force in the Second Ray. One of the key concepts of love is *allowance*. It is not within Saturn's agenda to permit this to occur. Now that Saturn has already done his job, it is within Jupiter's paradigm to move past the restrictive organization of personal goals and to expand them into the group goals potentially offered by Jupiter's placement. This is the beginnings of a move toward humanitarian consciousness for the *exoteric* native.

Jupiter's presence here will also tend to augment the importance level of the *exoteric* native's worldly aspirations and objectives to a point beyond the expectations of the average person. That is, they may become obsessed with "making a difference" or becoming wildly successful while gaining attention and recognition for being "special." This may have been trained into them through a constant diminishing of their worth and goals in their upbringing thereby encouraging them to over-compensate. The Sun's sign and axis position will tell what areas of life are brought into the mix and what they might provide. In this instance, the intention will be to "shine" in the eyes of the superiors and peer group to compensate for their perceived childhood diminishing. They likely may want to lead the group that would have them as a member. Whatever the focus of the *exoteric* native with this position falls on, or who, their desire will be "to get, have or to be" more than the common sense of their current life circumstances will reasonably allow.

Esoterically, Jupiter's "rulership" here is to bring an awareness of *love and wisdom* through and for the groups that the native chooses to involve themselves in. That is, he will use the group participation as a vehicle for making the *exoteric* native familiar with the concept of sharing, allowing and supporting. The inclination toward this will be provided by the energy of Jupiter emphasizing group dynamics and interplay while the native obtusely focuses on the personal gains that they will acquire from their participation. The end result may, hopefully, be an opening of the heart center with compassion and caring for the other members of the group.

SATURN brings the Third Ray energy of *active intelligence* to Aquarius and the eleventh-fifth house axis. *Exoterically*, his position here serves to organize, consolidate and structure how the native wants to be successful in the tangible world and what his or her projected path, conscious or not, is here to manifest. However, the lesson here is not so much what is accomplished according to the native's wishes and assumptions but what is learned along the way. Overall, this will teach the native the value of planning, discipline, patience and diligence.

In learning the tangible characteristics of Saturn and applying them, a knowledge of the Third Ray and of how things are connected through invisible energy lines in the tangible world will follow. This begins the activation of *active intelligence* which can be seen as a rudimentary awakening of our understanding of the patterns and cycles that the universe follows in order to manifest the universal *Plan*. There may be times where the native may confuse their own personal plans with "the goal" while simply being synchronized with the natural patterns and cycles of the universe. But even in light of their own egotistical view of the world and its mechanizations, there will still grow a slow underlying comprehension, conscious or intuitive, of the universe's laws on a much grander scale and the cycles and patterns they follow. The eventual result will, hopefully, be the *exoteric* native's recognition of their own history and the emotional and mental patterns that they are either aligned with or entrapped by. This alignment or entrapment can either be conscious or not. The sign and axis position of the Earth will give the native a hint as where to see the best example of where and how these personal patterns may be operating.

Saturn is very comfortable in this position and even with the native's expectation of their willing acclimation to the seriousness to be dealt with here, the overall lesson might be a little easier than Saturn's placements in other axis with the exception of the tenth-fourth house axis. Planning and organizing in the native's past lives may have been lacking or overly demanding. Saturn's presence here is also an attempt to rebalance their planned and daily tangible life goals with the recognition and acceptance of their intuitive abilities as part of their input.

Esoterically, the *aspirant* may capitalize on the discipline and organizational skills of the *exoteric* native but must also be able to assist them in connecting to their intuitive awareness of *active intelligence* as being the energetic and connecting fabric of the universe. In this placement, the *aspirant* has already come to understand their limits and potential in enabling the others to perceive on a more subtle level.

URANUS brings the Seventh Ray energy of *ceremonial order* to Aquarius and the eleventh-fifth house axis. Here Uranian eccentricity will make itself known within the *exoteric* native's connection and alignment with or against family, social and business groups.

We might assume that because conventional astrologers have ascribed Uranus as a ruler of Aquarius and the eleventh-fifth house axis that Uranus will provide comfort for the native in group participation. Comfort is not a quality to be ascribed to Uranus. If anything, he may provide excitement but not the stability that Saturn's rulership will tend to provide. Here, he will more than likely provide a chaotic and unpredictable atmosphere giving aspirations a boost in "innovativeness" but not a path for consistency. Remember, Uranus will always bring us back into alignment with universal laws and values. If the *exoteric* native's aspirations are geared toward circumstances that produce comfort and security rather than alignment with universal principles, they will more than likely fall way short of their expectations.

If we look at the "love received" aspect of this axis we should expect that any affection proffered though this house will be sporadic at best. It may also bring the energy from unexpected sources, which would be exciting, but likely inconsistent.

Uranus' presence here brings the message that perhaps past and present aspirations need to be revamped. If the *exoteric* native's aspirations are geared toward creating any kind of security or consistency that conflicts with the universe's natural flow of evolutionary change, it will be expunged. Although the Seventh Ray supports *ceremonial order*, that order is not necessarily aligned with personal needs or assurances. Our sense of balance in our connection to the universe occurs at the sacral center. Marial arts, dance, physics and healing are a few of the disciplines that normally align with universal energies and principles provided that support the natural *flow* of energy. Comfort and security are *exoterically* static and are usually set in place with the intent of corralling the natural flow of energy only within preferred limits that won't expose or terminate any compensatory behavior emanating from perceived feelings of inadequacy or the need to control. Uranus, especially in this position, will not allow us to stop the energy from evolving within us. *Reorientation* is its key word as it will always bring us back to what the universe deems as proper and aligned with evolution. "We can go willingly or kicking and screaming, but we *will* go."

Esoterically, the *aspirant* can assist the *exoteric* native through capitalizing on the Uranian expunging of their personal securities. As their securities are purged, the *aspirant* has the space to show them the options that they might have to redirect their objectives. Remember, the Uranian explosive quality brings opportunity and vision through the elimination of what we might become stuck on or obsess about. As in the tarot deck, once the smoke clears from the Tower Card's execution, the card that follows is The Star which gives vision and long-term potential. As long as we are open to abandoning our personal securities, or even after having them ripped from us, the changing future will provide unexpected avenues for our soul's universally aligned expression.

NEPTUNE brings a Sixth Ray energy promoting proper *ideals and devotions* to Aquarius and the eleventh-fifth house axis. *Exoterically*, Neptune would bring secrets or delusions, about ourselves or others, to this axis. Since he clouds or fogs the perception of the *exoteric* native, their focus on tangible goals and aspirations may reveal them as a *true believer*.

If the *exoteric* native is aligned with the universal energies, this positioning will give a tremendous amount of *devotion* and faithfulness to the *ideals* directing their quest. If not, they will be seriously deluded about what or who they may be devoted to. If they are spiritually immature, that is, locked in their need for security in a materialistic view of the world, they may not be fully conscious of the values that are behind the *ideals* they are devoted toward. In this they may be deceiving themselves or others about what they are attempting to promote. This unrealistic view of the world will make them eminently susceptible toward being manipulated by others, including groups, through their delusions or the ones provided by others.

Neptune's presence here may also create a condition of hypersensitivity, especially, when their goals and values are challenged. Remember that the Sixth Ray is connected to the solar plexus and that Mars is a co-ruler of the ray. That brings the possibility of action without thought when, again, the *exoteric* native's goals or values are challenged. When the vibration energizing the Sixth Ray is not on the *esoteric* level, there is a distinct danger that fanaticism, activism and hyper-religious movements will take place well outside the limits of common-sense reasoning and accepted social protocols. Drugs and substance abuse may also be involved and if not, simple dependency on the deluded lead of others for inspiration and direction may also be in play.

Esoterically, for the *aspirant* who has aligned him or herself within more universal guidelines and with whom or for what they devote themselves to, there will be more subtle potential for refinement in aspiring toward the truest and cleanest form of *ideals and devotion*. In finding this heart space themselves, the *aspirant* will find it easy to assist the *exoteric* native in gently aligning themselves with goals and ideals that are much broader than simply their emotionally secure egotistical survival.

PLUTO brings a First Ray energy of *will and power* to Aquarius and the eleventh-fifth house axis. Pluto's *exoteric* positioning here brings an intensity and depth to the issues of this axis. In some cases, the native may become obsessed about their aspirations, maintaining or avoiding group involvement and plans for future accomplishments. One of the most important aspects of Pluto's position here is that he influences the native's goals and directions through direct contact with the public whether physically, through media or any other tangible connection.

There is power in numbers. Will the *exoteric* native choose to follow the group or desire to lead them? If they choose to follow, they will most likely do it for safety in order to disappear from direct attention or even to "brown nose" their perceived image by the leader. Their perspective is that there is "safety in numbers." Those who wish to lead, and are able to, will see the group as an opportunity to facilitate their preferences through using them. Their perspective is that "it's better to lead the pack than be responsive to it."

Pluto raises and regenerates the energy of the sign and axis he is in much like an atomic stockpile providing almost limitless potential for action. The First Ray is representative of the crown center and poses severe danger for all concerned if misused. The native's group leaders will have a profound effect on their future desires and intentions. Their participation in groups may invoke one of two perspectives: they may be either energized by them or deeply frightened or paranoid of them. Since Pluto exhibits such a strong dominance within the unconscious, the group's affect will have a powerful influence over how the native thinks about him or herself, their goals and how they make decisions about their future. It is likely that they will react to group actions and directives without any awareness or understanding of what they, or the group's leaders, are actually doing. The *exoteric* native is eminently susceptible to the focus of Pluto's energy in the group. The key to regaining balance is in acquiring inner balance and awareness concerning our deepest motivations.

Esoterically, the *aspirant* may have the opportunity to sculpt the *exoteric* native's participation in the group that they might slowly influence the direction of the group toward supporting the highest-minded goals and actions possible for their structure and direction. The *aspirant* with this positioning is also in a prime position to do the same with the groups that they have a connection to or participation in. Since the First Ray is so powerful and, as yet, not fully manifested, it is imperative that the protocols for the other rays are solidly in place before anyone has the ability to be able to manifest its full power.

VULCAN brings the First Ray energy of *will and power* to Aquarius and the eleventh-fifth house axis. Remembering also that Vulcan is never more than eight degrees away from the Sun, we know that the Sun's position here or in adjacent houses will bring additional light to all the issues concerning the *exoteric* native's goals, aspirations and future plans. In doing so Vulcan will operate like a rotor rooter clearing a path for the Sun's expression.

Vulcan in this position will purge anyone or anything that is not in line with what the Sun is attempting to show us or teach us. If the love received desired by the *exoteric* native is received including emotional security that in any way denies the reality of the situation, Vulcan will eliminate it. If the group that the native belongs to does not align with universal principles, Vulcan will manifest a way for the disconnect if not for its elimination. However, if the love received or the group participated in contribute to the clarity and truthfulness of what is needed by the native to spiritually mature, they will be streamlined and strengthened to provide the most solid support that they can possibly receive from the universe. It will also allow them to influence both.

Generally, this positioning of Vulcan manifests as a constant thwarting of the *exoteric* native's plans and aspirations. No matter what they do, if they assert what they want with any protections or continuance of anything that doesn't line up with the reality of the universe, it will fall apart. Vulcan's major lesson is in part involved with "encouraging" the native to become independent of any behaviors or scenarios that may provide a path to avoid dealing with the universe as it is. Its second lesson is "forcing" them to become self-accountable for their conditions and circumstances. The method most commonly used is to "pull the rug out from under them."

Esoterically, and for the natives that have become accountable for and accepting of their conditions and situations, the next step is becoming able to forge a path that will allow them to work *with* the universal energy and its protocols. When they do, they often shine by building organizations and pathways that assist others in becoming "universal adults." Vulcan is the planet representing the action and energy that most resembles our perception of a "creator." The *aspirant* is aware of this use of energy and is extremely cautious *not* to assist the native through the encouragement of any goals that are egotistically motivated.

MOON brings a Fourth Ray energy facilitating *harmony through conflict* to Aquarius and the eleventh-fifth house axis. *Exoterically,* the Moon's position here is similar to Mercury's with the exception that the Moon makes a connection which is much more personal and emotional, especially, with the aspirational issues that this axis deals with.

The *exoteric* native's emotional expectations and desires will be brought to this axis as either their plans to extract from the world what they want or to join a group that promises to provide it. They will take personally any feedback that relates to their preferred group's perspective and the reactions that they receive to their own wishes and plans from others. The Moon's position here makes the world all about them. With the Moon's connection to the polarizing Fourth Ray and the root center, we can understand the dominance of a personal perspective.

The Moon's position here represents the group's emotional dynamics. It's as if the group itself had its own personality. An insult to the group is seen as an insult to the native. However, we also have to remember that the Fourth Ray Moon *esoterically* veils Vulcan, Uranus and Neptune. In this light we can understand that any group that supports tangible points of security held by self-deceptive natives will meet with either purgation (Vulcan), bursting (Uranus) or dissolution (Neptune) through reorienting egotistically based securities toward a spiritually mature universe.

Although we've only spoken briefly about *hierarchical* rulerships, it's important at this juncture to note that the Moon *hierarchically* rules Aquarius. In the simplest explanation of the Moon in this position, it will be sufficient to say that the Moon here is representative of groups that are totally aligned with universal law in that the manifestation of humanitarianism and brotherhood are exhibited here in their highest form. This will be the ultimate aim of any *aspirant* or *initiate* striving for spiritual maturity. *This* is actually what is meant when we speak of the Aquarian age.

PISCES & THE TWELFTH-SIXTH HOUSE AXIS

MERCURY brings the Fourth Ray energy of *harmony through conflict* to Pisces and the twelfth-sixth house axis of the unconscious. This axis will work a little bit differently from the other axes as only half of the influence will be conscious to the *exoteric* native and through the sixth house side.

Mercury's presence in this axis brings *harmony through conflict* but on an unconscious level. It will also register in its effect as a matter of survival through seeming like there is always an internal conflict that conflicts with the native's personal preferences that they just can't seem to get a handle on. Their thinking will always be polarized and produce an agitated approach to just about everything. Whether or not the native is predisposed toward talking about personal issues, the Moon's sign and axis position will show what areas of life will have the most dominance in conversation. It's also important to note that much of their communication will erupt without their conscious intention or filter.

If Mercury has a vent through a trine or sextile to another axis, much of the *harmony through conflict* pressure will be released through other areas of life. If not, the pressure is likely to erupt through health issues coming through the sixth house. The areas of life likely to be affected will be the root center, mental health, the nervous system or any functioning of the body that relies on internal transportation or communication systems. Other planets in the axis may either mitigate or augment the effects.

Esoterically, the best way to relieve or even prevent unconscious pressure from building is to participate in some form of meditation or vigorous physical activity that deflates the internal mental pressure such as martial arts, sports or any activity akin to channeling or releasing pent up energy. The *aspirant* is not only aware of this but will likely participate in activities designed to bring submerged energies to the surface without harmful effects. They may also assist the *exoteric* native along similar pathways.

VENUS brings the Fifth Ray energy of *concrete science* to Pisces and the twelfth-sixth house axis. *Exoterically*, Venus usually brings choice and prioritizing to the forefront but in this axis they may remain submerged. This axis will work a little bit differently from the other axes as only half of the influence will be conscious to the *exoteric* native and through the sixth house side.

The choice and the prioritizing will likely take one of two forms. First, the native's choices and priorities may simply "bubble up" and snap into consciousness without any forethought or reflection. Generally, this will likely be with natives who have trust and confidence in their personal abilities. The second option may be a bit more elusive. Since the native's choice making process is, essentially, unconscious, it may not find its way out into the conscious world. This will likely occur if the native generally lacks confidence or trust in their own abilities. If so, they may be fraught with indecisiveness out of fear of "being wrong" or being received by the world in a way that might embarrass them.

Venus' presence here also hides the *exoteric* native's self-image. Knowing who they are will have to be seen as a reflection of those whom they encounter. This position also hides their values from their consciousness contributing to their indecisiveness. For the *exoteric* native, *concrete science* will be representative of the world's view of their identity and external values that they feel that they must live up to. If Venus has an avenue through a trine or sextile to other planets, the axes they are found in will be able to provide the basis for how they identify themselves. If not, Venus will push through to the sixth house as ailments that reflect through the lower back, the kidneys (fear meridian), the throat (personal will center) and the diaphragm.

Esoterically, the native may acquire more subtle knowledge about themselves and their identity through the third eye. This will help them to see the world more as a unified field of energy rather than a polarized set of parts that are linked to and dependent on their *exoteric* security driven choices and priorities. Until the "self" is found and unified, the native will be subject to fragmentary glimpses of themselves through the reactions of others. The *aspirant* may assist the native in meditations or moving toward activities, like creative art or martial arts, that literally block out the world and its interpretation of them in favor finding talents and releasing their own susceptibility toward giving up their autonomy to others. This will assist them in "putting aside childish things" that link them to childhood authority and show them the necessity of, power in and availability of being accountable for their actions and circumstances. The "letting go" is the hardest part. The *aspirant* has done this and knows how frightening it can feel in trusting their "higher power" to lead them in choice.

MARS brings Sixth Ray energy of *ideals and devotion* to Pisces and the twelfth-sixth house axis. *Exoterically*, Mars will operate like an atomic stockpile from the unconscious. Impulse will appear to be the primary and observable driving factor in everything that they do. The Sixth Ray has a very strong current emanating from the solar plexus. There will be many urges emanating from the unconscious where the *exoteric* native has no idea where they might have come from. At times, this can be extremely frightening for the native. At other times, when they have been completely unconscious of their own actions, they may look back at their actions and ask how could they have even chosen to do what they did. In an extreme case, they may find themselves somewhere and not remember how they got there. This may even propagate situations that are dangerous for the native.

For the native that has a poor grip on their own confidence and *Self-Trust*, they may find their own behavior and urges puzzling, frightening and something to be guarded against. For them, it feels much like a different person is directing their actions. A savvy manipulator will find almost no resistance in getting the native to do what they want provided they find the right keys to unlock their active unconscious.

From a karmic perspective, the native may have been so neglective in thinking out their actions and consequences in past lives that Mars' placement here may have been to over-emphasize their lack of conscious directiveness so the native will recognize the lack and take steps to correct it. Remember, Mars simply acts. For Mars, the mind is not necessary. The reverse may be true where they might have been so karmically locked into limiting their actions with their insecurities and thinking that nothing ever got accomplished. The urges of Mars coming from the unconscious would tend to bypass these limits. Although there is a modicum of mental discipline that must be maintained to keep a balance in our daily action, a measure of impulse and intuition must be allowed to filter into our deliberations.

If Mars has a trine or sextile to vent these unconscious urges toward other axes, these areas of life may provide the native with a conscious theatre for their recognition where they can gain a conscious handle on reigning in the tendency to operate purely from impulse. If these are not available or more challenging aspects are present, Mars will create illnesses through the sixth house that match Mars and the mental, emotional and bodily functions that he rules.

Esoterically, the *aspirant* has been through dealing with the "absentmindedness" that appears as a result of this positioning. He or she may simply draw attention to the "absentminded" actions of the *exoteric* native and assist them in gaining a more balanced perspective in integrating mind, instinct and intuition.

JUPITER brings a Second Ray energy of *love and wisdom* to Pisces and the twelfth-sixth house axis. This is a very comfortable position for Jupiter to work through. He will elicit a strong sense of empathy and compassion from the native. In a strong native and one who is well grounded in their identity and *Self-Trust*, it will be a soft and positive flavor added to everything that is done by them. However, if the native is in any way lacking in confidence and *Self-Trust*, their insecurity and need for approval will lead them toward feeling obligated to apply that empathy and compassion toward everyone who shows signs of a perceived need. This will exemplify the expansive and enlarging quality that is so typical of Jupiter.

Since Pisces and the twelfth-sixth house axis works in the unconscious, there will be urges coming from the *exoteric* native that, to them, defy reason or even acknowledgment of the compassion that they *feel* is "demanded" of them. Their need to be of constant service and of being useful to everyone who requests it of them, let alone those who actually are in need is, essentially, an unconscious compensation attempting to verify their preferred valuation of themselves. Since their attempted validation almost never happens in a way that they can believe it of themselves, the need for the indiscriminate application of their energy never relents. As a result, they end up draining themselves through "giving away the store" in a vain attempt to simply feel worthy. Since their emotional psychological reasoning is unable to admit to themselves that they *feel* unworthy, the mental explanation that is substituted becomes either "they will be unable to do it if I don't help" or "if I don't do it for them, who will?"

Guilt is a powerfully negative emotion that is generated through and tied to Pisces and the twelfth-sixth house axis. If the *exoteric* native is the recipient of negative self-image reinforcement in their childhood, their feelings of worthlessness get tossed into the twelfth house refuse pile like every other part of their persona that they are unwilling or unable to deal with. It then gets fed into their emotional ego machine that either projects that unworthiness on others or forces them to become a "savior" for others. Either way, their self-image never recovers until someone or something shows them otherwise.

Jupiter's position here is designed to over-emphasize their perceived deficient self-image to a point where the *love and wisdom* of the second Ray can provide them a person or situation that brings their perceived unworthiness to consciousness in a way that that person or situation is able to show them that they are allowed to have compassion for themselves. Hopefully, Jupiter will have a trine or sextile to planets in other axes that will provide the stage for the manifestation of that compassion. If not, maybe the Second Ray's second heart center representative, the Sun, will show other options for rebalancing the twelfth-six axis issues. If other avenues are not available, or the native refuses to take them, Jupiter will manifest illnesses typical of Jupiter's bodily representations. This will force the *exoteric* native to deal with their misconceptions of themselves at the most basic level.

Esoterically, the *aspirant* has already arrived at a place where they can understand and accept that they are not to be the "saviors" who "fix" others and their personally generated issues. The universe has given Jupiter's compassion the complimentary force of accountability that allows for the proper discrimination of when to assist others and when to let nature run its course. This latter approach is often called "tough love." This is probably one of the hardest parts of letting the heart center do its work.

SATURN brings the Third Ray energy of *active intelligence* to Pisces and the twelfth-sixth house axis. *Exoterically*, his position here is probably one of the most difficult positions to deal with let alone to rebalance.

Saturn's position here puts and holds his discipline, pattern recognition, organizational ability and authority in the unconscious. Submerging the third Ray into the twelfth-sixth house axis removes these qualities from the *exoteric* native's conscious awareness. This means that the spiritually unactualized native will be unable to consciously recognize repetitive patterns whose recognition could easily provide a path for removing behaviors that severely limit their willingness to risk failure or even success in the face of authority or their peer group. As a result, they will project their fears outward by seeing the world as keeping them suppressed, immobile or silent.

In conventional astrology, Saturn's positioning here usually represents the absence of the father in their childrearing years. However, in *esoteric* astrology the significance goes much deeper than simply not having a father. The major qualities that the father would provide, how to relate to authority and how and *why* to discipline themselves, would also be absent from their awareness. This would create an emotionally stunted child who would likely become either rebellious or submissive depending on whether their early behavior had been strongly reinforced in feeling entitled or undeserving. In either case, having their early years absent of the Saturnian influence, they would not have learned or understood the abilities and advantages that discipline and proper recognition of *balanced* authority could bring. Remember, the Third Ray is connected to the throat center which is the human will center.

The absence of knowing or understanding the dynamics of authority could also make them eminently more susceptible to abuse through not learning the meaning of abuse as a child. They would then, if submissive, allow the limits of such abuse to go farther than what a child raised in the prevailing culture might have been taught to expect or tolerate. If they were rebellious in nature and felt the same abuse, they would have a much "shorter fuse" and there would likely be violent reactions to what they *felt* as abuse.

For the *exoteric* native that has Saturn in this position, any career that could provide a perceptual consistency in discipline and authority, such as the military or police force, could allow the native to gain an understanding an expectation and an ability to incorporate the qualities of Saturn. Karmically, it may be that the native could have abused their authority or ignored authority issues in their past life. The absence of Saturn's conscious qualities in this life would be likely to attract outside entities to "fill the gap" and to bring these issues to the native's awareness in order for them to become integrated and handled with balance. With the Third Ray "buried" in the twelfth-sixth house axis, their conscious understanding of how the universe is organized and connected in its diversity would be absent. This might open the door toward allowing the more intuitive faculties of the axis to come into play.

Lastly, as long as Saturn has a trine or sextile to planets in other axes, the native would have avenues to explore the qualities of Saturn in the areas of life that those axes represent. If not, illness would manifest through the sixth house relative to the bodily functions that the throat center and Saturn tend to represent. This would also include mental illness as the Third Ray rules *active intelligence.*

Esoterically, the *aspirant* understands the advantages of incorporating discipline in their approach to life. They also know that the authority that universe wields relates only to the dynamics of creation and not to any egotistically or security-oriented restrictions. The *exoteric* native's need to control or prevent what they perceive as personally restrictive circumstances are simply reactions to their own projection. The *aspirant* knows that the intention of prevention is a purely human attribute based on mental functioning and is related to the human ego. The most difficult part for the *aspirant* would be in showing the *exoteric* native that in their alignment with universal law the protection of their ego is, essentially, not necessary.

URANUS brings the Seventh Ray energy of *ceremonial order* to Pisces and the twelfth-sixth house axis. Here Uranian eccentricity will make itself *felt* within the *exoteric* native's connection and alignment with or against the world at large. However, it will remain mostly unconscious. There is also a very strong sense of intuition, but it will likely remain submerged as the *exoteric* native with this placement is largely petrified of appearing different to their peer group.

Whenever and wherever Uranus is in its *exoteric* expression, the native likely will appear different and separate from the crowd. This will be a way of standing out. This will fluff up the ego. In almost every house in the chart, the native will likely see this type of reception as being beneficial for their intended self-image and for the impressions that they wish to create on others. In the "conscious" houses, they believe that they have control. However, the twelfth house axis is a different story. Remembering that the twelfth house is the home of our repressed fears, the urge to be "different" will heighten their paranoia about being diminished or ostracized for being "different." For the native who wants to "fit in" and to be seen as their definition of "normal," any Uranian expression will be perceived as threatening to their preferred self-image. They believe that they will lose support, respect and acknowledgment. Yet, with Uranus in this position, the urges to be and feel different will continue to surface making the native afraid to express themselves in almost any way for fear that something might "slip out" exposing them as weird or odd.

Since Uranus seems to express unexpected creativity through his movement in simply returning the world to its natural state, his positioning in most houses can be considered and asset by most natives. However, when the energies actually change the native's experience without their intention or ability to control the outcome, the native can become paranoid and afraid to act. This dynamic is tremendously amplified when Uranus is in the unconscious twelfth-sixth house axis of the native. This will likely encourage the *exoteric* native to become a hermit limiting his or her exposure to the outside world for fear of "letting something slip" that would put them in a bad light. One of the saving graces will be if Uranus is in trine or sextile to other planets in other axes which can provide an avenue for the intuition and creativity to express itself. Yet, even as the native may still choose to work alone, they can be extremely creative and productive due to the immediate availability of their Uranian intuitive functions.

Being fearful of appearing "different" has a direct correlation to being raised in a way that our confidence and *Self-Trust* has been diminished. We then doubt our own adequacy and fear exposure. The universe uses Uranus in the twelfth-sixth house axis to impel the native to focus on these fears through drawing people to them who will tend to expose them and bring these fears to the surface. As the native's perception of control is shattered by Uranian forces, they realize that they are not alone when the smoke clears.

This then gives them an opportunity to deal with their fears openly in daylight. Slowly, in doing so the native begins to realize that he or she are not the only ones who fear being seen as "different." They come to understand that their connection to the *ceremonial order* of the natural universe is not always perceived in its clearest light. Hence, they are not actually "different."

Esoterically, Uranus in the twelfth-sixth house axis offers a unique opportunity to find balance with everyone else. Remember, Uranus *esoterically* rules Libra through partnerships. Being alone is, essentially, an illusion. Activities like meditation, martial arts and sports activate the sacral center which is "home" for the Seventh Ray in balancing our bodies with the rhythm of nature. Additionally, if Uranus is in Pisces or the twelfth-sixth house axis and since he *esoterically* rules Libra, those two positions are solstice points to each other manifesting the arts such as painting, music, photography, designing, etc. If there are planets in Libra or the seventh-first house axis, the aspects they form will create release points for Uranus.

NEPTUNE brings a Sixth Ray energy promoting proper *ideals and devotions* to Pisces and the twelfth-sixth house axis. Ordinarily, Neptune would bring secrets or delusions, about ourselves or others, to this axis. But due to the nature of the sign and the axis, most everything is already shrouded in secrecy and perhaps delusions. He will also bring a tsunami of sensitivity even bordering on paranoia. Neptune's presence here may be comfortable for Neptune but will likely produce tremendous confusion for the *exoteric* native. Things that are normally buried in this axis will become more difficult to reach let alone understand. Fears would likely border on the irrational.

In this position Neptune is likely to produce a fear of confinement if not claustrophobia. There may also surface a fear of becoming trapped in situations where the native sees no way out. The empathy and compassion that the native would normally feel as part of this axis would appear to be binding if not compelling leaving them to feel obligated to people not of their choosing.

On the contrary, Neptune's presence here might alternately cause of fear of things falling apart or *dissolving* leaving them feeling helpless to remedy the situations. In both the confinement aspect or the collapsing aspect, their imagination of what might happen to them could be voracious. The Sixth Ray's connection to Mars and the solar plexus may also produce extremes in action to overcome the lack of feeling in control. Mars' sign and house position will give added information about where action might prove useful to give the native a sense of control.

For the *exoteric* native, the *ideals and devotion* energized by the Sixth Ray may also manifest as a fanatic dependency on others for their values, direction and grounding. The dependency may even manifest as drug or alcohol abuse simply to escape the trapped feelings. They may also escape into activities, through the sign and position of Mars, that could produce enough sensuality to blot out their painful feelings.

All in all, Neptune in this position is extremely difficult to get a handle on, especially, since he is so antithetical to the material world and buried in the unconscious. Any career that would capitalize on art and the creative aspects of life might produce an avenue of expression that would give them some stability in the tangible world. If the native is unable to find avenues for expression through trines or sextiles to planets in other axes, Neptune will produce "non-descript" illnesses through the sixth house that may be undiagnosable to the average physician.

Of all the planetary positions that the *aspirant* might see in their travels, this one will be one of the hardest to assist with. Remembering that Neptune *esoterically* rules Cancer will give the *aspirant* insight on where to begin to help themselves or the native find a sense of usefulness and solidity in the tangible world. But it will be up to the *aspirant* and the native to choose to risk changes in spite of their imagined outcomes. Once the *aspirant* and the native have gotten a handle on their fears and imaginations, this positioning has the potential to develop a profound psychic ability and artistic sensitivity more than any other positioning.

PLUTO brings a First Ray energy of *will and power* to Pisces and the twelfth-sixth house axis. Pluto's positioning here brings an intensity and depth to the issues of this axis. In many cases, the *exoteric* native may become obsessed with their own empathy, compassion and sensitivities. Nevertheless, the regenerative potential for whatever is activated in this axis is unsurpassed.

In this positioning there is a unique connection to the unconscious. The *will and power* that are accessible from this axis far outstrips any conscious intention or directiveness. The more open the native is to shared empathy and their intuition rather than personal emotions or mental strategizing, the stronger the support that will come from the universe.

Pluto is the *esoteric* ruler of Pisces. It powers the empathy and compassion that should rise up from our unconscious and be applied to the public. Whether he or she knows it or not, the native with this positioning, *exoteric* and *esoteric*, innately has a finger on the pulse of the feelings that the general public emanates. However, the use of this capacity can be used in two ways. First, the *exoteric* native, aware or not, *will use* that sensitivity as a strategic advantage if they feel entitled with confidence and trust in themselves or they *will be used* by the public because they've been trained into believing that they are inferior to the public and *owe* them service. Second, the *esoteric* native will grow to understand that the application of that empathy and compassion must be deliberated patiently and carefully to know whether its application will do more harm than good. That is, should they actually apply assistance out of empathy and compassion or should they withhold, apply "tough love" and let nature run its course so the recipient will not lose the lesson being experienced? The choice must be made slowly and carefully.

There is tremendous *will and power* available through the empathy empowered through this placement. It is connected to our crown center and is one of the chief methods for wielding power from the universe. If we try to apply it to the plans we put into play that increase our material and emotional security, we will receive some support from the universe in a direction which will ultimately discourage the pursuit of personal security. If we apply it as a result of being directed by our hearts and without the thought of personal advantage, the support we receive will be tremendously powerful.

Whatever is in or emanates from the twelfth-sixth house axis will be regenerated. As with all energy, it has no mind. It simply augments the movement as it is directed. However, the reason that energy directed at personal advantage and security appears to be only partially energized is because energy directed in that fashion has a built-in polarization that conflicts with itself and wastes a portion of the energy through the native's opposition to what is not wanted.

In some cases, Pluto's placement may evoke fear of crowds, public places and the public in general for the *exoteric* native. In other cases, some may be drawn to them. In either case, Pluto augments the energy so these unconscious fears or attractions may be brought to consciousness so they may be rebalanced. If the native has trines or sextiles to planets in other axes, the dynamic producing *will and power* can be clearly seen and applied easily. If the native has, essentially, no "vent" and is unable to channel Pluto's tremendous reservoir of energy into a conscious endeavor, it may unwittingly be vented through the sixth house producing an illness that might be extremely difficult to overcome or recover from.

Esoterically, as the *aspirant* eliminates motivations of a personal nature, the empathic power and ability to recognize and use it is augmented. Rather than addressing the *will and power* aspect directly, the *aspirant* knows that encouraging a balance of empathy and compassion in the *exoteric* native between themselves and others will permit the flow of First Ray potential to the extent that is necessary to empower their spiritual maturity. *Will and power* in itself should never be the objective of any native who is or would like to be on the *aspirant's* path. Remember, it is not fully manifest because the human mind and emotions are not yet wise enough or loving enough to fully manifest, let alone, use it safely.

VULCAN brings the First Ray energy of *will and power* to Pisces and the twelfth-sixth house axis. Remembering also that Vulcan is never more than eight degrees away from the Sun, we know that the Sun's position here or in adjacent houses *is necessary* for bringing additional light and awareness to the motivations behind the *exoteric* native's unconscious issues which need to be tempered before *will and power* can be safely applied.

Vulcan's positioning here is completely antithetical to the energy the axis normally projects. Vulcan's energy and projection will include *no feeling or emotion*. Here, he operates simply as a tool for purging issues that have either been pushed into the unconscious without awareness or consciously been thrown into the "refuse heap."

His placement here is for the purpose of bringing to consciousness the qualities of self that have become unacknowledged or ignored. When issues get submerged, they leave a void and create a polarity that the universe fills with other people who have the same or opposing issues. The responses of other people are one of Vulcan's catalyzers. This eventually causes confrontation which, hopefully, leads to mediation or the elimination of useless egotistical polarities that interfere with the natural flow of universal energy. It is only then that Vulcan can forge the tools that move us in the direction of manifesting the *Plan*. If Vulcan has trines or sextiles to planets in other axes, the purging can be much more conscious. If not, then Vulcan's overwhelming cleansing may occur through the sixth house as a variation of collapsing emotional states and body functions.

For the few of us humans who have allowed Vulcan to dissolve the walls that bar our consciousness from our unconscious, this becomes a rare opportunity to tap into the *will and power* that emanate from within our collective unconscious. These are rare and, indeed, few individuals who have arrived on these shores. It is only then, when the unconscious has been made conscious, that it is only minimally safe for the human mind to wield the awesome *will and power* of the crown center and the First Ray.

Although there are only a handful known people who have "mastered" this skill, there are still many who remain hidden among us, whether they are conscious of it or not, who assist us in moving past our human frailties. But there is also a plethora of those who *believe* that they have mastered this skill, profess to know so and move in ways that deceive us and then plunge us further into being less aware. One of Vulcan's capabilities allows us to recognize these individuals by virtue of our having an uneasy gut feeling by those who are *not* listening or through the using of our intuition by those who *are* listening to our subconscious and misusing it.

Esoterically, and for the *aspirant*, it is imperative that the Second Ray of *love and wisdom* be used by the *aspirant* along with Vulcan in assisting the *exoteric* native into a place where they might feel somewhat safe and protected rather than just dumping them on the barren shores of logic and practicality ruled by Vulcan. Our fragility is highly emphasized when dealing with the twelfth-sixth house axis, especially, since this is one of the places where we depend on our security to be solid. Even though, according to the universe, that security is an illusion, we still need to believe and feel it as being so until we grow enough in strength and in trusting our true ourselves. Forging that trust in the reality of things is one of Vulcan's protocols.

MOON brings a Fourth Ray energy facilitating *harmony through conflict* to Pisces and the twelfth-sixth house axis. *Exoterically*, the Moon's position here is similar to Mercury's with the exception that the Moon makes the connection much more emotional and intimate. In this position the Moon may become hyper-sensitive. This may manifest as irrational fears or if the *exoteric* native has become comfortable in a fluid environment, it may allow them to take advantage of others through the many subtle recognitions that they have about them.

One of the negative manifestations of having the Moon in Pisces or this axis is that the *exoteric* native may play helpless by feigning illness in order to gain attention and favors through inducing guilt or pity in those close to them. This may also produce a projection of victimhood on the public playing on the sensitivities of others who might be susceptible to being manipulated as a result of their being raised to feel inadequate or obligated to others.

If the Moon has trines or sextiles to planets in other axes, it will first show the areas of life that will be perceived more personally than others and second, if recognized and accepted by the *exoteric* native, allow the "defusing" of the compensation that ordinarily ensues. If the Moon does not have any "vent points," her compressed energy is likely to produces illnesses through the sixth house that relate to the Moon's rulerships. It might be thought that oppositions might produce an awareness of these compensations, but what happens, more often than not, is that these compensations only become more intensified through the producing of a more strongly perceived resistance from any projected polarizations.

On the positive side, the *exoteric* native with this positioning often will have a sixth sense about the people they encounter. If they were raised to have confidence, *Self-Trust* and personal strength, others will tend to trust them without knowing why.

They might say," I don't know why I'm telling you this but..." If their hearts are in the "right" place, giving their refection on what they've heard can provide tremendous clarity from a more "objective" perspective than was originally perceived by the recipient. On the negative side and if they were raised with diminished confidence, *Self-Trust* and strength, they would likely use the opportunity to gain advantage through producing obligation through inducing guilt in the recipient.

Esoterically, we must remember that the Moon veils Vulcan, Uranus and Neptune. The Moon's intended placement here is that all the ploys that the egocentric Moon may resort to will eventually be purged (Vulcan), burst (Uranus) or dissolved (dissolved). The *aspirant* recognizes this necessity and does what they can to assist the *exoteric* native in perceiving both sides of their personally oriented emotional polarizations as a simple compensation for their own feelings of inadequacy and powerlessness. Emphasizing where they *do* have confidence, *Self-Trust* and personal strength often releases some of the pressure the native feels toward compensating. The Moon's partnership with Mercury and the Fourth Ray is an intended transfer of effect from the Moon's polarizing and strategizing tendency toward Mercury's intuitive capabilities. This generally minimizes the *harmony through conflict* that the Moon brings to bear.

SUMMARY OF PART II

The previous section may seem unduly negative in some of the renditions of potential behaviors that might be emitted by the *exoteric* native. But please remember that this complete section has been geared toward understanding some of the purpose and logic behind the "placements" of the rays and their planetary representatives. In most cases, slow improvement through the native's life is often the case. With many exceptions, lessons must be repeated over and over enough to make the *exoteric* native "sick and tired" of the frustrating obstacles that the universe often places in front of us encouraging us to seek alternate avenues for inspiring growth toward spiritual maturity.

It should also be understood that as humans, we grow very slowly in wisdom and awareness. This occurs through the slow and patient removal and replacement of childish behaviors with more sophisticated and emotionally protective strategies. The faster changes are usually more representative of *transits* through each axis. The longer and more intense and internal changes are representative of *progressions* through each axis. Every conventional dynamic can be perceived, intuitively, through a universal lens as a useful tool for our spiritual growth.

With patience and forged personal growth, all the conventional dynamics involved in reading the energies and their changes in our client's charts can be perceived with a universal purpose in mind. As we, the *aspirant* or, perhaps the *initiate*, work to understand our clients and the dilemmas that they face, the more we learn that they reflect what *we* ourselves need to perceive, accept and implement for our own growth. We must welcome the mysteries and conundrums as opportunities for the exploration of ourselves and the part *we* play in the universe and its poorly understood *Plan*.

References & Helpful Reading Material

Arroyo, Stephen, (1975). *Astrology, Psychology, and the Four Elements: An Energy Approach to Astrology and its Use in the Counseling Arts.* CRCS Publications, Sebastopol, Ca. ISBN# 0916-360-016.

Arroyo, Stephen, (1978). *Astrology, Karma & Transformation: The Inner Dimensions of the Birth Chart.* CRCS Publications, Sebastopol, Ca. ISBN# 0916-360-547.

Bailey, Alice A., (1936). *Esoteric Astrology: Volume III, A Treatise on the Seven Rays.* Lucis Publishing Company, New York, New York. ISBN# 978-0853-301-202.

Berne, MD, Eric, (1964). *Games People Play: A Basic Handbook or Transactional Analysis.* Ballantine Books, New York, NY. ISBN# 0-345-25480-5-195.

Davis, James & Raifsnider, John, (1977). *Astrology of the Seven Rays.* Infinity Books, San Diego, California. ISBN# 0877-072-051.

Koparkar, Mohan, (1977). *Lunar Nodes*. Mohan Enterprises, Roch, New York. ISBN# 978-0918-922-045.

Meyer, Michael R., (1974). *A Handbook for the Humanistic Astrologer*. Anchor Books / Doubleday, Garden City, N.Y. ISBN# 0384-057-296.

Oken, Alan, (1980). *Alan Oken's Complete Astrology: A Modern Guide to Astrological Awareness*. Bantam Books, New York, N.Y. ISBN# 0553-012-622.

Sasportas, Howard, (1985). *The Twelve Houses: Exploring the Houses of the Horoscope*. Flare Publications, London, Eng. ISBN# 978-1903-353-042.

Schulman, Martin, (1975). *Karmic Astrology: The Moon's Nodes and Reincarnation, Volume 1*. Samuel Weiser, Inc., York Beach, Me. ISBN# 0877-282-889.

Stahl, Carl W. (1972). *Vulcan, The Intra-Mercurial Planet*. Solunar Research Pubications, Bay City, Mi. ASIN# B0006X5SY4 (Amazon).

Weston, L. H., *The Planet Vulcan History, Nature, Tables*. American Federation of Astrologers, Tempe, Az. ISBN# 978-0866-901-963.

Wilson-Ludlam, Mae R., (1981). *Interpret Your Rays Using Astrology*. American Federation of Astrologers, Inc, Tempe, Az. ISBN# 0866-900-039.

Wood, Ernest. (1925). *The Seven Rays: A Theosophical Handbook*. The Theosophical Publishing House, Adyar, Madras 20, India. ISBN# 0835-604-810.

APPENDIX

SHORT HOUSE INTERPRETATION GUIDE

11	10	9	8
Friends, groups, organizations, hopes, aspirations, ideals, love received, 3rd & 7th child Aquarius – Fixed air Uranus – sudden & unusual change Saturn – stable, teacher	Career, what you aspire to be, achievement, you father & mate's mother Capricorn – Cardinal earth Saturn – stable, teacher, father	Philosophy, religion, long journeys, higher education, in-laws Sagittarius – Mutable fire Jupiter – expansion	Death, the occult, wills, sex, regeneration, other people's money & abilities, karma, 2nd & 6th child Scorpio – Fixed water Mars – Aggression, sexual energy, action Pluto – control, transform

12		7
Unconscious mind, institutions, karma, self undoing, secret enemies, initiation, sleep Pisces – Mutable water Jupiter – expansion Neptune – illusion, delusion, universal love	**DEFINITIONS** Cardinal – Self starting Mutable – Changeable Fixed – Unchangeable Fire – Idealistic Initiating Earth – Materialistic Spiritual Air – communicating Mental Water – Emotional	Relationships, open enemies, marriages, contracts Libra – Cardinal air Venus – love, enjoyment, choice & balance
1		6
"I am", describes the way you meet the world & your present situation, Will give a good description of you with the 2nd & 4th houses Aries – Cardinal fire Mars – aggression, sexual energy, action		Work, pets, health, work ideals, work environment, ability to discriminate, service to self & others Virgo – Mutable earth Mercury – thought, communication & exchange

2	3	4	5
What you value, house of judgement & preference, possessions, money, abilities, disabilities, resources & earning capacity, 4th & 8th child Taurus – Fixed earth Venus – love, enjoyment, choice & balance	Ability to speak & listen, siblings, neighbors, early education, short trips Gemini – Mutable air Mercury – thought, communication & exchange	Early home, psychic foundations, your own home, mother, father in-law, end of life Cancer – Cardinal water Moon – emotions, feeling, physical body, mother	Children, creativity, recreational sex, pleasure, gambling, how you give love, 1st & 5th child Leo – Fixed fire Sun – focus, soul, vitality

Family Members By House

FAMILY MEMBERS ACCORDING TO HOUSE

11 Mate's children and/ or 3rd, 7th & 11th child	10 Father, cousins on mother's side, mother in-law, mate's cousins on father's side	9 Mate's brothers, sisters and neighbors (in-laws)	8 2nd, 6th & 10th child
12 Father's brothers & sisters Mother in-law's brothers & sisters			7 Mate or partner Father's father Mother's mother Nieces & nephews Mate's father's mother Mate's mother's father
1 Father's mother, Mother's father Mate's father's Father Mate's mother's mother Mate's nieces & nephews			6 Mother's brothers & sisters Mate's father's brothers & sisters
2 4th, 8th & 12th child	3 Brothers, sisters & neighbors	4 Mother Cousins – father's side Father in-law Mate's cousins on mother's side	5 Children and/or 1st, 5th & 9th child

45 Degree Chart

01 Aries	16 Taurus	01 Cancer	16 Leo	01 Libra	16 Scorpio	01 Capricorn	16 Aquarius
02 Aries	17 Taurus	02 Cancer	17 Leo	02 Libra	17 Scorpio	02 Capricorn	17 Aquarius
03 Aries	18 Taurus	03 Cancer	18 Leo	03 Libra	18 Scorpio	03 Capricorn	18 Aquarius
04 Aries	19 Taurus	04 Cancer	19 Leo	04 Libra	19 Scorpio	04 Capricorn	19 Aquarius
05 Aries	20 Taurus	05 Cancer	20 Leo	05 Libra	20 Scorpio	05 Capricorn	20 Aquarius
06 Aries	21 Taurus	06 Cancer	21 Leo	06 Libra	21 Scorpio	06 Capricorn	21 Aquarius
07 Aries	22 Taurus	07 Cancer	22 Leo	07 Libra	22 Scorpio	07 Capricorn	22 Aquarius
08 Aries	23 Taurus	08 Cancer	23 Leo	08 Libra	23 Scorpio	08 Capricorn	23 Aquarius
09 Aries	24 Taurus	09 Cancer	24 Leo	09 Libra	24 Scorpio	09 Capricorn	24 Aquarius
10 Aries	25 Taurus	10 Cancer	25 Leo	10 Libra	25 Scorpio	10 Capricorn	25 Aquarius
11 Aries	26 Taurus	11 Cancer	26 Leo	11 Libra	26 Scorpio	11 Capricorn	26 Aquarius
12 Aries	27 Taurus	12 Cancer	27 Leo	12 Libra	27 Scorpio	12 Capricorn	27 Aquarius
13 Aries	28 Taurus	13 Cancer	28 Leo	13 Libra	28 Scorpio	13 Capricorn	28 Aquarius
14 Aries	29 Taurus	14 Cancer	29 Leo	14 Libra	29 Scorpio	14 Capricorn	29 Aquarius
15 Aries	00 Gemini	15 Cancer	00 Virgo	15 Libra	00 Sagittar	15 Capricorn	00 Pisces
16 Aries	01 Gemini	16 Cancer	01 Virgo	16 Libra	01 Sagittar	16 Capricorn	01 Pisces
17 Aries	02 Gemini	17 Cancer	02 Virgo	17 Libra	02 Sagittar	17 Capricorn	02 Pisces
18 Aries	03 Gemini	18 Cancer	03 Virgo	18 Libra	03 Sagittar	18 Capricorn	03 Pisces
19 Aries	04 Gemini	19 Cancer	04 Virgo	19 Libra	04 Sagittar	19 Capricorn	04 Pisces
20 Aries	05 Gemini	20 Cancer	05 Virgo	20 Libra	05 Sagittar	20 Capricorn	05 Pisces
21 Aries	06 Gemini	21 Cancer	06 Virgo	21 Libra	06 Sagittar	21 Capricorn	06 Pisces
22 Aries	07 Gemini	22 Cancer	07 Virgo	22 Libra	07 Sagittar	22 Capricorn	07 Pisces
23 Aries	08 Gemini	23 Cancer	08 Virgo	23 Libra	08 Sagittar	23 Capricorn	08 Pisces
24 Aries	09 Gemini	24 Cancer	09 Virgo	24 Libra	09 Sagittar	24 Capricorn	09 Pisces
25 Aries	10 Gemini	25 Cancer	10 Virgo	25 Libra	10 Sagittar	25 Capricorn	10 Pisces
26 Aries	11 Gemini	26 Cancer	11 Virgo	26 Libra	11 Sagittar	26 Capricorn	11 Pisces
27 Aries	12 Gemini	27 Cancer	12 Virgo	27 Libra	12 Sagittar	27 Capricorn	12 Pisces
28 Aries	13 Gemini	28 Cancer	13 Virgo	28 Libra	13 Sagittar	28 Capricorn	13 Pisces
29 Aries	14 Gemini	29 Cancer	14 Virgo	29 Libra	14 Sagittar	29 Capricorn	14 Pisces
00 Taurus	15 Gemini	00 Leo	15 Virgo	00 Scorpio	15 Sagittar	00 Aquarius	15 Pisces
01 Taurus	16 Gemini	01 Leo	16 Virgo	01 Scorpio	16 Sagittar	01 Aquarius	16 Pisces
02 Taurus	17 Gemini	02 Leo	17 Virgo	02 Scorpio	17 Sagittar	02 Aquarius	17 Pisces
03 Taurus	18 Gemini	03 Leo	18 Virgo	03 Scorpio	18 Sagittar	03 Aquarius	18 Pisces
04 Taurus	19 Gemini	04 Leo	19 Virgo	04 Scorpio	19 Sagittar	04 Aquarius	19 Pisces
05 Taurus	20 Gemini	05 Leo	20 Virgo	05 Scorpio	20 Sagittar	05 Aquarius	20 Pisces
06 Taurus	21 Gemini	06 Leo	21 Virgo	06 Scorpio	21 Sagittar	06 Aquarius	21 Pisces
07 Taurus	22 Gemini	07 Leo	22 Virgo	07 Scorpio	22 Sagittar	07 Aquarius	22 Pisces
08 Taurus	23 Gemini	08 Leo	23 Virgo	08 Scorpio	23 Sagittar	08 Aquarius	23 Pisces
09 Taurus	24 Gemini	09 Leo	24 Virgo	09 Scorpio	24 Sagittar	09 Aquarius	24 Pisces
10 Taurus	25 Gemini	10 Leo	25 Virgo	10 Scorpio	25 Sagittar	10 Aquarius	25 Pisces
11 Taurus	26 Gemini	11 Leo	26 Virgo	11 Scorpio	26 Sagittar	11 Aquarius	26 Pisces
12 Taurus	27 Gemini	12 Leo	27 Virgo	12 Scorpio	27 Sagittar	12 Aquarius	27 Pisces
13 Taurus	28 Gemini	13 Leo	28 Virgo	13 Scorpio	28 Sagittar	13 Aquarius	28 Pisces
14 Taurus	29 Gemini	14 Leo	29 Virgo	14 Scorpio	29 Sagittar	14 Aquarius	29 Pisces
15 Taurus	00 Cancer	15 Leo	00 Libra	15 Scorpio	00 Capricorn	15 Aquarius	00 Aries

Directions: Start at any position. The first box to the right is 45 degrees from the origination point. Keep counting to the right. When you arrive at the last column, wrap around to the first column on the same row to continue until you've ascertained all eight phases.

Phase Wheel

00
45
315
New
Moon
Emergence
Balsamic
Moon
Release
Crescent
Moon
Assertion
3rd Quarter
Moon
Reorientation
90
270
1st Quarter
Moon
Action
Disseminating
Moon
Synthesis
Gibbous
Moon
Expression
Full
Moon
Fulfillment
135
225
180

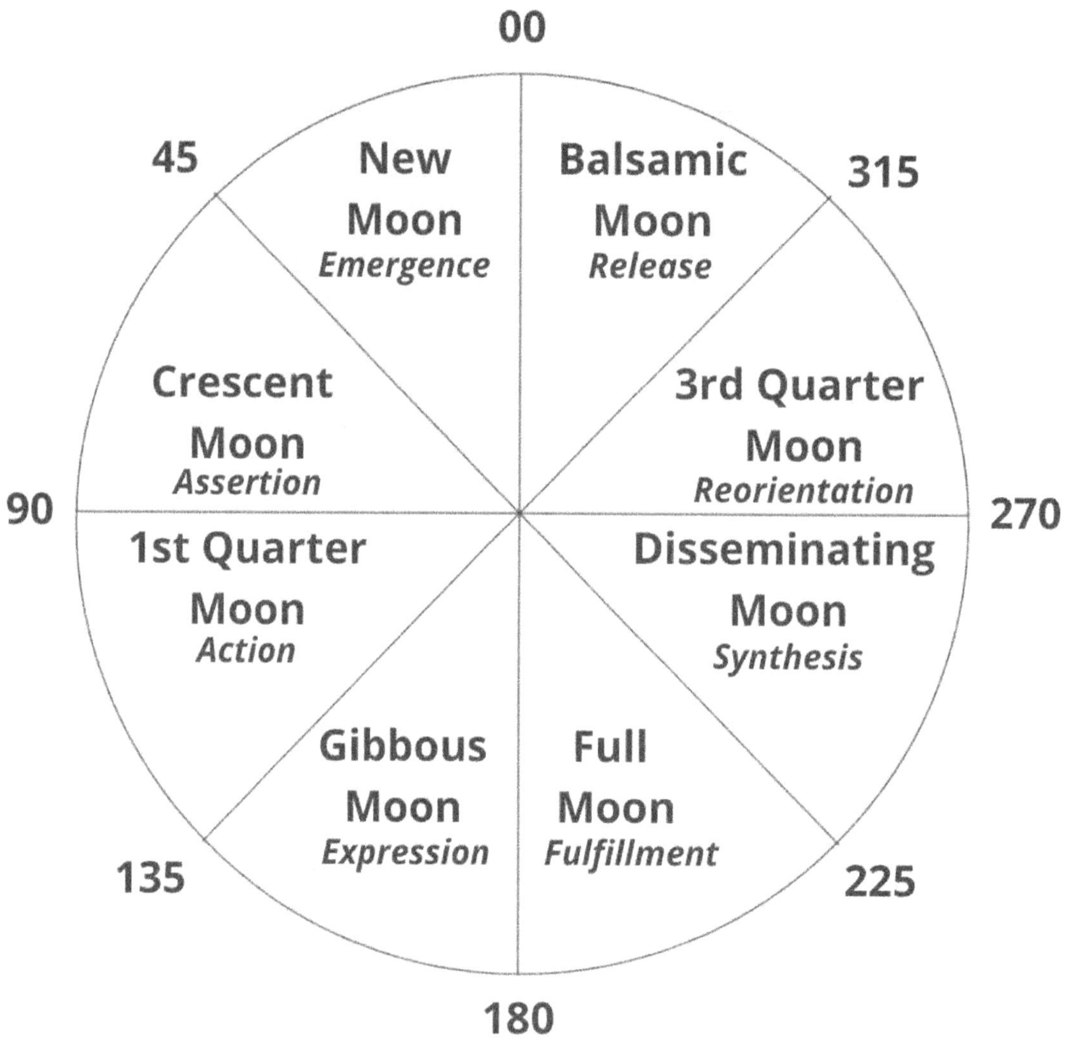

		Signs	Exoteric	Esoteric	Hierarchy	Aspects	Center & Gland	Master & Angel	Stones
1	⯛ Will & Power ♇	♈ ♌ ♑	♂ 6 ☉ 2 ♄ 3	☿ 4 ⛢ 7 ♄ 3	⛢ 7 ♆ 6 ♀ 5	Conjunction ☌ 00 Degrees Synthesis	Crown Pineal	Morya Michael	Diamond Rock Crystal
2	♃ Love & Wisdom ☉	♍ ♊ ♓	☿ 4 ☿ 4 ♃ 2	☽ 4 ♀ 5 ♇ 1	♃ 2 ⊕ 3 ♇ 1	Opposition ☍ 180 Degrees Awareness	Heart Thymus	Kuthumi & Djwal Kuhl Jophiel	Sapphire Lapis Lazuli Turquoise Sodalite
3	♄ Active Intelligence ⊕	♋ ♎ ♑	☽ 4 ♀ 5 ♄ 3	♆ 6 ⛢ 7 ♄ 3	♆ 6 ♄ 3 ♀ 5	Trine △ 120 Degrees Ease of Flow	Throat Thyroid	Paul the Ventian Chamuel	Emerald Aquamarine Jade Malachite
4	☿ Harmony Thru Conflict ☽	♏ ♉ ♐	♂ 6 ♀ 5 ♃ 2	♂ 6 ⯛ 1 ⊕ 3	☿ 4 ⯛ 1 ♂ 6	Square □ 90 Degrees Developmental Tension	Root Adrenal	Serapis Gabriel	Jasper Chalcedony Agate Serpentine
5	♀ Concrete Science	♌ ♐ ♒	☉ 2 ♃ 2 ♄ 3	⛢ 7 ⊕ 3 ♃ 2	♆ 6 ♂ 6 ☽ 4	Quintile ✩ 72 Degrees Creative Transformation	Third Eye Pituitary	Hilarion Raphael	Topaz Citrine Steatite
6	♆ Ideals & Devotion ♂	♐ ♍ ♓	♃ 2 ☿ 4 ♃ 2	⊕ 3 ☽ 4 ♇ 1	♂ 6 ♃ 2 ♇ 1	Sextile ✶ 60 Degrees Production	Solar-Plexus Pancreas	Jesus Uriel	Ruby Tourmaline Garnet Carnelian
7	⛢ Ceremonial Order	♑ ♈ ♋	♄ 3 ♂ 6 ☽ 4	♄ 3 ☿ 4 ♆ 6	♀ 5 ⛢ 7 ♆ 6	Septile ✡ 51 25' Degrees Occult Direction	Sacral Gonads	St. Germain Zadkiel	Amethyst Porphyry Violan

ABOUT THE AUTHOR

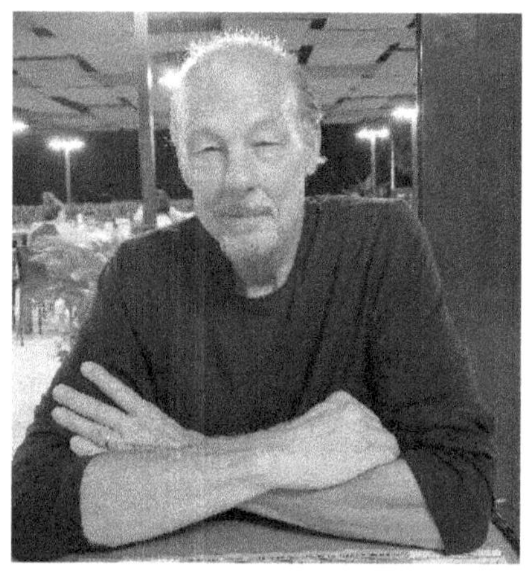

John Lawrence Maerz is an author, instructor, professional speaker and coach with specializations in metaphysics and psychology. His extensive background includes astrology, tarot, numerology, I-Ching, energy work, martial arts, psychic development and mediumship.

John has worked as a counselor and case manager with teen substance abuse, in child protection services and is a seasoned personal coach and adviser with diverse experience in the field of human potential. He incorporates and integrates personality influences, shadow work, nutritional needs, creative expression and personal desires while uncovering his client's innate abilities and potential.

John co-owned and successfully ran Starchild, a metaphysical bookstore in Port Charlotte, Florida, from 1995-2005. He also co-owned and ran the Astrological Institute of Integrated Studies begun in Bayshore New York, a school teaching a multitude of metaphysical subjects from 1983-1989 and in Florida from 1989-2005. He is dedicated to raising awareness and sharing his own unique perspective and understanding about life's journey and its meaning. He recognizes and emphasizes the importance of having balance and accountability. He challenges his students and clients to keep fulfilling their spiritual potential through their own individual experiences.

Over the years, John has produced a series of books, workshops, lectures and seminars presenting different metaphysical topics in print and on MP3. These materials are available on JohnMaerz.com. He is also a voracious writer and has written more than 85 articles on many thought-provoking subjects which are also available on his site. He has also published fifteen books on metaphysics and psychology. **You can contact John at (941) 286-1562 or JM@JohnMaerz.com**

Books by JOHN LAWRENCE MAERZ

- **TAROT**: *The Astrological Layout*
- **CYCLES**: *The Application of Energy Within the Natural Cycle*
- **IS ANYONE THERE?** *Reaching Across the Veil in Mediumship*
- **ENERGIZING SELF-TRUST**: *7 Steps for Reclaiming Your Power*
- **OUT OF THE BOX**: *7 Elements for Raising a Self-Directing Child*
- **SIGNS & PORTENTS**: *A Reader's Guide for Combining Psychic Tools*
- **PLOYS FOR DOMINANCE**: *A Guide for Recognizing & Disarming Manipulation*
- **NUMEROLOGY**: *Life's Mirror of Vibration*
- **ASTROLOGY 4 PURPOSE, POWER & PERSPECTIVE**: *A Primer for the Seven Rays & the Work of Alice Bailey*
- **IN THE WORLD BUT NOT OF IT**: *Heaven, Hell & the Many Faces of Enlightenment & Ascension*
- **UNWINDING THE KARMIC WHEEL**: *The Journey from Survival to Compassion*
- **CORE VALUES**: *Recognizing & Surviving the Global Assault on Our Personal Autonomy*
- **UNCOILING THE SERPENT**: *Kundalini & the Dynamics of Spiritual Maturity*
- **SELF-WORTH:** *It's Origins, Faces & Remedies*

www.ingramcontent.com/pod-product-compliance
Lightning Source LLC
Chambersburg PA
CBHW080251030726
47593CB00009B/2450